India and the West

Books by Barbara Ward

THE WEST AT BAY

POLICY FOR THE WEST

FAITH AND FREEDOM

THE INTERPLAY OF EAST AND WEST

FIVE IDEAS THAT CHANGE THE WORLD

INDIA AND THE WEST

THE RICH NATIONS AND THE POOR NATIONS

BARBARA WARD

INDIA

AND THE

WEST

Revised Edition

W · W · NORTON & COMPANY · INC · *New York*

Library of Congress Catalog Card No. 64-14852

1256158

The preparation of this book has been made possible by a generous grant from the Carnegie Corporation. The Indian Planning Commission and the Indian Commission General for Economic Affairs in Washington have given unstinting assistance. The Bombay Council for Economic Education has generously given permission for the reproduction of the first three chapters in the section entitled "After China's Attack." And the book would never have been written at all, had it not been for the knowledge, counsel, patience, and unwearying help of two friends to whom this book is most gratefully dedicated:

TAYA *and* MAURICE ZINKIN

Contents

PART

1

The Revolution of
Economic Growth

Chapter One

The Issue

INDIA, today, is engaged in a vast experiment to bring its giant economy into the main stream of modern life. Even if this effort of economic expansion concerned only the Indian people, the scale and vision of the attempt should still catch the imagination of the world. To create the conditions of modern living for over 400 million people, to rescue from extreme poverty nearly half the inhabitants of the free yet underdeveloped world, to bring into the age of atomic energy and outer space one of the most ancient of the world's great civilizations—all these are stirring adventures of the human spirit in their own right. But the significance of India's plans extends beyond the frontiers of India. They are a vital, perhaps a decisive, chapter in the wider history of modern man.

India is undergoing the profound process of economic

change and development which began in the West about two hundred years ago—the process of applying savings and science to the earning of man's daily bread. First launched in Britain, the movement spread rapidly to communities which resembled Britain in wealth, background, and institutions: the neighbouring lands of Western Europe and the countries of European settlement overseas. Thus, with few exceptions, the first general move of modernization occurred round the shores of the North Atlantic ocean.

It was—inevitably—a revolutionary change. Men cannot transform their methods of work, their relations with each other, the centres of power and influence in their society, without unleashing forces of unsettlement and fear, and hence of violence as well. As Western society grappled with the problems and upheavals of the new economics, it produced two broad versions of modernization; some states achieved their transformation within the framework of decentralized power and free institutions, others were driven by the stress of change to maintain—or lapse into—dictatorial rule. Among these latter communities, Communism has provided the basis for the most thorough and enduring experiments in tyranny.

The economic revolution was not long confined to the Atlantic arena. By trade and investment, the Western Powers carried its methods and aspirations all round the world, linking the most distant lands with the Atlantic base, involving them in the new opportunities—and uncertainties—of a world-wide market. The effect of this stimulus varied, naturally, with local conditions. Generalizations are a little dubious; but perhaps it is safe to say that the economic consequence of the Western impact was everywhere to set in motion the disintegration of the traditional economy—but nowhere to establish decisively the pattern of the new. Only in Japan, from which direct Western influence had been excluded for two hundred years, did the local leaders carry through the full process of modernization. Today, most of the world outside the Atlantic arena is still in the process of creating the effective framework of a modern economy.

For this reason, the ultimate political framework of these new economies is also still in doubt. So far, the only fully modern economy—that of Japan—has undergone a series of metamorphoses, veering from feudal to militarist to parliamentary back to militarist again, and under the impact of defeat, to pacifist and democratic as well. The changes have been too sharp and too dependent upon outside influence for any future pattern to seem secure. Among the still developing economies, the issue is undecided. China, by choosing the Communist route, has recreated in Asia the dramatic Western division between freedom and dictatorship as the organizing political principle of the modern community. India alone has the political scale and historical influence to offer the counterpoise of economic modernization conducted within a liberal framework. If its experiment succeeds, one may guess that Japan's wavering allegiance to free institutions will be safely anchored and that the pattern of decentralized power and political elbow room in Asia will be secure. Equally, a failure in India would bring with it disillusion with the methods of freedom throughout Asia and probably in other developing continents as well.

One could go further and argue that, for free government everywhere, the proof that its principles applied only in the Atlantic world would be a crippling setback. True, free government has hitherto been the privilege of a minority of men in time or space. But the scale of its operations has increased over the centuries—from Greek or Italian city states to constitutional monarchies of the scale of Britain and on to a vast continental federation in the United States. The next extension of freedom as the organizing principle of government must be intercontinental in scope. Nothing less is physically sufficient in the age of instant communication and supersonic flight. Nothing else is spiritually flexible enough to contain peacefully the clashing faiths, the contradictory purposes, the vitalities, insights, and visions of protean human nature. Deny this possibility and freedom loses its creative role in building a political framework for the coming world society.

Communism, on the contrary, accepts—or rather seeks—the opportunity. Mr. Khrushchev proposes to himself nothing less than a world over all of which waves the flag of Communism. He, at least, does not believe in the survival of a world half-slave, half-free. But if freedom is to maintain its hold on men's hopes and allegiance, it cannot accept a shrinking role. The capture of another vast society by Communism, a further lurch to the side of tyranny, yet another suggestion that freedom belongs with the setting, not the rising sun—these possibilities would so weaken Western confidence and staying power, so increase Communism's overweening confidence and ambition, lead to such an access of that dizziness through success against which even Stalin warned his people, that the outcome could be to precipitate the ultimate struggle from which neither the Communists nor the West nor indeed the world itself would emerge in any state save that of annihilation. It is therefore not a metaphor but sober truth to say that India's experiment of economic growth within the framework of political freedom can be decisive for the whole future of mankind.

In the pages that follow the attempt is made to document more fully the dramatic significance of the Indian plans. They cannot be properly assessed in isolation. They belong in the mainstream of three great contemporary revolutions—the development of the mixed economy and of welfare-capitalism in the West, the counter-revolution of Communist ideology and State capitalism in Russia and China, and the unavoidable duel between these two revolutions for influence in the excolonial and uncommitted world. Without this wider context, the Indian experiment, vital though it is in its own right, loses its extra edge of worldwide significance. The first section of this book, therefore, attempts to set the scene and sketch the fateful dialogue between Communism and the West before bringing India to the centre of the stage and examining more closely the background, inspiration, obstacles and achievements of the Indian plans.

Chapter Two

The First Breakthrough

IT IS not always easy for
people in the West to grasp that the aim of the Indian
plans is to achieve for India the processes of growth and
modernization which Western society has already undergone. The initial Western time of strain and saving has
passed into history. And in some of the key communities
of the West, the economic revolution did not have to be
planned at all. A fortunate conjunction of circumstances
made it happen in a sort of spontaneous combustion. In
Britain, where the modern economy first emerged, the
three or four decisive changes which must occur in every
country in the course of modernization had been gathering momentum over several centuries, before their general acceleration at the end of the eighteenth century produced an economy which was new in kind. To understand what these changes are one must look at the typical

organization of the economy before the advent of modern science and technology.

This economy is parochial, based on an economic unit often no bigger than the village or the estate. Its wealth is primarily in land; but agriculture is a way of life, not a market activity. Whatever the type of farmer—feudal landholder, peasant owner, tribal cultivator—they all produce for themselves and not for sale to others. The artisan and the merchant tend to play a marginal role. They lack prestige compared with the men in government, religion, or agriculture. Literacy is largely confined to a small class of rulers, priests, and scholars. The whole range of economic activity is limited by relatively narrow possibilities of technique and manufacture. The merchant can often become rich; but he is then an easy prey for the royal taxgatherers. His instinct is therefore to consume rather than to save, or to acquire status by acquiring land. In any case, the amount of capital he can employ is restricted, like his merchandise, by the limitations of pre-scientific technology. The speed of a horse, the skill of a hand, the heat of charcoal, the force of water or wind—these are the limits of innovation until, in the seventeenth and eighteenth centuries, science begins to batter the barriers down.

Such societies do some saving. Saving is, after all, simply not consuming. If a community were to consume everything it produced, it would be reduced to hunting or food gathering. Once farming is the dominant mode of life, men must put by seedcorn for the next harvest, they have to clear land, mend drains and ditches, and prepare the fields for resowing. All this amounts to saving and investment; but in static, traditional society the level is probably below 5 per cent of national income each year and does little more than keep the economy moving from harvest to harvest. In fact, the only large innovations possible in traditional agriculture are to clear more land or to make more effective use of water power; and neither has a cumulative effect upon general investment.

Irrigation does indeed require capital, effort, and organization on a considerable scale; and it seems likely that man's first more elaborate experiments in civilization occurred in the great river valleys—along the Nile, the Euphrates, the Ganges, and the Yellow River—where waterpower was used as the basis for ambitious irrigation. But neither irrigation nor land clearance sets in motion a progressive process of expanding saving and investment. Once the limits of land or water are reached, there is nothing more to be done; and this fact is undoubtedly at the root of much of the recurrent turbulence in man's unquiet history.

If population increases beyond available resources, the outcome is the old fatal cycle of China: peace encourages births; births press on the available land; the peasants fall into debt and starvation; banditry and civil war follow; peace vanishes; population falls; and then, after the restoration of new imperial leadership, the cycle begins again. When the alien Manchus established the Ching dynasty in the seventeenth century, the population of China was probably some 60 million souls. Two centuries later, the figure had multiplied five times. The Emperors did what they could. More land was cleared on the frontiers of the Empire, and before their dynasty fell, the Manchus could claim to have undertaken two-thirds of all China's irrigation. But the inexorable tide of births continued to rise. By 1850, the phase of disintegration had begun again.

The Chinese cycle is the most ancient, the most continuous, and the most documented illustration of the limits of the old technology. But other societies have dissolved under similar pressures and wherever today subsistence farming still remains the basis of society—as it does, for instance, in many parts of India—the pressures can revive with, if anything, more virulence than ever, since populations now increase more sharply and the old fatalism of static societies is eroding away.

But in Britain, long before the eighteenth century, the hallmarks of traditional society had begun to vanish. The small parochial unit of economic activity began to be replaced by a national framework forged in the military struggles with France and Spain, and in competitive merchant ventures against Portugal and Holland. All our evidence suggests that the first stages of economic development demand such a national setting. These new techniques draw the whole community into their operations, and they require for efficiency a larger communal unit than the old village economy. At the other end of the scale, vast societies like the Indian or Chinese lack the needed sense of purpose and cohesion; and in any case, they are in economic reality only congeries of tiny local units.

Thus the nation-state seems to have been the first political unit both cohesive enough and wide enough to incubate successfully the forces of economic growth and the division of labour needed for modernization. Certainly in the hundred and fifty years since British society underwent its transformation, the connection between nationalism and modernization has been almost one of cause and effect; nothing spurs the desire for development more than the sense of being a national community.

The passing of the parochial economic unit had other aspects. By the eighteenth century, British agriculture had long ceased to be based on subsistence and prestige.

Landlords first turned to the market at the end of the
Middle Ages when they began to enclose the old communal lands of subsistence farming and turn them into
sheep runs for the production of wool for sale. In the
eighteenth century, another great wave of enclosures
marked the development all over Britain of scientific
farming based on new techniques, new crops, and new
livestock for the market; Bakewell experimented with
sheep breeding, "Turnip" Townshend with winter feed,
Coke of Holkham with marling and crop rotation.

In Britain, too—as in much of Western Europe—the
merchant had long enjoyed an honourable and influential
position. In the great cities he could rise to responsible
government; there was never an Asian equivalent of Lord
Mayor of London or Bürgermeister of Ghent. The opening of trade with the Orient and the discovery of the New
World enlarged his opportunities enormously. He was
able to accumulate wealth without inhibiting fear of arbitrary royal confiscations. His Protestantism taught him
the value of hard work for profit, and discouraged him
from spending the result in riotous living. His private
savings were made more effective and investable by the
growth of a modern credit system. Modern banking had
come into being in the great cities of Europe two centuries and more before the industrial revolution. In the
eighteenth century, the spread of country banking
throughout Britain extended credit to a new range of
entrepreneurs.

Manufacturing had taken widespread hold in Britain
even before the eighteenth century. Sea coal came by
ship from the North to London, iron ore was smelted in
charcoal furnaces, the water power of the Pennines began
to be used to provide power for cloth mills. What the
eighteenth century did was to provide an active tribe of

potters and ironmasters and millowners with new possibilities of securing credit and with massive openings for technical innovation. And since, in a culture based on popular reading of the Bible, a very wide level of literacy had existed for some centuries, the artisan class had an indispensable tool at hand to help it grasp the new opportunities.

Here we touch upon the profoundest element of change. When after the bitterness of Europe's religious wars men's minds turned from theology to the natural sciences, a host of experimenters and inventors arose in Britain who were driven by the desire to experiment and innovate and to break down technical barriers to greater efficiency and productivity.

One man can be taken as typical of them all: John Wilkinson, who devoted his life to a visionary and single-minded development of the uses of iron. He made iron ships, iron bridges, iron docks, even an iron church; and he had himself buried in an iron coffin. His enterprises spread from Creusot to Cornwall. He was one of the first of the large entrepreneurs, uniting in a single business system mines and foundries, wharves and ships. And he was only one in a whole generation of new men, also experimenting, seizing on the experiments of others, developing new inventions and patents, investing in their hunches, drawing golden profits one year, straining credit to the limits of bankruptcy the next—and all the while, without conscious plan but with irresistible effect, setting in motion the transformation of the whole economy.

British society had thus been diverging from traditional patterns for some considerable time before the second half of the eighteenth century. Why, then, should one speak of a revolution or a "breakthrough" or, to use Professor W. W. Rostow's vivid metaphor, a "take-off" into a new kind of economy? The reason is fundamentally a question of scale and interaction. The changes had all begun to occur before; but after 1750 they all came together, expanded together, acted upon each other, and stimulated further joint development. The analogy of "take-off" is helpful, since it gives the impression of the whole economy, like an aircraft on the runway, gathering sufficient momentum to leave the old limitations behind and operate in what was in fact a new type of economy. Each change by itself would not have had this effect. The crucial point is that the changes were cumulative.

Agriculture has to be transformed to produce for the market. Otherwise there is not enough bread and meat for the new cities, with their expanding industrial sectors which produce no food but must be fed. Equally, agriculture must, in countries of relative underpopulation such as eighteenth-century Britain, yield workers to the urban sectors and still produce more food. Output and productivity both need to go up on the farms. But productivity is a matter of better methods, more science, more experiments, more machines; and many of these changes demand a growing industrial sector where the fertilizers and the improved implements can be produced. The "industrial revolution" is thus a somewhat misleading term with which to describe the changes that must precede modernization. Farming and industry alike have to be transformed by the new technology and the new openings for investment.

With industry, too, the cumulative effect is equally striking. By the late eighteenth century, inventions were beginning to come in great clusters, each making possible new developments in other fields. The steam engine could not have been technically improved without new methods of iron-making. It would have been useless to apply the new power engines to manufacturing if the old system of roads—neglected, pot-holed quagmires—had kept the new flow of goods immobilized at the factory gate. New canals were dug, energetic turnpike trusts remade the roads, coastal shipping grew, docks were built—thirty acres of docks at London alone before 1810, making it the greatest port in the world. The stage was then set for the most vital of all the early technical innovations, the development of railways, which in country after country was to prove a major factor in the early stages of growth, mobilizing capital, bringing country and town together in a common national market, stimulating coal mines and steel-making, extending the engineering industries, and allowing bulk trade in raw materials to expand all round the globe.

Much of this expansion could not have occurred otherwise than in the middle of a general revolution of economic growth. The basic capital of an industrial society—the "infrastructure" or overhead in the shape of railways, roads, docks, industrial housing, mechanics' institutes, the first schools, power installations—all entail a heavy investment and one which does not always promise quick returns. Moreover, few of these investments can begin in a small way and expand as demand expands. They have to be complete or they are useless. A railway from London to Manchester cannot stop at Rugby and still serve the same purpose. So savings absorbed in the basic services must be provided in large sums. They presuppose a certain wealth; yet they are the precondition of further wealth. Only development with a marked rhythm of expansion can finance them and still provide capital for further advance.

Scale affects development in another way. One isolated factory cannot endlessly expand its product—say, of calico cloth—because its own workers will soon be supplied and other groups may not be earning the rising wages which permit them to buy more cloth themselves. But a whole group of industries can shop with each other, expand with each other, and add to each other's success by pushing up demand and production to the point of maximum efficiency. This expansion of the whole system is exactly what occurred at the end of the eighteenth century.

The nature of the breakthrough to modernization can be expressed in another way. As we have seen, the limitations of traditional prescientific technology set a low ceiling on investment. It was, after all, no use devoting work and saving to techniques which in the end made the investor no better off. But the revolutionary change brought about by the development of scientific techniques is that it enormously increases the number of ways in which both food and other resources can be produced in greater bulk with less work, time, and effort. For the same reason, it frees resources for further expansion, so that the process can become cumulative. When Coke of Holkham gave his tenants long leases on the condition that they practised a strict rotation of crops, the output of food increased sharply. Thus, without additional work, there was food available not only for Coke and his tenants but also for the stream of Irish labourers who were swarming over to build the Duke of Bridgewater's canal. The canal in turn halved the cost of coal delivered in Manchester. With the added margin, Manchester artisans could experiment with new textile machines. Once the machines had cut the cost of cloth, the labourer after buying his overalls, had a little money to spare for his children's shirts as well. The savings made on one improved technique could thus be invested to improve other techniques. The beneficent change moved round the whole economic chain, each expansion helping all the rest.

With so many new opportunities for profitable invest-ment, the amount invested rose steeply. As it rose from 5 to 10 per cent of national income and climbed onward to 12 and 15 per cent, the volume became sufficient to cover the increase in population, leave some margin for increased consumption, and yet each year add to the re-sources available for still more saving. At a rough esti-mate, a 3 per cent increase in capital is needed to produce a 1 per cent increase in income. Thus, when new capital investment passes the level of 12 per cent of national income, it begins to produce a steady increase of at least 4 per cent in national income, a figure well beyond the most rapid increase likely in the growth of population—the biological maximum appears to be about 3 per cent a year. The old locked and guarded door—the threshold where population reaches the limit of resources—is burst open. Beyond it, mankind begins to experiment in new realms of growth.

Yet the leap in capital investment from 5 to 15 per cent of national income is formidable. A fully developed economy, equipped with basic services, with a network of transport, with cities built and machines installed, with an educated population and widespread facilities for re-search and further scientific innovation—such an economy can, if it manages its investment program sensibly, both save and consume comfortably on the basis of its sub-stantial existing resources. If its population is stable, it can probably prosper on annual savings of less than 12 per cent. The level is not absolute. A 15 per cent figure only suggests the scale required in the early stages of develop-ment, when population is still growing sharply. But how can this original momentum be achieved? The effort has to be large, interlocking, and sustained. However unwill-

ingly, nature must be made to take a jump. By definition
the underdeveloped economy is relatively poor. How can
it mobilize enough resources to force the breakthrough,
to reach the acceleration needed for take-off into future
growth?

To mobilize resources means not to use them for current consumption, but to devote them to instruments, procedures, and work which increase a later flow of goods.
For the wealthy this is not too difficult, since they have
margins from which to supply capital while still maintaining their habitual standards of living. But in no society have the monied group alone had enough resources
to set in motion the really massive saving that underlies
the transformation of a static into a dynamic economy.
Not all the merchants and bankers in the City of London,
not all Britain's dukes and country gentlemen, not all the
hard-fisted, cost-conscious artisans of the northern towns
had enough spare resources to finance unaided the revolution in which they were all engaged. The surplus had to
come from savings imposed on the mass of the people.

Their consumption did not rise—it may even have
fallen—as the new methods released new resources for
human use. Thus the bulk of the additional wealth was
available for further investment. To the workers in the
villages and cities went little more than was needed to
keep them and their families alive; and a child of eight,
working in mill or mine, does not need much to keep it
alive. The labourers had no vote. If they tried to combine
in unions to improve their lot, they were shipped off in
convict ships to Australia. Not until the middle of the
nineteenth century did the vast productivity of the new
industrial machine begin to spill its benefits over into
greater mass consumption. Not until the 1860s did industrial unions begin to exercise real influence. In the first

bleak decades of industrialization, the new wealth enriched its organizers and expanded the whole base of production. But the labouring poor in slums and hovels paid a large part of the bill.

These, then, were the conditions of the first decisive transformation of a traditional economy into the new pattern of dynamic growth. All later efforts of the same kind have occurred under the same conditions: the growth of nationalism to form a coherent self-conscious national unit; the emergence of new leaders bent on development; the spread of literacy; a transformation of agriculture from subsistence farming to production for the market; a powerful thrust of industrialization which, beginning in one or two sectors, supplies the impulse for general expansion; and a massive original effort of saving, which usually entails great hardship, but which nonetheless provides the underlying energy for the primary drive to growth.

Since the British breakthrough, nation after nation has drawn its anchor up from the sands of an unchanging agricultural past and set out on the open, hazardous seas of growth and change. As might be expected, the societies that were most akin to Britain made the passage first —Western Europe, North America, the overseas territories of British settlement. For all of them, the journey was in one sense easier than it had been for Britain. A chart, however rough, was in being, the British chart. But each society has its own rocks and shoals to pass.

Lack of national unity held Germany and Italy back until late in the century. The French Revolution removed France's feudal superstructure but left peasant agriculture intact; today, nearly two hundred years later, agricultural output is still impeded by tiny farms, divided holdings and inefficient techniques. Even in North America where the way was eased by vast national resources, by an almost total lack of feudal or subsistence farming, by enterprising men, a growing labour supply and capital from abroad, some areas were resistant to change—the plantation system based on slavery in the South, French peasant society in Quebec. In Southern Europe, whole regions, such as Sicily and Spain, were moored so deeply in a feudal past that the ship groaned and strained but stayed at anchor.

Outside the Atlantic area, the roots have proved even deeper, the break from immobility even harder to make. The whole drama of India's plans lies precisely in both the ambition and the strain of the attempt. But the process has begun. Just as millennia ago, agriculture gradually drove the hunters and nomads to the fringes of settled land, so now the new society based on science and technology has begun to supersede the old world of subsistence farming and limited trade. The aim is everywhere the same. The profound differences spring from the variety of local traditions and resources and increasingly from decisive differences in the techniques of expansion.

Chapter Three

Growth by Trial and Error

THE FRAMEWORK of economic expansion is determined at every turn by politics. Once the whole modernized aparatus with its cities, schools, factories, power stations, roads, and railway tracks has been constructed, it is no longer an end in itself. It becomes an instrument of the community's social and political purpose, a sort of machine in being which can be used for all manner of ends, good and bad—and it is politics that determine what these ends will be.

For this reason, we can leave out of account some of the most economically resourceful but politically barren of the economic breakthroughs which followed after the Britain experience. In Germany, Russia, and Japan—all in the closing decades of the nineteenth century—the traditional leaders of society, the feudal lords, the military cadres, the Court, and the higher officials, launched their societies into economic modernization. What chiefly impressed them about the British model of economic expansion was how vastly it had increased Britain's national power, prosperity and prestige. They set out to achieve the same, putting most of their emphasis on power: in other words, on a modern military establishment. Since modern arms require iron and steel, improved transport, heavy industry, technicians, and literate conscripts, militarization is a potent form of modernization; and in a few years, the three societies were well on the way to economic growth.

It is also just conceivable that if war could have been avoided, the sheer extension of their economies would have brought into being a professional and middle class influential enough to substitute more civilized economic and social purposes for the government's overwhelming preoccupation with power. Between the wars such a group did appear and briefly dominate politics in Japan. But at the end of the nineteenth century, the modernization, under largely feudal and traditional leadership, coincided with the decay of three ancient empires— Turkey and its old opponent Austria-Hungary in Europe, China in the Far East. Into this vacuum of power the emergent nations were violently drawn in 1914, largely to keep each other out. And since, after four years of suicidal conflict, the old vacuum very largely remained, while the victorious Powers made a Gadarene rush back to the "normalcy" of pre-1914, it was only a couple of decades before the conditions which had created 1914 returned and plunged the world once again into virtually the same war.

The political consequences of militarized modernization were thus almost wholly evil. The nations in a sense recognized this fact themselves; and after each struggle, they attempted to create the framework of more liberal politics. The economic consequences proved more complex. The wars undoubtedly illustrated the appalling destructiveness of modern industry and science when applied to arms. But they also suggested the extraordinary expansion of production that could be achieved if all labour and all saving were dedicated by the government to the tasks of war. Total mobilization passed into history with far-reaching results. Nonetheless, the human cost of such an effort made it unlikely that it could be permanently incorporated into the working institutions of mankind. Outbursts of total military violence are not, after all, new. The Assyrians, the Mongols, the Nazis each in turn have proved that total aggression, however mobilized, ends by defeating itself.

The decisive patterns in economic growth must be looked for elsewhere in the mixed experimental societies of the West and the planned ideological societies developing under Communism. This is the significant distinction, this is the real drama of opposites on the world's stage; and it has been inherent in the processes of growth ever since the two possible patterns began to exercise their direct and potent influence upon the shape of politics.

Among the early political economists, Marx above all had the insight to see how deeply contemporary changes in economic organization would affect the balance of power in the political community. The pattern he foresaw of slavery giving way to feudalism, feudalism to capitalism, and capitalism to communism was too total and too apocalyptic to fit the facts about everyday divergent humanity. But it contained a core of truth: that political dominance in society shifts when new levers of economic power come into new hands, and the old rural parochial economy, with its emphasis on self-sufficiency and status, gives way to a nationwide market based on competition, ambition, profit, and skill. The new men feel the old methods and patterns as intolerable restraints, the old leaders fear and resist changes which erode their power. Everything at this point depends upon the flexibility and elasticity of minds and institutions in the community. If there is no "give" in the political structure, if the old rulers entrench themselves and make no concession, the impatience of the newcomers is inevitably channelled into violent and apocalyptic visions of what must be done to break down resistance. If no part of the old order can be touched, the alternative seems inescapably to lie in sweeping away the whole structure and beginning again. Equally, if accommodations can be made and the processes of reform at least begin, the radical temper lacks the incentive to seek total solutions. Men are content to wait and change and reform, share power, and extend their influence gradually.

In the first stages of modernization, Britain and France provided models of these two opposite possibilities. The French political system remained a rigid exclusive oligarchy too long. Reforming energies turned to violent visions of the scale of change that would be needed in order to change anything at all. Jean-Jacques Rousseau produced his fantasy of society remade by the uncorrupted will of the whole people—a General Will in whose name government could create a new ideal condition purged of the encrusted evils of the past, a condition in which mighty absolutes—absolute Liberty, absolute Equality and absolute Fraternity—would be achieved in one great act of political destiny. When the Revolution at last broke out, this mood, not the more modest reforming tendencies of the unfranchised middle class, swept the country into the new tyranny of a total mass state.

In Britain, on the contrary, flexible institutions and a more moderate spirit of reform interacted upon each other to produce not a single violent revolutionary upheaval, but a steady process of accommodation. It must be remembered that Britain in the eighteenth century was still very far from being either a liberal or a humane society. Its parliamentary system and civil liberties were essentially limited, and had been largely designed to safeguard the wealthy and influential citizen against the actions of government. They did not protect the mass of the people. Most men had no vote. Some of the laws governing the poor—property laws, game laws—were profoundly oppressive. Men might endure the horrors of deportation to Australia in floating Belsens simply for the theft of a shilling's worth of cloth. Without reform, such a society would have headed toward uncontrollable violence. But the ideal of the citizen's rights and of limited government proved sufficiently flexible to incorporate the rising interests of the new men. Enough of the old rulers—Whig magnates or Tory gentlemen—had the instinct of sound government: which is to know when to concede. The Reform Bill of 1832 set in motion the extension of the rights and liberties of the few to the people at large.

The mood of concession also reflected the relative moderation of the reformers. The spirit of the enlightenment in Britain did not turn to extravaganzas of total change. The radicals, the Tory reformers, the evangelical leaders attacked abuses in particular, not some graven image of Abuse. They reformed the economics of government, the legal system, the lunacy laws; they set up sanitary commissions; they examined the fixed habits—and undeniable evils—of government in the light, not of the New Jerusalem, but of cool reason and utilitarian principle. What they sought—the greatest good of the greatest number—was radical enough in the context of the times. But it was not irrational. It did not claim to bring a new heaven and a new earth. It did not threaten present rulers with extinction, and, as a result, they responded by permitting flexibility and "give" in government. Thus constitutional government based on ancient liberties fused with reforming liberalism to provide a plural, decentralized, libertarian framework for the new economy. Britain cleared without catastrophe the first hurdle of development: a head-on collision between the old, agrarian, conservative and ruling class and the new men bent on innovation and reform.

Other societies had similar good fortune, among them, European communities such as Switzerland, the Low Countries, and Scandinavia which combined strong traditions of civil liberties with very little feudal superstructure. The United States was in a sense "born free," inheriting Britain's constitutional system and no feudal class or tradition at all; other overseas communities of British settlement also enjoyed similar political foundations. But in few other areas could this particular pattern be repeated. In all of Asia, India alone has had anything comparable in the way of a lengthy liberal indoctrination. And especially where strong feudal structures or ancient traditions of despotism provided the background for modernization, the apocalyptic tendencies of change by violence remained strong—as they do to this day.

The nature of the political settlement in 1832 had profound consequences for the next phase of economic development. The men who began to share parliamentary power after the Reform Bill represented the new spirit of reform. Few decades have seen so much practical, rational change of institutions and customs as occurred in the 1830s. But the attitudes of these men included the belief that in the new developing economy the most rational way of running the economic system was to leave it to run itself. This conviction about the beneficence of *laissez faire* had many strands. The instinct to limit government as such had a deep hold on British constitutional tradition. In the particular context of the economy, many rising businessmen felt they had to battle their way through a maze of bureaucratic controls, mercantilist restrictions, monopolies and special interests in order to get a clear run at the market. Their vision of government was that of Dickens in *Little Dorrit:* a vast Circumlocution Office full of Tite Barnacles practising the dedicated art of seeing that nothing ever got done.   1256158

But the chief reason for their faith in *laissez faire* lay in the fact that in this first British version of the world's revolution of modernization a sudden vast expansion of wealth and power did follow from men pursuing profit in the open market. There might be other ways of achieving that result. But no one knew what they were. In the first half of the nineteenth century there was thus only one working model of rapid expansion; and it was grounded in *laissez faire* and the profit motive.

The new men—industrialists, aspiring artisans, small traders, the host of rising entrepreneurs of the new order —were not in their own way of thinking launching a revolution. They were making money, as much money as they could. It was the country's good fortune that this policy should also have been the one most likely, in the new environment of scientific and technological opportunity, to produce the maximum expansion in the output of wealth.

Profit represents the difference between the real resources invested in the production of an article or a service and the real resources a purchaser is prepared to give up to secure it. In a relatively wide and unrestricted market —the market, for instance, of eighteenth-century Britain, organized as a nation state and increasingly unified by better transport—the man who made the largest profits was the man who, while using his resources most economically, still satisfied his customer and made a sale. The greater his capacity to cut costs, to combine his resources in the most economic proportions, to foresee taste and anticipate needs, the greater his profits; and from his profit margin came not only his own reward but the expansion of capital needed for further investment and hence for further growth.

Nor was profit, then or now, simply a guide to the market. It also creates a broad system of priorities. If between two or three alternative methods of production, or two or three alternative types of product, one promises to earn the larger profit, this becomes the best guarantee that resources are being used most economically and devoted to the needs that are making themselves most urgently felt.

The capacity to seize such opportunities in the present market and to look with shrewd calculation into that pit of uncertainty which is a future market demands special gifts: a spirit of experiment and perseverance, an accurate capacity for estimating future returns, a certain resilience after defeats and setbacks. For this reason, the entrepreneurial talent which began to flourish so widely in Britain as the revolution of growth took hold was more than mere money-grubbing. Men who only wanted money could go on being what they had always been—speculators, gamblers on the market, hoarders, landlords gobbling up rents, merchants intent on cornering supplies for a quick sale. The true entrepreneurs were men like John Wilkinson, experimenting passionately in the uses of iron, and building around his experiments the organization of a whole new industry. A sense of enterprise, a sense of achievement, ability to create an organism that would last and work through time—all these entered into the entrepreneurial drive for which profit provided reward and zest and further scope, but not the only motive.

Thus, in the first decades of the new economy, the profit motive seemed an almost miraculous instrument of growth. It enormously reinforced the belief that a man must be pursuing the common good most efficiently when he pursues his own. The poet, Pope, speaking for all eighteenth-century optimists, had been right. "Self love" and "social" were the same. From this it was only a short step to the argument that any interference with the free movement of the market, any modifying of the iron laws of supply and demand, would inevitably break the delicate central mechanism by which entrepreneurial energy flowed through the whole vast and growing system. *Laissez faire* not only worked. Alternatives to it might not work at all.

The miseries of the poor, the wretched labours of little children, squalid slums, desperate outbreaks of industrial unrest, the disproportionate growth of wealth among those who were wealthy already—they were simply costs, regrettable perhaps but inevitable, that had to be paid in return for the increase in power and wealth of the community as a whole. This attitude was not all hardness of heart or social complacency. There never had been a human society in which the workers, especially in the cities, had not lived very near the edge of misery. Private charity might relieve individual want, but "the poor ye have always with you." Only visionaries had the idea that the new machines might bring a modest comfort within reach of all; and the language of some of these visionaries—one thinks of Fourier's phalansteries and free love—was not precisely convincing. In fact, few people felt that they knew how the system really did work. They stood around it like inexperienced mechanics, uncertain whether any tinkering with the engine might not bring everything to a standstill with a last, melancholy, expiring spurt of steam.

That men who were doing well out of the system should want no change is understandable. But theorists and philosophers, as well as thrusting industrialists, felt deeply the danger of playing about with the workings of ineluctable economic law. Richard Cobden and John Bright were men of conscience and integrity. But they still thought child labour laws and factory regulations endangered the whole free enterprise system; and this conviction was destined to survive long after their generation and even after it became clear that the system was much more tough and resilient than its apprehensive supporters supposed—and still suppose.

Such views may seem fantasy to-day. Yet in the context of the first economic breakthrough, they had a rational base. The profound belief in the indispensability of *laissez faire* simply reflected the success of the system and the lack of any known alternative. But as the century developed, the picture grew less clear. From the first, the economy showed signs of instability. It proceeded in irregular spurts—the ups and down of the business cycle— and since banking was still relatively disorganized and limited liability did not become the basis of business enterprise until the mid-nineteenth century, the downturns of the cycle brought bursts of bankruptcy and intense financial instability. And there were deeper uncertainties. Once the first burst of saving and investment had created the framework of a modernized economy, what forces would sustain continued momentum? Would the profit motive be enough? Would it function with the old efficiency? It was not wild-eyed revolutionaries who asked these disturbing questions, but sober fathers of political economy such as Adam Smith, Malthus, Ricardo, and John Stuart Mill. And their answers were not altogether reassuring. They saw a number of convincing reasons why, beyond a certain point, the rhythm of expansion would slow down and even stop.

There is a limit to the labour and resources that can be devoted to any one enterprise. After a certain point, extra investment of work or saving does not give an equivalent increase in profit. The entrepreneur then has no reason to push expansion further. One can imagine a total economy in which every sector has gone through a cycle of growth and consolidation. The general momentum would then be bound to slacken unless a whole new range of inventions and demands came into being. And it was not easy to tell in advance if this would always be the case.

This was not the only trend making for slower growth. The labour which could be drawn into new industries from agriculture, urban unemployment, petty trading, or domestic work was not unlimited—at least in the West. Once there were more jobs than workers, the men would bid up the price for their labour, especially if politically they had earned the right to combine in trade unions.

The same pressures could be exerted by scarcity of land or other resources. Once the economy needed more of these than might be available, their prices, too, would rise. The difficulty could become especially acute in the case of food in Britain. By the end of the Napoleonic Wars, the demand for food was already outrunning output on British farms. Ricardo's picture of cultivation be-

ing expensively extended up the hillsides and food costs
rising catastrophically seemed real enough before overseas investment opened up the breadbaskets of North
America and the Ukraine.

Caught between higher costs for labour and higher
costs for resources, the entrepreneur would find his margin
of profit whittled away. He might prefer not to undertake
the work, the anxiety, the risk of a new venture at all if
the final result would no more than cover his costs—and
if it might not even do that. For a time, no doubt, buoyancy could be maintained by investing abroad in territories where land and labour were still abundant. But at
some point a tendency toward stagnation might become
inescapable. Fresh investment would no longer be undertaken in the "mature" economy; and incomes, employment, prospects, hopes would all alike slip into stagnation.

This stagnation might not even occur at a particularly
high level. Although there was room for a definite increase
in general living standards in the first stages of growth,
there could be no guarantee that reductions in the rate
of profit might not set in long before the bulk of workers
and farm labourers had reached a level of income covering more than their ordinary needs. And at this still low
level of purchasing power, markets would be unlikely to
keep up with the steadily increasing productivity and
output of the new machines. The risk of "over-production"
—which was really under-consumption—would intensify
the entrepreneurs' lack of confidence. The whole economy
would tend to settle at a level of output far below either
industry's capacity to produce or the people's potential
capacity to consume. Yet a solution could not be found
solely through the operations of the profit motive. It was
precisely the low level of profit that had produced this

situation in the first place. Thus, at some stage beyond the original breakthrough to steady growth, far from profit providing the guarantee that the best use would be made of scarce resources, the economy's primary reliance on the profit motive could easily become the reason why so many resources were not being used at all.

The early political economists—with the vigorous exception of Karl Marx, whose strictures will be examined later—had no positive answers to give to these possible risks. It was not entirely unjust to accuse them—as they were accused—of evolving "a gloomy science." And in some measure the next phase in the West's economic revolution bore out some of their more discouraging predictions. As community after community came to the end of the primary thrust of growth and acquired the institutions and techniques of a well-developed economy, there was a perceptible slowing down in the momentum of growth, followed not too long after by the first signs of stagnation. The tempo of British development began to slacken toward the end of the nineteenth century; and after an interval of feverish expansion and destruction during the First World War, the whole of Western Europe slowed to a standstill, the failure of each country's economy further depressing the prospects of its neighbours'.

The most disturbing feature of the stagnation was the emergence of massive unemployment, which left the resources of the community consistently under-utilized. To this problem, as the early political economists had foreseen, sole reliance on the profit motive was no answer. Depressed markets produced low profits and low profits helped to perpetuate depressed markets. When, in the 1930s, Keynes published his *General Theory*, he pointed out that the supposed classical equilibrium between de-

mand and supply was based on the belief that the flow
of goods generated by the economy would be absorbed
by the consumption and saving to which they gave rise.
But if low profit margins discouraged the entrepreneur
from investing, if he preferred to hoard his savings instead
—in short, to save without investing—the balance was
destroyed and the economy, far from achieving a real if
fluctuating advance, might bog down at a level well below its productive capacities and even decline. Here in
fact was practical proof of the old fear that, beyond a
certain point, the free economy would cease to generate
its own powers of expansion. Since, in Keynes's day, the
banks were full of deposits and the streets with men on
the dole—and no human wit appeared able to bring these
two surpluses of capital and labour together—it was not a
very revolutionary conclusion to believe that the main-
spring of the classical economists, private profit, was in
need of repair. A more radical view of course was that it
should be dropped altogether.

Even the most generously endowed economy of all—
the United States—seemed to fall into a sort of immobility in the 1930s. The talk was all of the closing frontier,
of the problems of maturity—or, less politely, of stagnation—and the impossibility of moving the becalmed ship
back, at least by any customary or accepted compass, into
the main stream of hope and growth.

Yet today, this same Atlantic world has moved onward
to standards of mass prosperity undreamt of by even the
most optimistic nineteenth-century visionaries. How were
the forecasts of the gloomy science thus disproved, the
rigidities and inevitabilities overcome, the iron ring of
immutable economic law broken, just when it seemed to
be about to close? The answer is: not one thing, but many
things. Just as a series of unrelated pre-conditions oc-

curring together in the single community of Britain launched the whole experiment of modernization, so another set of conditions, not formally related to each other and scattered over the Atlantic arena, have set the stage for a new surge of economic advance.

Chapter Four

The Mixed Economy

THE NEW pattern reflects some vital changes within the framework of private enterprise. Two, in particular, had pervasive and radical effects. The early fathers of political economy could hardly have foreseen what the enormous expansion of scientific research would do both to productivity and to new inventions in agriculture and industry. There is room for rising profits and rising wages provided new techniques continue to increase output per man hour. And there seems no end to the innovations—in materials, in methods, in products, in salesmanship—that new research can produce year after year in a developed economy. The doors of technology were not so narrow as the early economists supposed. Certainly, these men would have totally disbelieved the phenomenon of the American farmer steadily producing a higher crop from a smaller acreage.

Another decisive change in the structure of industry began with Henry Ford's Model T, which foreshadowed the age of mass production of consumer goods going far beyond the old range of food, apparel, and household needs. Ford's decision to pay wages high enough to create a new market for such goods and to recoup profits by a small return on a vast turnover also had revolutionary implications. He proved that moderate profits need not deprive industry of its essential incentive, provided the operations were on a sufficient scale. Thus he showed a way around the old roadblock of profitability falling as labour and materials rose in price.

There is a perhaps apocryphal story about a similar time and theme in Europe. The directors of a successful Italian firm of automobile manufacturers were informed that their cars had the competitive edge on any other make in Europe. "Good," they replied. "Halve the output and double the price." In terms of immediate returns, this answer may well have been more profitable than Henry Ford's. Only their way was the highroad to stagnation, his was not.

But the decisive changes were political. In the West, the constitutional system continued to prove its flexibility by absorbing the aims and ambitions of new groups and interests thrust forward by economic development. Throughout the nineteenth century, qualifications for voting were widened, more and more of the population secured enfranchisement, a mass electorate came into being. And since in any society the poor outnumber the well-to-do, the interests of the workers could not be neglected by parties in search of a majority.

To the mechanics of politics should be added a profound and widespread sense of social concern. From the earliest days of industrialism, the argument that men should not interfere with the laws of supply and demand had been countered by appeals to higher laws of justice and charity. Christian reformers such as Lord Shaftesbury were pioneers in securing government action for factory reform and the limitation of working hours. When men spoke of the evils that might flow from impeding the workings of the market, the reformers replied, in terms of moral judgment, that for children of six to fall and die in the machines they were tending was an evil before God and man that no economic theory could warrant, no economic gain redeem.

The rising middle class, more comfortable and influential as each decade went by, had their consciences continuously disturbed by a whole literature of protest. Charles Dickens's masterpieces—*Bleak House, Hard Times, Little Dorrit*—showed them an aristocratic society in decay and a new inhuman materialist industrialism growing like a cancer within it. But perhaps no words Dickens wrote in his novels evoke so vividly the hopelessness of the very poor as the terrible description of a slum in St. Mark's, which occurs in one of his letters to Baroness Burdett-Coutts.

In a broken-down gallery at the back of a row of these [wooden houses] there was a wan child looking over at a starved old white horse who was making a meal of oyster shells. The sun was going down and flaring out like an angry fire at the child—and the child and I and the pale horse stared at one another in silence for some five minutes as if we were so many figures in a dismal allegory. . . . Lord knows when anybody will go into the child, but I suppose it's looking over still—with a little ivory head of hair, as pale as the horse, all sticking up on its head—and an old weazen face—and two bony hands holding on the rail of the gallery, with little fingers like convulsed skewers.

Yet the context of the letter is significant. It was written to the heiress of a great banking fortune; Dickens was advising her how best to spend her wealth in aid of just such waifs and outcasts as the pale child in the forgotten slum. Devoted and dedicated men and women buying up derelict properties, building "model dwellings for the labouring poor," opening church schools, founding hospitals, and encouraging thrift and self-help, were pioneers and pathfinders for the day when the governing groups, prodded by the reformers and conscious of the new political power of the mass vote, came surely if reluctantly to the conviction that "the greatest good of the greatest number" is ultimately the concern of the state.

The extension of the idea of the "general welfare" from Disraeli's first experiments in urban housing to the state's manifold responsibility for the citizen's well-being in modern democracy has had two vital consequences in the context of economic growth. The needs of the mass of the people for welfare services could only be financed by rising taxation. A progressive income tax, redistributing income from those who might save to those who would be sure to spend, checked the prewar propensity of entrepreneurs to "over-save" in the Keynsian sense. At the same time it provided the free market with a floor of which the importance came fully to be realized only after the Second World War. Welfare payments and insurance schemes of all kinds, public and private, pretty well maintain the level of consumer spending even during the downturn of a business cycle. Throughout the three or four post-war recessions in America, consumption has actually increased. The old fatal mechanism by which unemployment in one sector quickly spreads to others by the sharp fall in the purchases of the workless seems to have been effectively checked. This maintenance of the market has proved more influential for growth than any supposed deterrent to investment caused by higher taxation.

Even so, the early reforms designed to produce the beginnings of what one might call "welfare-capitalism" were not enough to ensure full employment and steady growth. During the first three decades of this century, further reform was checked by a profound disagreement on the measures that should be taken next. The old division between apocalyptic reformers and resistant conservatives which had shaken Western Europe in the first decades of the nineteenth century reappeared in contemporary politics, the men of the left arguing that only total state ownership, state intervention, planned expansion, massive public works, and the abandonment of the profit motive would create an abundant community, the men of the right asserting that any such attempt would create such concentrations of state power that all liberty would be lost. In this division, one must of course distinguish between the genuinely apocalyptic thinkers—the Communists—who worked for the total overthrow of the system, and the more moderate socialists who believed in securing changes by the ballot box within a democratic framework. But even between moderates, the deadlock seemed complete; the socialists equated private enterprise with stagnation—which was not too far from the truth, and the conservatives equated complete state control with tyranny—which was not altogether untrue, either.

Western economies broke out of this trap largely as a result of the Second World War. Total mobilization doubled the size of the crucial American industrial sector in only four years. New techniques, new inventions— nuclear energy, electronics, mechanical industry—received an enormous boost from war's massive investment. The socialist point was underlined that government action in the shape of public works on a vast scale—for this is, in one sense, what a war effort amounts to—can take up the slack in an economy. But the conservatives could show that such a mobilization does not require total public ownership, since private enterprise, operating in an atmosphere of expansion, functions better than any large centralized public bureaucracy. In short, the socialists had to admit that private enterprise is compatible with full employment and a growing economy, and conservatives that public action is needed to ensure high activity and sustained growth. From these pragmatic conclusions has emerged the new concept of a mixed economy, part public, part private, which is now the dominant form of the free economy in the West.

The validity of this new concensus underwent a conclusive test within two years of the end of the war. Its fundamental principles—that governments must be ready to keep the whole economy buoyant, and, if necessary, use their powers of taxation and credit creation to that end—had barely won recognition in the domestic economy before they were challenged suddenly and sharply in a new field.

Hitherto, the workings of the international economy had been largely unregulated and unplanned. A *laissez faire* of nations in the world market matched the *laissez faire* of individual enterprises in the domestic market, and for much the same reason. It was assumed that each country pursuing its own interests would unconsciously produce the good of the whole—not entirely an irrational belief for, as we shall see, the expansion of the Atlantic area did for a time act as a mighty stimulus to economic development elsewhere. It was not wholly fanciful to regard the Atlantic nations as so many leading sectors in a new worldwide economy, with their growth sparking expansion in other undeveloped lands.

This dream faded after 1929 when, in nine short months, international trade fell by two-thirds, international lending ceased almost entirely, and even the wealthy West could not break from relative stagnation. The rest of the world was in even worse plight. Within the developed economies, there were at least institutions, policies, and some sense of community and purpose to offset the miseries of depression. After 1932, for instance, the British Government set to work to build houses, and a measure of well-being returned as a result of this practical plunge into public works. But there were no responsible international institutions, no active elements of supranational government, no general sense of community working to mitigate the evils in the world at large. Colonial governments adhered almost universally to the principle that local costs must be covered by local taxes. Britain's first colonial welfare funds were not fully established until the 1940s. The League of Nations had neither powers nor funds to act in the economic field. Thus the 1930s were a time of almost worldwide stagnation unrelieved by any new hope or initiative. Not by any flight of imagination or perversion of history could such a condition be confused with a functioning world economy; and the argument gathered strength that any such system would require a stronger, more consistent, and more organic base than unalloyed national self-interest. If the nations pursued only their own aims, they could no more create a stable and peaceful world than could each individual business unit build a rich and expanding economy solely by pursuing its own profit. The calculus did not work out. The *laissez faire* of national self-interest was no more self-regulating than the *laissez faire* of unadulterated business interest. Nations needed to work within a wider framework of political institutions, human solidarity and conscious social goals. Within that framework, both instincts —national self-expression, economic enterprise—were no doubt valuable, indeed, indispensable sources of variety and dynamism. Without it, they could run amok. For a decent human order, more was needed than exclusive worship at the shrines of either "the idols of the market or the idols of the tribe." Such was the lesson of the inter-war years. The question in 1945 was whether the powers could learn it in time.

Not even the minimal institutions of international solidarity were in existence. The groundwork of a community had to be created from scratch. But by 1945, the nations, however hesitantly, were going to work. The worst devastations of the war were made good by the United Nations Relief and Rehabilitation Administration, whose efforts for the war-torn nations were financed by a contribution of one per cent of national income from the wealthier and less devastated lands—an epoch-making precedent, since it established for the first time in concrete form in world society the principle that the rich should tax themselves for the poor. True, the Powers conceived the experiment in temporary terms, and America and Britain voted it out of existence in 1946. But the precedent had been established; and meanwhile other more permanent international agencies were being brought into existence.

While the peaceful settlement of disputes remained the chief function of the United Nations, many of its own departments, as well as the specialized Agencies—the Organizations for World Health, for instance, or for Food and Agriculture—had a wider concern with the economic

and social substance of a world society. Two of these institutions in particular—the International Bank for Reconstruction and Development and the International
Monetary Fund—suggested that the nations were no
longer content wholly to rely upon the automatic workings of the economic system to carry out such vital functions as ensuring the international flow of capital or
evening out the ups and downs of international trade.

Yet the resources allotted to both institutions also suggested that the powers still very gravely underestimated
the scale upon which the new policies and new institutions would need to work. The original capital of the
International Bank was ten billion dollars, whereas in few
postwar years has the international transfer of capital
through public institutions been less than $4 billions a
year; and this figure is probably half the sum that could
be usefully absorbed. Similarly, the original funds at the
disposal of the International Monetary Fund amounted
to $2 billions, but in 1947 alone, Western Europe's trade
deficit with the United States reached $9 billions. The
problems facing the Atlantic world clearly were on a scale
which, during the postwar years, the Powers were largely
unprepared to handle.

The test came, therefore, when, after two years of
rather haphazard reconstruction—UNRRA working in some
countries, military government funds propping up others,
an American loan vanishing at lightning speed in Britain
—the full scale of the postwar crisis was revealed. No
country in Western Europe had the working capital, the
functioning equipment, the exports or the domestic
product to pull itself out of the gulf of wartime disloca-
tion. The situation was, if anything, worse than it had been
in 1919; and what threatened in 1947 was not so much a
major slump on the model of 1921, but total collapse.

There were no answers to this risk in the orthodox vocabulary of economic policy. If the nations of Europe could not secure goods and supplies from America—the one great economy to survive the war not crippled but vastly reinforced—they could not restore their own productive machines. But without a functioning economy, how could they export goods to secure American supplies? The deadlock was complete.

When it was broken by the great and imaginative American gesture of the Marshall Plan, more was achieved than simply a physical restoration of Europe. Western Europe itself was rebuilt in such a way that it could never again be the same type of society. New principles were introduced into international relations which at least promised to be applicable over wider areas and longer stretches of time. And perhaps the most vital consequence could not be expressed in physical terms at all: this was a new dimension of freedom and spontaneity in the relations of nation with nation, of man with man.

The basic element of the Marshall Plan was, inevitably, a transfer of resources from America to Europe. In the four years between 1948 and 1952, the United States government made some $13 billions available in free grants with which the European nations were able to secure food and materials for their current functioning and invest in new machines and processes for the future. But the manner in which the aid was given went far beyond a simple reconstruction of past wealth and capacity. The really creative element was that the Plan changed a static into a dynamic pattern of growth.

In 1947 the Western world was still in the cramp which gripped it in the Great Depression. During those years, each country, with the United States at their head, had tried to protect its own economy by higher and higher tariffs while seeking simultaneously and irrationally to increase its sales overseas. From this ludicrous effort of everyone to sell and no one to buy the world derived one thing only—a virtual standstill in international trade. The habit of protection was thus strong in Europe, even without the aftermath of the war. But the six-year conflict had blocked old outlets for trade, destroyed stocks, liquidated working capital. The margins were so small that governments felt they had to operate under a series of bilateral agreements designed to balance exactly purchases and sales; and this reduced the trade of a developed continent to a system of barter only suitable for trade in a subsistence village.

By insisting that aid should be given not to each nation separately, but to the whole group of nineteen, the American government began to undermine the inward-looking policies of each of them. By pressing steadily and vigorously for the restoration of multilateral trade and a wider payments system, the Americans ensured that the reviving dynamism of each separate economy assisted and enhanced the neighbouring economies as well. For the downward spiral of contracting trade, they substituted a beneficent cycle of growth sparking further growth. The movement did more than secure a freedom of trade unknown since 1914: it also encouraged a more radical desire to remove all barriers to trade and to gain the full advantage of a unified market for nearly 200 million people. Thus did the spirit of the open market and free trade revive, confirming at an international level the paradox clearly at work inside the postwar economies, the paradox that judicious government action does not repress, but is on the contrary a precondition of vigorous private enterprise.

The clearest case was that of France, where stagnation

had been peculiarly bitter and prolonged. Part of the funds which the French government secured by selling America's free gifts of food and raw materials—the so-called counterpart funds—were devoted, under government direction through the Monnet Plan, to reorganizing and modernizing France's basic services—power and transport—and to an attack upon the problems of France's most backward sector, peasant farming. The Monnet Plan included efforts to consolidate holdings, to introduce mechanization, to improve techniques, and to draw especially remote and isolated rural communities into some contact with the market.

All these efforts, some brilliantly successful, some handicapped by tradition and suspicion, especially on the land, nonetheless recreated the spirit of French enterprise. After thirty years of high-cost stagnation, the French economy moved forward into the new world of scientific production and modern technology. The face of France began to change, even in areas once remote from bustle and growth. Beside the little farms of Bearn and Bigorre grew up a symbol of French revival, the fantastic domes and spheres and cylinders worthy of some futurist community in the space age—the installations and settlements on the great gas fields of Lussagnet and Lacq.

This combination of a widening market, high investment and new technology began to work the change in Europe that had already occurred in America; the shift to a mass economy of high consumption. Within a decade, there was no escaping the evidence. The era of the popular car and the petrol station, the television set and the supermarket, of mass holidays and mass travel had opened. Under the impetus of the Marshall Plan, Europe had begun to escape from the old cage of limited profits, low productivity, depressed employment, and economic stag-

(55)

nation. Thus the greatest achievement of the Plan was one that had not been foreseen at all. It did not simply restore Europe, as its authors intended and hoped. It went much further and remade it in a new image.

Naturally, in a single decade, the process is not complete. The drive of some Marshall nations to achieve a more complete fusion of their economies in a single "common market" has left others uncertain and outside. But the general result is not in doubt. Europe has crossed the perilous divide at which it halted after 1919. It has achieved the momentum of a new stage of growth.

The consequences are far more than economic. The Plan restored a feeling of scope, possibility, and achievement, after three decades in which the dominant mood had been one of closing horizons and all doors locked against further progress. Now all was reversed. Europe has risen a phoenix from its old ashes. The triumph for the present is great. But the implications for the future might be greater still. If a crisis on the scale of Europe's collapse in 1947 could be overcome by vigorous, purposive intergovernmental action, a precedent had been set, a tool invented for working on other possibly more intractable problems in other areas of the world economy.

Chapter Five

Politics of the Apocalypse

WHILE free society struggled to combine liberal politics with the unfolding dilemmas and opportunities of economic growth, a parallel effort was being made by the Communists to create a total and apocalyptic version of the same process. It is this intense contrast of ideals and practice applied to what is in essence a similar transformation that gives such dramatic edge to the struggles of our times. Freedom and tyranny, pragmatism and fanaticism, the spirit of compromise and undeviating ideology are equally at work to build a functioning society out of the new materials of science, technology, and economic expansion. The performance of each thus acts as a commentary on the performance of the other. The context of competition is completely inescapable. And since the outcome touches on the deepest needs of humanity and involves the entire globe, the duel has

(57)

overtones of fate and vision and historical destiny unique in the record of mankind.

Both traditions are profoundly rooted in the Western world. Indeed, neither can be found anywhere else. Only Western society produced from its classical and Christian tradition the ideas of limited government, responsible citizenship, and a community ruled under law. Elsewhere the tradition was one of despotism somewhat modified by custom. And only Western society brought forth the vision of humanity progressing toward some great act of historical judgment, after which it would emerge, redeemed and transformed, to crown history with a glorious and timeless millennium. All other civilizations saw the fate of man as a repetition over endless ages of the great cycles of birth and death, a "melancholy wheel" allowing no hint of deliverance save for those who could wean themselves from earthly things. The thought that human society might be perfectible and humanity redeemable belongs to the Jewish and Christian tradition alone.

The vision first appeared as a political force still in a religious setting. The Anabaptists of Münster in the sixteenth century spoke the language of Christianity and revolution. So did the Levellers in Cromwell's army. By the time of the French Revolution, the apocalyptic mood had become secular. A great act of political redemption was now expected to "put down the mighty from their seats and exalt them of low degree." And the greatest of all the revolutionaries, Karl Marx, based his apocalypse on the strictest rejection of its religious roots. Yet the vision and the passion are wholly derived from a religious past—from Christian faith in redemption, from Jewish outrage at exploitation and injustice, from nearly two thousand years of the belief, found only in the West, that the poor, the rejected, and the oppressed will go first into the kingdom of heaven.

Nor does this end the debt Marx owes to other sources. His philosophy he derived from Hegel, his politics from contemporary French thought, his economics in large measure from the first great classical school in Britain which included Adam Smith and Malthus, his direct experience of society from the early stages of industrialism in France and Victorian England. But this dependence on others is not the theory's main significance. Every system of ideas must be in some measure derivative. The decisive point is its new effectiveness and power; and here there can be no doubt about the profoundly creative nature of Marx's synthesis.

He wrote at a time when all the ancient landmarks of settled, traditional society were beginning to be violently disrupted by the new economic forces of technology and science. Men simply did not know what was happening to them or how to think about the changes that all around them undermined old familiar things and set up strangeness and novelty in their place. The mind demands some sort of answer and cannot be for long content with confusion. Thus the grandeur—and the risk—of creative ideas consists in their ability to order dim and disparate facts in such a way that men feel they understand them and thus recover a sense of mastery. They no longer look out on a scene of chaos. They discern roads and guide lines, patterns and possibilities. In every beginning is "the Word."

Times of upheaval and violent change enormously reinforce the potency of ideas. The component molecules of established order fall apart under the revolutionary bombardment. They become free elements waiting to be combined in new patterns—and ideas provide the patterns. Then, established as a new mode of seeing reality, ideas mold men's aims and actions and enter as an active force into history. In this sense, there is truth in Goethe's variant: "In the beginning is the act."

Marxism's strength lies in the degree to which it created a new way of looking at the world when the old certainties were beginning to dissolve. Its tragedy is the degree to which the analysis, for all its power and brilliance, failed to conform to the facts. The original error was Marx's assumption that the first hard years of early industrialism in Britain represented the final and only form capitalism would ever take in Western society. The late 1840s—when his Communist Manifesto appeared—came toward the close of the first phase of capital accumulation. To secure savings on a sufficient scale for continued expansion, the organizers of the new industrial system controlled and used virtually the whole surplus produced by the new machines. The workers—ignorant, bewildered, disordered, herded in slums, dazed by the new factory disciplines—earned a subsistence wage and no more. For this they had to work as many as sixteen hours a day, six days a week, in conditions of overcrowding, filth, disease, and neglect—not worse, perhaps, than the old rural poverty, but more unfamiliar, more impersonal, and so much more inhuman. A glittering edifice of expanding wealth might be erected on the groundwork of their gruelling days. But for them, there was only one reality—poverty and exploitation.

This was the world to which Marx applied his powerful mind; and he must be counted one of the greatest of the early political economists. He saw more clearly than any of them that the investment of savings in a whole range of technological innovations was creating a decisive break with all previous modes of production. The capitalists were building a new society for which a quite new analysis would be needed; and many of Marx's insights were very near the mark. He was after all not alone in prophesying uncertain prospects for the new economy. His contemporaries believed that at some point rising costs of labour or land might limit profits and slow down the growth of the system, even if they did not, like Marx, foresee a total and catastrophic collapse. He realized, perhaps more clearly that anyone else, that under existing conditions too little of the gains from the expanding industrial system would be distributed to the mass of the workers; and as a result their purchasing power would be insufficient to clear the market of the fabulous flow of goods pouring out from the new machines. In this he foresaw both the fluctuations of the business cycle and the future decades of stagnation, even if he missed the breakthrough to mass consumption on the further side.

But the core of his analysis led him directly away from reality. It persuaded him to prophesy increasing poverty and misery for the workers just at the moment in the 1860s when, after the first rigorous period of massive saving, the benefits of the new system began to trickle down to the mass of the people.

In part, his reasoning follows from a curiously unreal and unconvincing economic analysis. Marx believed all value was created by hours of labour. Competition in a disorganized, overcrowded labour market would keep wages down to the number of man-hours needed to earn a bare subsistence. Over and above that minimum, the men would be working solely for the capitalist, creating his profits, his surplus, providing him with the fruits of exploitation. Since, by Marx's definition, profits could only be earned from the unpaid work-hours of the labour force, the introduction of more and more machines would not help the entrepreneur. Machines were, in Marx's strange analysis, simply congealed labour time and, as such, "machinery creates no new value." Only in collaboration with workers working unpaid hours could machines give rise to profit. But the essence of the new machinery was that it was labour-saving. Some men would lose their jobs and would not be re-employed. The remainder would have to work longer hours to make up for the unpaid hours no longer worked by the unemployed.

Marx also thought capital—the machines, the installations, the whole physical apparatus of production—would become more expensive, the more capital there was in existence. This is the old classical argument that after a certain point more investment brings in a smaller return. The only way to counter this rising expense would be to squeeze the workers' wage bill still more sharply. As a result, the more fully an economy became industrialized, capitalized, and mechanized, the worse the pressure on the mass of the workers would become.

At the same time, fierce competition for shrinking profits and shrinking markets would reduce the number of entrepreneurs, wipe out small businesses, eliminate the middle class, and lead to the creation of giant monopolies and trusts. Then at the apex of society would stand the few monopolists; at the base, the vast proletarianized masses. Once they became conscious of their numbers and their strength—in a word, class conscious—the masses would take over the economy, and, "expropriating the expropriators," build the new Jerusalem of a classless, propertyless society.

However, the labour theory of value was wrong. Value springs from a hundred things; scarcity, consumers' whims, good luck, sudden discoveries, intelligent anticipation, superior powers of organization, the play of the market. And investment in new equipment can be far more than labour-saving. It saves capital as well. A breakthrough in technology can be productive enough to allow the entrepreneur to make a bigger profit even while wages are going up. There is no iron economic law that dictates the inevitability of the poor becoming poorer; and in Western society, politics and social policy saw to it that they did not. At this point, Marx's errors go deeper than mere faults of economic theory. These might have been corrected, for at least part of his analysis conformed to the facts. But he could not admit that parliamentary tradition and social conscience might contradict the law of progressive impoverishment. If he had done so, the entire foundations of his system would have been swept away.

He needed the inevitable, self-caused collapse of capitalism in order to round off his bold vision of the dialectics of history in which, over the millennia, feudalism had risen from primitive communism, and capitalism from feudalism—each stage thrust forward by internal contradictions and class struggles rooted in the uneven distribution of property. Now, in the latest unfolding of the historical process, capitalism's internal contradictions and increasing concentration of economic power were themselves creating the propertyless proletarians who would take over the system and establish at last a society without private property—and hence, by definition, without contradiction or strain, a classless millennium. In this scheme of things, impoverishment and growing despair, progressive ruin and class war were needed to round off the vast historical drama. Without catastrophe it might lose its crowning denouement—and no author willingly sacrifices his last act.

Its inevitability was also vital to Marx's belief that he had uncovered the scientific laws of historical develop-

ment. Since men and women had begun, a century before, to devote more and more of their thought and interest to experimenting with the behaviour of material things.
the notion of discovering the precise scientific laws
governing all phenomena had gathered fascination and
strength. If precise, measurable, verifiable laws controlled
the behaviour of solids and gases, why should not similar
laws be found to control the behaviour of men and society?
These Marx believed he had discovered in the unchanging
laws of the historical dialectic, laws which reflect the
material substructure of human existence. Ultimately all
its phenomena—from art and philosophy to individual
canons of behaviour—can be traced back to modes of
production and class relations based on property-holding.
Here is the solid, material base from which immutable
laws can be deduced—positivist, objective laws from
which all traces of sentiment or heritage or tradition have
been cleansed. Marx's most serious claim for himself was
that his was "scientific socialism"; and if one thing is certain about a scientific fact, it is that it cannot be repealed
by act of parliament.

If capitalists are compelled by scientific necessity to
exploit their workers, and government by an equal necessity simply reflects capitalist interests, then, by definition,
parliament cannot improve the lot of the worker. If it
could, the underlying unchanging laws of capitalist society would be shown to be quite simply false. According
to Marx, government had to conform to the interests of
the property-owning capitalists. It could only be "the
managing committee of the bourgeoisie," for it belonged
to that superstructure of politics and ideas which is derivative and must reflect the underlying play of productive
forces. At first, in the early days of industrialism, dogmatic respect for the workings of the market did very

largely check legislative reform. For Marx this was proof of his theorem that a bourgeois government could not reduce hours of labour and thereby reduce the only source of bourgeois profit. The trouble began when the government took to regulating hours and inspecting conditions of work. The supporters of *laissez faire* wailed that it undermined their system. They were wrong. The system it undermined was that of Marx.

By the end of the 1860s—when *Das Kapital* started to appear—the British economy was over the first testing stage of initial capital investment. The workers had begun to share a little in the new wealth and to protect both their share and their prospects through the organization of trade unions. The disorganized labour market had given place to groups of men ready and, up to a point, able to defend themselves. At the same time, industrialization had greatly increased the numbers and prosperity of the professional and managerial groups. The middle class was expanding proportionally faster than any other.

These economics and social changes were reflected in politics. Leaders realized they could enhance their own power by enfranchising new groups, and that if they did not, others would do so. They began to heed the general demand for an extension of the vote. By the time adult male suffrage was secured in the 1880s, the vote had begun to transfer political power to the majority—who, in any society, are bound in the main to be poor. Public action to relieve poverty followed inevitably on electoral reform—not a very surprising result, save for the Marxists who had to believe that economics determine politics and never the reverse.

Thus ended the first phase of Communism's dialogue with the West. It proved conclusively that however much Marx had sharpened the tools of economic analysis

and contributed a new dimension to men's thinking about
the impact of economic change on social institutions, the
ultimate rigidity of his thought prevented him from
seeing the opposite impact of ideals and politics on economic development. Yet in the liberal West, the last word
was to lie with politics. On an analysis mainly derived
from the first stages of Western capital accumulation,
Marx built up a whole theory of historical change and
human destiny. At that point, Western capitalism, react-
ing primarily to profound political and social pressures
and beliefs, moved to a new stage, which faulted the
Marxist analysis. The decisive question after the 1860s
was thus whether Communism would be modified to
conform to reality, or whether the idea of Communism
would be cut loose from the restraints of fact.

Marx himself found no way round the dilemma. He died,
leaving *Das Kapital* unfinished, at a time when working-
class politics were dominated by moderate Socialist
leaders, who were more interested in improving the workers' conditions at once than in any ultimate goal of total
state ownership. And these men believed that a better
society could be achieved peacefully through the ballot
box, without a total revolutionary upheaval which they,
with a growing stake in society, did not relish at all. The
balance of power on the left remained with the more
moderate men.

The next turning point in Communist development
came in 1902 with the publication of Lenin's pamphlet
What is to be Done? In it Lenin set Communism firmly
on the path of fantasy and myth. In effect he declares
that the Western working class has "enslaved itself to the
bourgeoisie." The proletarians will not produce the revolution because better wages, better prospects, and the
vote have taken away their revolutionary drive. The only

course open to convinced Communists is therefore to prepare for revolution, even if the masses do not want it. Communism must co-operate with the working class; but if class consciousness recedes and the workers are not ready for the decisive struggle, then they must be brought to it by force and fraud.

Thus the stage was set for conspiracy. The revolution which was to have been produced by the ineluctable forces of history had now to be imposed by the force of a single, dedicated Communist minority. This by definition meant dictatorship. But it is one of the oldest sophistries of human thought to believe that if you have the right ideas, you have the right to impose them. The false scientificism of Marxist theory encouraged this trend. The scientific laws of history demand a revolution. Hence to be opposed to revolution is to be opposed to science and so to objective truth. As Auguste Comte remarked: "Men are not allowed to think freely about chemistry and biology. Why should they think freely about political philosophy?" No one, the dogmatist argues, can wish to be in error. Therefore truth is what men really want, even if they do not recognize it. Give them truth and you give them what they really and objectively desire. So truth makes them free and dictatorship is liberty—the old, old syllogism in whose name the unnumbered crimes against liberty have been committed.

The Leninist phase of Communism opens with the concept of a conspiratorial group using any and every opportunity to seize power and impose the Communist pattern by force. The traditional liberties and safeguards of the citizen—the right to be heard, to criticize, to choose or be rid of a government, to enjoy safety from arbitrary arrest, and due process under law, safeguards worked out painfully and pragmatically over the centuries in free men's struggles against the tyrannies of old—these were now to be stripped away in the name of a new freedom achieved through Communist truth. And by a grim paradox, the new system began to take shape just as the first law of Communist "truth," the law of increasing misery, had been found to be completely false. But Lenin dropped the pretence that Communism was closely related to reality. It was now a weapon to conquer reality, not a philosophy to reflect it. And in accordance with this concept, the seizure of power by violence or deceit, not by consent, became the dominant Communist procedure. From the first seizure of power by the Bolsheviks in Russia in 1917 through the revolutions of the next forty years, there was one chief route to the establishment of Communist government: armed intervention, violence, infiltration or fraud; and only one attitude toward its maintenance: to remain in office permanently, if necessary by force.

When the Communists took over power for the first time in Russia in the October Revolution, the coup had little or nothing to do with any pre-ordained Marxist pattern. Here was no highly evolved, highly industrialized community with a vast mass of despairing proletarians and a small dominant group of monopolists at the top. Even before the war, Russia had barely completed the first stages of economic growth. It had a small modernized economic sector, a very limited industrial working class, a basis of modern communications, and a vast peasant society still only partially drawn into the modern economy. Its structure of government had also remained very largely traditional. Representative institutions had barely been attempted. Czarist autocracy was virtually intact. Even without a violent war, Russia must have continued for some time to be a very unstable society in which modern economic forces would undermine, without replacing, older forms and traditions—a society, in short, in which apocalyptic versions of politics would stand an excellent chance of catching men's minds. But in addition to this preliminary weakness, three years of total war had rained hammer blows of disruption and despair on the collapsing state. In 1917, the revolutionary masses were not proletarianized workers taking over an advanced industrial system, but war-weary soldiers and peasants demanding peace and land in a totally demoralized community. It was Lenin's supreme tactical achievement to see that the new revolutionary situation, even though it in no way resembled Marxist predictions, had created conditions fluid and plastic enough to allow any determined group of men to impose on them the stamp of their will and purpose. For this type of revolution, his minority group of Bolsheviks were better fitted than any other. They had the discipline, the will to power, the coherent ruthlessness needed to turn chaos to their own account. This they did in 1917, establishing the first Communist regime, not in an advanced industrial society, but in a ruined and still primitive autocracy on the brink of total dissolution.

The coup could hardly have been less in keeping with Marxist theory. But it underlined a profoundly relevant fact: that Communism exercises its most potent influence in the earliest stages of modernization, during and not after the breakthrough to sustained economic growth. This is the time of maximum political and social instability. If, in addition, the emergent society becomes involved in war, the resulting chaos gives a highly disciplined revolutionary minority its surest chance of seizing power.

However, the first consequence of taking control in a society which in no way fitted the Marxist analysis was that the Communists had very little idea of what to do next. The truth is that Marx had never described his classless millennium. He asumed that the revolution would occur first in a highly industrialized society in which Western capitalists would have already built a full productive apparatus that anyone could run. The only question would be the distribution of its fruits—and common ownership would take care of that.

Lenin, too, thought the entrepreneurial function could be carried out by cooks or carpenters. But the experiment of putting workers in charge of the factories—the brief period of War Communism—soon discouraged him. By 1921 the Bolsheviks had on their hands a moribund economy, shattered by war, disorganized by revolution, producing little food and fewer manufactures. For a few years, the machine was kept in motion by a policy of encouraging peasants and traders and small businessmen to make money—Lenin's New Economic Policy—but this development was soon seen to be leading directly to the creation of new self-reliant classes, especially on the land, a trend which might have led to the expansion of the economy but equally would have brought about the extinction of the dictatorship. The Communists naturally decided to save the dictatorship.

The solution imposed by Stalin was to set about building, under total state control, a fully modernized, industrialized system. Its models were the developed industrial communities of the West and particularly the experience gained by them during the First World War, when they had started to mobilize men and capital on a complete and planned basis for the expansion of heavy industry and the production of arms. But the fundamental model went back even further, to the grim period of primitive capital accumulation in Britain on which the original Marxist analysis had been based. Then the ability of the industrialists to devote nearly all the savings of the new industrial machine to further saving had been the precondition of the breakthrough to sustained growth—even though it had left the workers, in factory or farm, living more or less at subsistence level. National savings had risen to a steadily higher proportion of national income—at cruel cost to mass consumption—but the process of modernization was achieved.

In Soviet Russia the savings imposed by Stalin under the first Five Year Plan proved infinitely more merciless. The mobilization of peasant labour in such vast new industrial centres as Sverdlovsk cost, according to witnesses, as many victims as the bloody Battle of the Marne. Perhaps ten million political prisoners were set to work virtually as slaves. In towns bleaker than Victorian slums, in conditions of unparalleled hunger and poverty, the factories went up, the coke ovens were heated, the steel mills began to roll. And if workers in the town were miserable, the farmers were destitute. For a decade virtually the entire agricultural surplus was removed from the countryside by forced levies at derisory prices. The drive to collectivize the farms and the deportation of resisting peasants killed millions and undermined productivity in Soviet agriculture for a generation. But out of all the suffering and saving, capital investment increased far beyond any earlier percentage of national income. It edged up to 25 per cent and more. Industrialization under forced draft succeeded. By 1939 Russia had forged the armature of a modern industrial state.

This breakthrough was to become Russia's most significant achievement. Had Communism remained as Lenin left it—a political dogma of common ownership and social equality applied somewhat uncertainly to a stagnant economy—it would probably have proved as ephemeral as earlier experiments in egalitarian rule—the Anabaptists of Münster, Cromwell's Levellers, the Paris Commune. But under Stalin, the total discipline of a ruthless revolutionary party showed what it could accomplish in societies as backward or stagnant or disorganized as Russia had been. Using the techniques of mobilization and planning of a war economy, he thrust Russia through a second take-off by means of forced saving, forced labour, and savage discipline. He carried his country from the wooden plough to the atomic pile in forty years. Thus he not only gave Russian society the sheer brute strength to survive in an angry world, he also provided an alternative blueprint for economic growth in any society too caught in its own contradictions, divisions, or poverty to achieve development by more spontaneous methods. Thus the modern industrialized world offered two possible patterns of economic growth: the informal, experimental Western mixture of market forces and government direction, relying on a considerable degree of decentralized decision-making and local initiative; and Russia's total state plan imposed from above by iron political control.

Indeed, since the Second World War, it can be argued that the chief significance of the Russian experiment for the outside world lies in its forced achievement of rapid modernization. It has yet to prove that it can provide an economy as abundant and various as the new mass consumer economies of the West. Large bureaucracies, however much the attempt is made to decentralize them on a regional basis, seem to lack the flexibility and inventiveness shown by private enterprise in meeting the infinite variety of human needs and tastes. There may, too, be some political inhibitions standing in the way of making the consumer supreme. The system works well enough when it is a matter of military strength, of centralized scientific experiment on a vast scale—moon probes and rocketry—or of a steady expansion of large industries which can be developed on massive lines. For all these things Soviet methods are efficient, although no more so than are Western economies when mobilized under central command during war. It is the civilian economy which lags behind in the Soviet experiment; and in spite of Mr. Khrushchev's protestations that he will catch up with America in a generation, there is little guarantee that he can in fact succeed—for this to happen the assumption must be made that Western growth and variety will meanwhile peter out.

But in the matter of reorganizing stagnant or chaotic economies for the achievement of modernization, Soviet methods have not only been shown to work in Russia. They can now be purposefully exported to other bewildered or recalcitrant nations. The Soviets are wealthy enough to finance their own exports of capital; and when their assistance is invited, they can combine instructions on the techniques of economic growth with lessons in the arts of political repression. The more disorganized the society in which they operate, the greater the chances of infiltrating their own pattern of control. Thus the present duel between Western and Communist methods does not really concern the future shape of advanced societies. It is profoundly and urgently engaged at the point at which emergent societies seek to set in motion the processes of economic growth. And since at least one-third of humanity is engaged on just this task, the area of competition encompasses the whole world.

Chapter Six

Lenin on Imperialism and War

IT IS about the uncommitted and largely ex-colonial world that the Communists have evolved some of their most persuasive theories. As a firm historical starting point they have the fact that until the day before yesterday most of the world outside the Atlantic area was under one form or other of Western colonial control. Strangely enough, however, the Communist theory of imperialism has a quite different point of departure: not the fact of colonialism, but the breakdown of Marx's law of increasing impoverishment.

Lenin had shown in 1902 how Communists could use the technique of conspiracy and dictatorship to get around the awkward fact that the bulk of Western workers were not revolutionary. But he had not shown why such a state of affairs could have come about. This breach in Marx's iron law could not simply be by-passed. It had to be explained in order to preserve the system's aura of scientific accuracy, and this Lenin set out to do in a book published in 1916, the darkest year of the First World War. *Imperialism: the Highest Stage of Capitalism* seeks to explain in Marxist terms the workers' disaffection from Communism. But it also explains practically every current phenomenon of that violent epoch, and its compelling synthesis still profoundly influences men's minds.

Lenin's starting point is one of the issues with which the classical economists had been concerned—the tendency of profits to fall and business to stagnate after an early surge of investment. Marx had said that the failure would be catastrophic. It had not proved so but no Marxist could admit that political or social forces had mitigated an iron economic law. Somewhere an explanation had to be found in terms of the economics of exploitation, and Lenin looked for it abroad.

In the classical analysis, there is a perfectly reasonable explanation for the tendency of entrepreneurs to extend their investments overseas. As the nineteenth century advanced, wages were rising at home and resources were becoming more expensive. In undeveloped economies, labour could still be hired for more or less subsistence wages, and resources were still untouched. The lure of profits was thus quite obvious, especially in the abundant, temperate lands. But Lenin followed Marx in dismissing a possible rise in wages. He argued instead that stagnation in the home market, due to insufficient purchasing power, drove capitalists to look for openings for investment elsewhere.

Up to a point Lenin's analysis of the need to invest abroad follows an earlier attempt to explain the competitive colonialism of the European Powers at the end of the nineteenth century. J. A. Hobson in his book, *Imperialism*, comes to much the same conclusion about the motives dominating investors at that time. But Lenin draws much more far-reaching conclusions from his analysis. Once exploitation—in the strict Marxist sense—had begun in territories overseas, the workers at home gained, in Lenin's view, some margin of the prosperity which had been sweated out of the kaffirs and coolies abroad. How they did this, given the capitalists' supposed habit of securing the whole surplus, is not explained. But Lenin claims that they became involuntary rentiers; and their abandonment of Communism is simply one more sign of the corruption into which they had fallen. They live, like bourgeois, by the exploitation of others.

This theory, which had begun by explaining the disaffection of Western trade unionists, developed into a new painting of the whole Communist world picture; and Lenin's version, far more than Marx's, still dominates Communist thinking to-day. The monopolists, Lenin argued, would not simply seek to invest abroad. In their dislike for competition, they would insist on exclusive rights of exploitation and attempt to establish imperial control. Nationalism would be exacerbated at home to support their claims. Force would be used abroad to defend them. These exclusive attempts to dominate markets must lead to conflict between rival imperialists and hence to the risk of war. Nor would there be any end to the jostling and the aggression, for different nations would reach the stage of monopoly capitalism at different times, and would launch new imperialist drives to secure a redistribution of existing markets, again by force. This, said Lenin, was the frightful circuit of violence in which the world of 1916 was caught; and there could be no breaking out of it until capitalism itself was destroyed and the consequences of exploitation, at home and abroad, liquidated forever. Thus Lenin tied every contemporary phenomenon—nationalism, capitalism, colonialism, exploitation, aggression—into a single comprehensive, worldwide sequence of cause and effect.

There should be no doubt about the power and persuasiveness of his synthesis. To this day it is profoundly believed by millions in the Communist world, and still exercises formidable influence on leaders in ex-colonial lands. Its continued hold reflects in part the elements of truth in it, in part the degree to which new lands and new leaders, jolted out of their traditional patterns of thinking, have seized on a thesis which appears to give so all-embracing an account of their predicament. Yet Lenin's theory of imperialism is in reality quite as unsatisfactory as Marx's law of impoverishment from which it was derived—and it is unsatisfactory for the same reasons. It describes a particular phase in Western capitalism as though it were the immutable archetypal shape of capitalism and entirely neglects essential political differences and developments which later transformed the system into totally new patterns.

The law of progressive impoverishment was derived by Marx from the first three or four decades of primary capital accumulation in nineteenth-century Britain. The law of imperialism was derived by Lenin from the phase of capitalist expansion in the three or four decades immediately before 1914. Neither phase was destined to last. Both were totally transformed by politics, above all by the politics of freedom and welfare. But Communism could not admit the change without abandoning infallibility. And if it did this, it would no longer be Communism.

Between 1880 and 1914, the world gave some support

to Lenin's analysis. Outside the Atlantic arena, most areas were under one form or another of imperial control. Britain and France, two established industrial systems, competed malevolently for influence and investment in the Far East, in North and West Africa, and along the Nile. Germany, the latecomer in European industrialization, tried the pressure of her growing armaments to stake out exclusive spheres in Africa and China. Japan, barely industrialized, plunged into the Far Eastern rivalry of the Powers to carve up a crumbling China, fought a war with Russia, and lopped off Formosa and Korea.

Meanwhile, Germany and Russia watched with growing apprehension and cupidity the simultaneous weakening of both Austria-Hungary and Turkey and the resulting power vacuum throughout the Balkans and the Eastern Mediterranean. The question whether pro-Russian Slav or German influence should be predominant seemed to threaten the whole balance of power in Europe. The Russians believed they could not afford to allow Germany the addition of the strength that Balkan dominance would imply. In this, Russia was supported by the French. But Germany believed its security depended on no further Slav encroachments, and therefore backed Austria-Hungary. Again and again, between 1908 and 1914, Balkan conflicts between local supporters of Slav or German influence threatened to precipitate a general struggle. At last the terrible spiral into war could not be checked, and the Powers behaved as Lenin later argued they must behave—their rivalries and competitions drove them inexorably into an imperialist armageddon.

Yet even in 1914, many of the pieces in the Leninist jigsaw puzzle would not fit. The two chief agents in the drama, Russia and Germany, were not late monopoly-capitalists. Germany had only recently forged a modern economy, Russia was barely out of the first stage of growth. Britain, the most mature of Europe's economies, attempted with all its energy to stay out of the conflict. The United States, the chief economy which included large trusts and great monopolies, almost contrived to avoid the war altogether. Nor, in fact, did the struggle turn on the issue of colonies. Lenin argued that colonies would be seized as exclusive areas for investment, and that rivalries for them would lead to conflict. But the great bulk of investment from industrialized Europe before 1914 had gone either to other developing European nations or to the temperate lands of European settlement overseas—to North and South America, to Australasia, and to South Africa. And here there were no exclusions or barriers to the investment of any government or enterprise that wished to take the plunge. Even in so vast a dominion as India—a colony acquired by Britain not as a result of late capitalism but in the first days of its economic expansion—the total British investment in 1914 after a hundred years of empire was not much more than a tenth of Britain's investment overseas; and if other nations had wished to invest, no one would have prevented them. Thus, *pace* Lenin, the bulk of the investment went to lands which were not colonial and were barely involved at all in Europe's pre-1914 rivalry. Even in the areas where imperialist rivalry most resembled Lenin's prescription—in Africa and China—war was avoided. In Africa, the powers patched up a working agreement; and in China, they accepted the American policy of an "open door" which explicitly prohibited exclusive spheres for outsiders.

It is important to grasp this point: massive Western investment did not necessarily imply either imperial control or involvement in imperial struggles. To this day,

the chief emphasis in Communist propaganda to underdeveloped lands is that Western investment must be the
entry point for colonial control and is the chain which
ties a country to the imperialists' chariot wheel. The conditions under which trade and investment may lead to
colonialism will be examined later. Here it is only necessary to stress the lack of inevitable connection between
investment, colonialism, and war even in the late nineteenth-century heyday of Western imperialism. Colonial
rivalries did at that time add to tension and distrust between the powers; but they did not precipitate the final
struggle. This was fought, as so many earlier wars had
been fought, over an issue which predates Marxism by
centuries, the issue of the European balance of power. To
equate it with the rivalries of "late capitalism" is as sensible as to describe Napoleon or Louis XIV or Gustavus
Adolphus or the whole succession of Habsburgs or even
Charlemagne as early capitalists. By trying to explain
everything, Lenin, like Marx, ended by explaining too
much and blaming on one brief historical phenomenon
—prewelfare capitalism—all the ills to which human flesh
is heir. The very ambition of the analysis, which gives it
its exhilarating power over questing minds, ends by destroying its rational ground.

Between the wars, however, the power rather than the
irrationality of the thesis seemed more apparent. The
idea attracted the attention of small intellectual elites in
non-Western lands at once. Many of the Communist
leaders of to-day—Chou En-lai, for instance, or Ho Chi-
minh—were formed intellectually by the pure gospel of
Lenin just after the First World War; and it is still through
Leninist spectacles that they look at the contemporary
world. But the synthesis gained wider currency once the
Great Depression had devastated Atlantic society. Then

it did not take too great an exercise of intellectual ingenuity to fit the Leninist analysis to current facts. There was profound stagnation within home markets of the West. Nationalism was raw and resurgent in Germany, Italy, and Japan. They did claim a redistribution of the old colonial world. They did threaten to launch aggression. To equate fascism with late monopoly-capitalism, to define the issues as a struggle between rival imperialisms, to look to a Communist future as the only alternative to the collapse of Western bourgeois society—all these attitudes were not so remote from the dreary facts of depression and aggression as to exercise no fascination on minds looking vainly for some wider vision and brighter hope. On young people, especially, the Marxist combination of supposedly scientific analysis and burning moral condemnation of the evils of Hitlerism, Fascism, imperialism and colonialism had an almost hypnotic effect. These were the years of Popular Fronts, of Left Book Clubs and popularized Marxism, of the Spanish Civil War and the brief flirtation of many fine and dedicated minds with a Communism they regarded as the only alternative to the Nazis' triumph.

Yet the analysis was in fact now more astray than ever. No monopolists or capitalists were striving to preserve or extend exclusive spheres of investment. In the general stagnation, international movements of capital had come virtually to an end. Late-capitalist America proclaimed its universal neutrality. Imperialist Britain began to consider giving colonies away to appease the Nazis. Imperialist France thought of little beyond avoiding war. No one checked Italy's Abyssinian adventure—and what was Italy doing masquerading as a late monopoly-capitalist with its small, largely state-owned, industrial sector? No one stopped Japan as she moved on to swallow up China, a process she began not in the heyday of late capitalism but before she had even completed her first take-off into industrial growth. Even Nazi Germany could hardly be fitted into the pattern. The industrialists who supported Hitler before his rise to power found, like Frankenstein, that their monster was uncontrollable. Not the economic drives of monopoly capitalism, but the crazy impulses of blind nationalism and atavistic race instinct drove the German community on to aggression and conquest. And when war came, once again it came not over colonial escapades but over European hegemony, the old central issue of the balance of power. Twist events as one would, turn them upside down and inside out, still they did not add up to the consistent pattern of an imperialist struggle launched by the innate contradictions of late capitalism. In 1941 even the Communists gave up the attempt. The moment Hitler's troops invaded Russia, the struggle was turned into that very old-fashioned and traditional type of conflict, a patriots' war.

After 1945, the last vestiges of fact to back Leninist theory vanished. Inside the Atlantic arena, the new mixed economies achieved a transformation which even Lenin had admitted would endanger his analysis. At the beginning of Chapter IV of his *Imperialism,* he had written:

It goes without saying that if Capitalism could develop agriculture . . . if it could raise the standard of living of the masses who are everywhere still poverty-stricken and underfed, in spite of the amazing advance of technical knowledge, there could be no talk of superfluity of capital. . . . But if capitalism did these things, it would not be capitalism.

In the 1950s Lenin's impossibility occurred. The booming domestic markets of the West absorbed more and more capital. Far from industrialists eagerly seeking investments abroad, private international capital had become

(82)

scarce throughout the ex-colonial world. Only continued investment in oil prevented the flow of private Western capital to underdeveloped areas from falling to little more than a trickle.

The political transformation was even more startling. In ten short years the Western powers liquidated virtually the whole of their colonial system in Central and South America, in Asia and in the Middle East; in Africa the areas remaining under Western control were, in the main, countries with special problems of European settlement, such as Algeria or the Rhodesias. Elsewhere, independence, however precipitate, was all but complete.

And yet day in, day out, the Communists still plug the theme of colonialism and the danger of Western investment leading to infiltration and control. As the Chinese paper *Red Flag* put it—just before the collapse of the Summit Conference—"Communists believe in the absolute correctness of Lenin's thinking; war is an inevitable outcome of systems of exploitation and the source of modern wars is the imperialist system." Why is this? The short answer is because the ex-colonial lands represent the largest contemporary area of the West's unfinished business. It is here that economies have been brought to the most vulnerable stage of economic development and then all but abandoned with the job half done. The Communist attack on all forms of Western investment and assistance represents their shrewd assessment of what is most likely to lessen Western influence—and the ex-colonial areas' stability—at this crucial stage.

The long answer entails looking at the now all but completed history of Western colonialism and seeing why it is that on the one hand Communist analysis has been so faulty, yet on the other still demonstrates such potent appeal to non-Western minds.

Chapter Seven

The Colonial Pattern

T HE HISTORY of the West's colonial drive conforms to no tidy pattern such as the Marxists suggest. Just as the thrust of economic growth and investment takes different forms in a liberal or a feudal or an autocratic society, so in the world at large the economic energies of the West, first in trade and later in investment, were shaped at every turn by political facts, and—however unpalatable this may seem to the ideologue—by political chance as well.

Europe has always needed to trade. It lacked all the early definitions of wealth—jewels and precious metals, spices and silks—and from the earliest times sought them in the fabulous Orient, sending back bullion in exchange. The Moslem conquest of the Levant cut Europe's direct links of trade with Asia; and it was in a determined effort to outflank the hated Arab middleman that Portugal and

Spain unlocked the doors of Europe, opening up the sea route to India and discovering the Americas while they were looking for Cathay.

This release helped to unleash formidable energies in Western Europe. The rivalries of the traders enhanced a sense of separate nationalism. Gold and silver from the New World helped to capitalize a whole new class of merchant adventurers. Direct links with the Indies drew the boldest spirits into trade. The scale of the discoveries encouraged the mood of exploration, questioning and experiment. All these changes helped to undermine traditional feudal society and prepare the way for the dynamic market economy. In the same measure, they caused the Western communities to diverge more and more sharply in cutting edge and power from the magnificent but static civilizations of the East.

In the three hundred years of thrusting advance that followed, economic interest provided the propulsive energy of the West; but war politics determined the pattern of its impact. The rise and fall of the nations' fortunes within Europe decided their effectiveness overseas. The Dutch destroyed Portuguese dominance. They in their turn were largely eclipsed by the rivalry between Britain and France. And Britain achieved its Eastern supremacy by finally defeating France in Europe.

And all the Europeans were in their turn influenced and limited by local conditions. As a rough generalization, one can say that the outward thrust of the Europeans produced three different results, according to the nature of the local community. Where the land was underpopulated, or barely peopled at all, and the climate temperate, the Europeans set up overseas settlements, from the vast expanse of North America down to such tiny pockets of temperate, fertile land as the Highlands of Kenya. In most of these territories it was possible to reproduce the political institutions of the mother country and to advance steadily to full self-government.

Where the area was tropical, and—as often as not—highly populated as well, and where in addition local authority seemed too precarious to provide stable conditions for trade, the Europeans took over local government and provided their own order. Indonesia in the seventeenth century, India in the eighteenth century, large parts of Africa in the nineteenth, and China in the twentieth all suffered a collapse of internal authority and had to accept an order of security and control imposed from outside. Since Western incursions and rivalries were in themselves a potent force for disruption, local anarchy proved more typical than effective local government; and for this reason, by 1914 most of the world had come under Western control. Lenin picked on only a partial explanation for Western colonialism, the desire to invest. Actually, colonialism sprang primarily from the interaction between Europe's desire to trade and the non-European areas' internal instability. But this is a refinement, to the non-Westerner. He is chiefly impressed, like Lenin, with the fact of colonial control.

But there were exceptions. China maintained some sort of authority until the late-nineteenth century; Japan's government never collapsed at all. The Monroe Doctrine kept the Europeans out of Latin America once the Iberian colonies had declared their independence. And some states—Persia, Afghanistan, Siam—even contrived to survive precariously as buffer states between rival imperialisms. Even so, before 1914, perhaps only Japan can be said to have been in full control of its own destiny. Even where the forms of political independence remained—as in most of Latin America—economic dependence upon the developing West amounted almost to a colonial relationship.

When one turns to the economic consequences of the Western impact, comparable distinctions reappear between the temperate areas of European settlement, the colonial territories, and Japan. In North America, in Australasia, South Africa, and the more southerly parts of Latin America, land, fertility, climate, and entrepreneurial skills combined to encourage a repetition abroad of much of what was happening in Europe—and European investment provided the spur. By the chance of history, Britain, the first economy to industrialize, a small island "composed of coal and surrounded by fish" but otherwise not very amply endowed, had to begin early in the day to look for food and raw materials abroad. Its investment opened up mines and established the farms and granaries of the New World, built export industries, and financed the railways and ports needed to transport the goods overseas; and in a few decades had given the first impetus of growth to a whole new ring of temperate and developing economies.

According to Professor Nurkse, Britain in 1870 had $2,800 millions invested abroad, all but 20 per cent of it in Western Europe, America, Argentina, and the temperate lands of the British Empire. By 1913 the figure had risen to $11,200 millions, and the share of the temperate, developed lands was still 70 per cent. So much, then, for Lenin's theory of investment as a primary reason for colonialism. These figures also illustrate the extent to which the endowed and well-favoured regions received the bulk of the capital needed to make them wealthier still.

Since many of these regions had mineral reserves for a developed industry and traditions of enterprise and saving inherited from Europe, the spur of outside investment sparked internal expansion and diversification. They began to cross the threshold of full modernization, and joined Western Europe to form a new elite of wealthy communities, trading primarily with each other, investing in the main in each other's markets. As early as the 1880s, inter-Atlantic commerce covered between 60 and 70 per cent of world trade. Nor, to this day, has the proportion changed very much. Thus the experience of economic development in the Atlantic world has certainly done little to contradict the law of unregenerate nature by which "to those who have shall be given over and above that which they have."

And the experience of the highly populated tropical colonies has confirmed the pendant truth, that the needy tend to receive a lesser share. Europe's interest in the East began in trade, from the urgent need of the sunless, spiceless, silkless Northern climes for Oriental luxuries. And pre-industrial Europe had little to send in return. It is still possible to sympathize with the dilemma of a young factor of the East India Company trying to sell Yorkshire woollens through a monsoon summer in Madras. In the early stages, therefore, the chief emphasis in trade lay on what the West could buy. After the economic breakthrough to modernization, concern shifted to the manufactured goods, especially textiles, which Western traders hoped to sell. Now it was the turn of Asia to see whether it had anything to sell in return; and one of the things that made Far Eastern trade a mirage that drew European merchants deeper and deeper into China was the fact that three hundred million potential Chinese purchasers had nothing commensurate to offer in return; not "all the tea in China" could fill up the balance. Yet, in attempting to provide Asia with goods to sell, European capital did repeat in some measure the processes of investment that had opened up the temperate lands. They established exports industries—tea, jute, coffee, sugar, copra, rubber, tin—to serve the Atlantic world's rising needs. They put in some of the infrastructure of transport, ports, and harbours. They began to educate a small Westernized elite. They brought into existence a group of local entrepreneurs. They wove a web of commerce stretching from Savannah to Singapore, and created the first rough sketch of a world economy with the Atlantic world as its leading sector and the rest drawn in varying degrees into the processes of modernization. This world market in fact somewhat resembled the early stages of any domestic economy in which some sectors are fully developed and modernized, with a high degree of technological skill and trained manpower; while, at the factory gates, a cottage industry may still produce with methods unchanged for centuries and out in the countryside farmers still work for themselves and their families and never enter the market at all.

But the effect of the Western impact and investment did not on the whole draw the colonial territories through the decisive sound barrier of modernization. Where land was abundant and resources rich, wealth increased sharply and enriched the local community as well as the foreign investors who had financed the development. Tin and rubber in Malaya, tea in Ceylon, cocoa in Ghana are solid bases of national wealth. Per capita income, local services, prospects for investment, and many other indices of development have all increased sharply as a result of the colonial experience. But the general impact—which will be examined more closely in the crucial instance of India —fell short of successful modernization. Export industries and their contingent infrastructure of transport and power did not set in motion sustained local development

in countries where other resources were meagre, entrepreneurial talents slight, and the great mass of the people
worked in subsistence agriculture. And colonial governments did not in the main consider it their responsibility
to foster development which private interests were not
prepared to undertake. This was still the epoch of *laissez
faire.*

Moreover, all Europe's dependencies became involved
in the relative stagnation of the interwar years when investment virtually ceased and the bottom fell out of international trade. These years of stagnation had a particularly dire effect in colonies already tending toward overpopulation. The peace imposed by colonial control, and
the health measures introduced as Western influence increased led almost everywhere to a sharp spurt in the
growth of population. But no comparable economic development accompanied and supported it. This was to
prove one of the most fateful consequences of Asia's experience of partial modernization.

The notion that metropolitan governments might have
direct responsibility for growth and development in their
colonies really only appeared after 1945. In Africa, in
particular, the first postwar decade saw a spectacular increase in French and British investment in a series of
planned expansions of local services and resources with
capital provided in the main by the taxpayers at home.
This extension of what one may call the welfare principle
to colonial areas was, of course, a logical extension of the
acceptance of the same principle at home. But when it
came finally to be adopted, colonialism, by an irony of
history, was virtually at an end.

How far the Western incursion failed to provide a decisive spur to general modernization can be illustrated by
the one country which effectively kept the Europeans out.

For two hundred years, the Japanese excluded all foreign traders; when, after 1850, they realized they no longer had the power to exclude external influence, they allowed the Americans and the British the typical commercial concessions of the day—the right to trade, the right to free zones in treaty ports, the right to jurisdiction over their nationals—rights which in less united communities soon led to internal disruption and Western encroachment. But the Japanese authorities also set themselves systematically to create the apparatus of a modern state.

The result was a tour de force of effective modernization under government initiative and control, an experiment preceding Russia's by sixty years and carried out under, if anything, even more unfavourable conditions; for in 1868 Japan, already densely overcrowded, was held fast in a decadent frame of feudalism, lacked most of the resources for a modern economy, and was beset by all but irresistible Western pressure from outside. But Japan also possessed a small group of men who in their way were as determined and single-minded as Lenin's Bolsheviks in 1917 and—in the short run at least—considerably more skilful.

The Meiji reformers abolished feudal tenures, gave the farmer the land, introduced modern agriculture, more than doubled farm output in the first decades, and, while taking two-thirds of the surplus by way of the land tax, still left the farmer more prosperous with the remaining third. Compensation to the feudal Samurai and Daimyo in the shape of government bonds provided, together with the agricultural surplus, the funds for the new industrial sectors; and the feudalists themselves joined the officials and entrepreneurs of the new economy. Men were sent overseas to be trained; government financed and launched the new industries before selling them back to the clans and private industrialists; modern textiles replaced old handicrafts; cottage industries were linked as suppliers to large scale enterprise; and new leading sectors followed one after another—shipbuilding and coal mining after textiles and silk, cement and glass and building materials after textiles, and thereafter power and steel and heavy industry and all the apparatus of a modern industrial economy. By the end of the nineteenth century, Japan received the accolade of modernity. The Western powers gave up their special concessions. By 1914, she was dominant in the Far East.

Yet the political price of this economic achievement proved disastrously high. Japan's contact with the West began at a time when the Western powers were passing through the most aggressive and illiberal phase of their overseas expansion. The Western traders who were carving up China by force, and who had compelled the weakening empire to submit to the opium trade, to open its ports to Western commerce, and to give concession after concession to the West's insatiable pursuit of the Chinese mirage of unlimited trade were not attractive models of Western civilization. If Japan saw only the force and the cupidity, can it really be blamed? And Japan's own traditions were wholly militarized and despotic. It was inevitable in these circumstances that Japan should build a destroyer as soon as a textile mill, and use universal education in the first place to produce literate conscripts. The progression of violence—from the first attack on China to the crowning blow against Pearl Harbor—was inherent in the first acts of modernization. Japan entered the contemporary world at the point of the sword and all but perished by it.

Nonetheless, the community has not been wholly without liberal tendencies. The triumph of Western democracy in 1918 encouraged the middle and professional classes in Japan to assert their influence; and in the twenties parliamentary institutions and representative government took a certain hold, until they were eclipsed by the stagnation of the world after 1929 and the rise of Fascism. And after 1945 the Allied victory, occupation by American forces, and the imposition of an American-inspired constitution have reinforced the liberal elements, however precarious they still remain.

Where the effect of Japanese militarism was wholly and decisively disastrous was in China. China's experience of the West in the nineteenth century proved discouraging enough. As its central government disintegrated, it had to submit to near-partition at the hands of the Western powers. But in the next fifty years, any advance that it might have gained from the contact—in partial modernization, in education, in national coherence—was nullified by the steady encroachment of Japanese imperial power. By 1945, China had been at war with Japan— with some interruptions—for half a century. Continuous conflict had shattered all hopes of modernization under moderate leadership and kept to a minimum the development of any indigenous institutions of a modern stamp. Even more than in Russia in 1917, the Chinese community had been reduced to near-dissolution, its soldiers hungering for peace, its peasants for land. In this condition, Mao Tse-tung, like Lenin before him, had the wit to see that the peasants, not the workers, were the spearhead of revolution, and to advance from his agrarian base to the capture of the whole empire.

It should now be possible to define rather more clearly the "unfinished business" of Western colonialism. Outside the temperate lands, the impact of the West stimulated only one thorough breakthrough to modernization—in

Japan—and there it occurred in tough opposition to Western encroachment and advanced under the star of militarism and war. Elsewhere the processes of modernization stopped short of a breakthrough; and it is still to be proved that any ex-colonial territory can reach effective economic strength within a liberal framework. Moreover, it is not at all certain that the Western nations feel any further responsibility for their former colonies' future advance. The last ten years have seen an ever speedier liquidation of most of the old colonial relationships. The Indian struggle for independence, the longest, severest and most deeply engaged, ended in success in 1947. Thereafter the transfers of power have followed with ever-increasing speed, until, as in the Congo or Somalia, it has been all but flung at peoples whose readiness to receive it was doubtful, to say the least.

True, these transfers are a response to desires and demands which Western education has itself implanted. However precipitate, the granting of independence fits into the broad pattern of Western development already carried out inside domestic society. First the leading entrepreneurs of the West drew their own masses into the web of a developing economy where, for a time, the poor lived and worked without representation or influence. Then, when pressure for enfranchisement gathered strength, the vote was steadily extended, admitting a new estate to power in the realm. As a result, its needs and desires became the concern of government; and welfare, full employment and economic expansion had to be transferred from wholly private control to the supervision, and, where necessary, the intervention of the state. This, broadly speaking, is the domestic cycle in the West which has brought the Atlantic world from the first difficult beginnings of primary accumulation to the wealth and elbowroom of the modern mass economy.

But the analogy can be applied to the world at large only up to a certain point. The peoples of other lands have been drawn into the world economy created by Western enterprise. As their involvement increased, they, like the workers of the West, demanded enfranchisement and are now receiving it. But the last act is missing. There is no guarantee that after receiving the freedoms of the modern world, they will share more fully in its benefits. On the contrary, the first consequence of enfranchisement may well be to bring to an end even the remarkable chapter of direct assistance to their colonies which the Western powers began in 1945. Independence may well entail less stability, less prosperity, less work, less promise. It may end by being not the crown of a fruitful association but the signal of an increasing relapse.

Even if such a possibility meant no more than a sorry end to the whole colonial experiment, the Western nations, at the moment of their greatest prosperity, should surely not be indifferent to the risk that the lands they dragged up to the fringes of modernization may now slip back again for lack of continued Western support. But the issue is in fact more pointed and dangerous. Almost without exception, the ex-colonial territories have reached what is perhaps the most vulnerable phase of economic development. Their old ways of living and working—subsistence farming and marginal trading under the institutions of chieftaincy or feudalism—have been stirred and weakened by Western forces of economic change. Sectors of each community—usually the export sectors—have modern forms and aspirations. Yet the modern element is isolated and held back by what is traditional and unmodernized. The impatience of the innovators clashes with the fears of the older men. It is the classic recipe for radical resentment and disorder; and if the struggle is sharpened by lack of external capital and by a falling off even in the degree of progress achieved so far, internal pressures may increase to the point where Communism, with its total discipline, its offers of aid and its pattern of forced growth appears the only alternative.

So far, the outcome of Western colonialism has been in the main to leave the old world dying, but to create no new world in its place. This is the West's great unfinished business, the division which splits the planet into "two nations"—of the rich and the poor—the gap which should challenge the conscience of the wealthy fully as urgently as any domestic miseries of early industrialism, the gulf of potential despair and violence into which—now as then—the whole of society may still be drawn. And this, too, is the context within which the greatest of all the ex-colonial territories—India—is making its experiment in economic growth within a liberal frame.

PART

2

The Indian Plans

Chapter Eight

Conquest in India

THE BRITISH never set out to conquer India. They first came as traders in the seventeenth century, establishing modest centres of commerce at a number of points along the coast where, by permission of the central authority of the Moghuls, they were allowed to trade with Indian merchants, build lodgings for their men, berths for their ships, warehouses for their goods, and live more or less under their own laws and fiscal arrangements. The East India Company had three principal "factories"—at Bombay, at Madras, and at Calcutta; and for a century, the directors and factors of John Company carried on their business in the main peacefully enough, without excursions into local politics.

Such a pattern was not confined to India. In the seventeenth and eighteenth centuries, Western traders played quite as restricted a role in other Eastern lands. Only the

(99)

Dutch were permitted to trade with Japan; and they had
to agree to close confinement on the small offshore island
of Deshima and to humiliating visits to Kyoto to make a
formal annual submission to the local rulers. Any Western
merchant—British, French, American—wishing to open
trade with China could do so only by establishing himself
in Canton, dealing with a carefully selected and limited
group of Chinese middlemen—the Hong merchants—and
accepting sharp restrictions on his own activities. He
might not bring his wife with him, he might not employ
a Chinese servant. He might not even go for an evening's
row on the river. It was made perfectly plain that the
Westerners were the petitioners and the trade accorded
them a privilege for which they had to pay. In return,
however, they were not subject to the confiscatory whims
of the local governor who in Asia had always tended, as
one young Civil Servant of the East India Company described it, to "look on the growing riches of a subject as
boys look on a bird's nest. He eyes their progress with
impatience, then comes with a spoiler's hand and ravishes
the fruits of their labour"—one reason, incidentally, for
the absence of a general spirit of entrepreneurial activity
in the Orient.

Yet by the end of the nineteenth century most of Asia
and Africa had come under Western control. The process
by which this came about—a process which still profoundly colours the thinking of all ex-colonial peoples—
can be followed very clearly in India, although India did
not provide the first instance. The Dutch in Indonesia
enjoy the equivocal distinction of being the pioneers.

Three elements were chiefly at work in the transfer of
power: an undeviating Western desire to trade, bitter
rivalry between the different groups of European merchants, and—the decisive factor—the local collapse of

effective authority. Without the third, the other two elements would have had little effect. The European nations chased each other around the Eastern oceans for over a hundred years, pursuing their monopolies and practising every form of violence and piracy against each other; but their landborne activities remained largely peaceful wherever the writ of the local princes still ran.

In the eighteenth century the Moghul Empire began to dissolve, and India plunged into an anarchy of which there is little other example in its entire history. Local viceroys attempted to turn their imperial offices into hereditary fiefs and fought for their claims, while rivals sprang up to dispute their authority; in the resulting atmosphere of divided loyalties and civil war, lands were left untilled, education languished, superstition and obscurantism overtook religion. Life and limb were in danger, trade declined. And at this point the most fateful consequence of disorder made its appearance—the foreign merchants began to intervene. When local disorder broke out, they could hardly avoid defending themselves. If, in the course of the troubles, they had their storehouses burnt, their ships confiscated, and their records destroyed, commerce, to say the least, was not likely to prosper. In our own day the breakdown overnight of the prosperous Congo into fighting factions is a reminder of how completely economic activities depend upon pre-existent law and order—a condition the wealthy West has tended to take for granted. If, as happened in Calcutta under Suraj-ud-Daula, the local authorities march in, pillage the factories and murder the inhabitants, some instinct of self-preservation can hardly fail to be aroused. Again and again in the history of Western colonialism, the first inroads were not premeditated encroachment but a defensive effort to create a shield of security round a threatened outpost, and to restore enough orderliness for trade to be carried on. And the more grievous the surrounding disorder, the larger the Western merchants felt their bridgehead needed to be.

But this was not the only spur to action. The Western traders lived with one eye over their shoulder to see what rivals might be maneuvering to take their place. As far as profits and monopolies were concerned, they had always been perfectly ruthless with each other—a reaction which is perhaps a little less surprising when one remembers the appalling risks of navigation in those days and the scale of profits (5,000 per cent on a single shipload of nutmeg) which would accrue to the lucky merchant who made landfall in Europe. In India in the eighteenth century the British and French settlements kept an anxious watch on each other. The French had an organizer of genius at Pondicherry in the person of Dupleix; as the post-Moghul anarchy spread and rival chieftains disputed its inheritance, he sought to reinforce French power by the widely-used Western expedient of backing the claimants who made the best terms with France. The British at Madras who supported their own candidate, Mohammed Ali, found an organizer of equal brilliance in young Robert Clive; they defeated France's claimant, Chanda Sahib, at the siege of Arcot. Mohammed Ali duly succeeded as Nawab of the Carnatic, but now he was a puppet and the British ruled.

Thereafter, by a series of actions designed either to check local anarchy or to counter the French, with whom the British were repeatedly at war until 1815, or to do both at once, as in Bengal, effective British rule was extended—overtly or by puppet governors—from the original settlements to all Bengal and Bihar, then to the dominions of the Mahrattas, then to Delhi of the Moghuls;

and at last, after ninety years of expansion, to the whole of the Indian subcontinent.

Yet the scale of the conquest reflected more than local anarchy, and was already a warning to all Asia of the new and formidable quality of the Western incursion—a warning the Japanese were to heed and the Chinese rulers totally and disastrously to neglect. The little groups of Europeans already belonged to the modern world, the world of nationalism and rationalism, of modern accountancy and technology, of modern weapons and modern machines. They were very few, so few that Suraj-ud-Daula is supposed to have believed that all Europe contained no more than ten thousand men. But they held together in the new unity of exclusive nationalism. Their leaders and lieutenants pursued British—or French or Dutch—interests with ruthless tenacity. No one deserted, as the Maharatta chief Holkar did at the crucial battle of Panipat; no one betrayed his side for money or power. They combined adventurousness and panache with the most careful and systematic attention to their records and their account books. And increasingly they were better equipped and armed. When the Portuguese first appeared in Eastern waters at the end of the fifteenth century, they already enjoyed some technical superiority—better arms, more maneuverable ships. Thereafter the disparity increased as Europe began to undergo the scientific and technological revolution and the East did not. With better weapons and better discipline, the tiny European bands could by the middle of the eighteenth century rout large Asian feudal levies. All the British wars in India were fought with minute proportions of British soldiers. Increasingly they trained and officered Indian men.

A hundred years later, the full industrial revolution made the Westerners virtually irresistible in military terms, as China and Japan were to discover. But already in India the writing was on the wall, and the Indians themselves were aware of a new and menacing quality. A contemporary historian, Sayyid Ghulam Husain Khan, wrote thus of the British in his Commentary:

They join the most resolute courage to the most cautious prudence nor have they their equals in the art of ranging themselves in battle and fighting in order.

But he went on to add:

If to so many military qualifications they knew how to join the arts of government, if they . . . exerted as much ingenuity and solicitude to relieving and easing the people of God as they do in their military affairs, no nation in the world would be preferable to them or prove worthier of command.

This, he concluded, they did not know how to do—and through "apathy and indifference . . . reduced their people everywhere to poverty and misery."

These strictures applied to British rule in Bengal in the first decades of British conquest when a troop of traders and adventurers were let loose, under the East India Company's vague authority, to make their own fortunes at the Indians' expense. This they did handsomely, until strong protests in parliament in Britain and the reforming government of such great proconsuls as Warren Hastings and Cornwallis began to create the framework of more enlightened rule. But even though—as we shall see—the longer record in India went very far to disprove the censure that the British lacked "the arts of government," the strictures must be remembered. It is the mixture of chicanery and highhandedness marking so much of the Western record in Asia that haunts the minds of men in ex-colonial and uncommitted lands to this day.

They remember—and Communist propaganda quotes

Lenin strenuously to remind them—that Western control was first imposed to protect Western commercial interests, and that to do so, the Westerners played one local leader off against another and supported the man who was ready, if necessary, to put foreign interests before local needs. The process began in Indonesia. It was carried forward on the largest scale in India. All through the nineteenth century, the pressures and rivalries went on, the Manchus having to repeat India's concessions, Britain and France renewing their rivalry in Africa, Germany jostling its way to the top of the queue, and even the supposedly anticolonial Americans maneuvering themselves into control of Cuba and the Philippines. Such memories are too recent to be exploded yet, even if the Communists were not constantly reviving them. The enormous head of emotion generated over the possibility of Katanga breaking away from the Congo federation and engrossing—with Belgian help and with control of the Belgian-run mines—well over half the federation's potential revenues has roots in over a hundred years of colonial domination in which again and again the Westerners have seemed to the local peoples to safeguard their own tough economic interests by skilful manipulation of the local political scene.

This is not the whole story of Western colonialism and the British record in India provides an infinitely more complex and constructive record. But force and fraud certainly belong to its beginnings and reappear as continuous strands in its history. And today they are very far from being banished from the picture of colonialism held by leaders in emergent lands.

Chapter Nine

The Political Heritage

UNDER the surface of anarchy, what kind of a community had the British come to control? Like all traditional societies of the East—or indeed any civilized society before the impact of Western ideas—India's unity lay in culture, not nationalism; and this culture was sacred and hierarchical. The Indian imagination was molded by the great Hindu epics—the *Ramayana* and the *Mahabharata*—just as the Bible and the classics suffused the Western spirit. And in India hierarchy reached its most complete form in the institution of caste, by which the work, family life, marriage, and social intercourse of virtually everyone were fixed in a pre-determined place in the religious and social scale. Over three hundred castes limited and underpinned the people's life, giving them at the same time security and immobility. At the top of the ladder stood scholars and warriors,

Brahmins and Kshatriyas. At the bottom, below all caste, were the millions of untouchables. No society in history has ever pushed hierarchy so far.

Beyond this hierarchy, the spirit of government was largely arbitrary and rested on the whim of the sovereign. Yet it was limited by the immemorial customs of the people. Around the Court and the imperial entourage, absolute government was the rule. But royal power hardly penetrated the villages; and there a myriad tiny societies—the largest experiment in organized anarchy known to history, as Professor J. K. Galbraith has described them—governed themselves through their own committees of elders—*panchayats*—on the basis of customs which did not change.

These little republics were also the basic units of the economy, for they were villages of cultivators, and the land contributed the overwhelming share of the community's subsistence. Nobody owned the land, anymore than to-day anyone owns the open sea. A large variety of people had rights in it. The king had his share—the land revenue; the clients, officials, and courtiers to whom he gave a share in the revenue—the Zamindars, the Jagirdars—had their portion; the peasant families or clans or brotherhoods who cleared the land and established the villages took their share in return for cultivating the land; and families had continuing rights in their separate strips. But the land reverted to the commune for redistribution should the family die out. Village servants, weavers, accountants, watchmen, scavengers, got their portions, too. In addition, the village as a whole might have common lands for grazing and perhaps some woodlands for fuel.

It was so stable a system that it allowed the Gangetic Plain to be cultivated continuously for five or six thousand years. But it had no reserves against external disaster. If the monsoons which bring India all its rain in four months between June and September failed, there was famine which no power on earth could mitigate so long as the bullock, eating almost the weight of grain it could carry, was the only means of transport. And the system could not cope with the consequences of population rising beyond the available supplies of land. So long as peasant families could move on and open up fresh land, they did not need to fear either falling productivity or external extortion. The Indian farmer preserved his light friable soils for millennia by careful fallowing. Only if the land became overcrowded, did the fallowing time have to be cut and the family strips reduced in size, with a consequent fall in fertility. Nor could the Zamindars or the king's revenue officers or the local money-lenders squeeze the cultivator too hard so long as he could pull up stakes and go off with his family to find new land. But, like all traditional, static, subsistence societies, India could not avert disaster once the land had filled up.

Apart from the land, other sources of wealth were negligible. There were artisans in the villages, and more elaborate establishments in the big centres organized by merchants who could amass considerable fortunes. European traders enriched this class still further once they arrived to organize large-scale trade with the growing Western markets. Like the later compradors in China, Indian merchants around Surat and Bombay and Madras and Murshidabad acquired considerable fortunes. However, they did not gain comparable political influence. Leadership, the dominant values, prestige remained with the noncommercial groups—the scholarly Brahmins, the rulers, Moslem and Rajput, and their retainers, the princes, the Zamindars, the warrior castes. Toward trade they had the attitude of the gentlefolk in Victorian England. It was not quite respectable to devote one's life to acquiring wealth.

In such a society, there could be no indigenous forces making for constitutional government. At the head was the emperor; and of him Sir Thomas Roe, one of the first British visitors to India, had written in the early seventeenth century: "The King by his own word ruleth," and the Indians "have no written law." Below the Court all was fixed by caste rules and tradition down to the *panchayats*—where local autonomy combined with the all-pervasive force of tradition kept the village baked hard in the cake of custom. The forces which had made for liberal rule in the West—the vision of human equality inherent in the Jewish and Christian tradition, the classical concept of citizenship under law, the medieval division of power between Church and State from which the concept of plural, decentralized authority could be derived, the early power and influence of trading cities with their respect for the merchant and their scope for the professional and middle classes—of all this, there was virtually no trace in the vast, hierarchical, undynamic Indian polity.

And these same forces—arbitrary government, monarchs and their taxgathers watching wealthy merchants like boys after birds' nests, the disrespect felt for trade, the merchants' lack of influence, a static agriculture, and a society profoundly oriented away from innovation, science, and technological change—prevented the emergence of any of the impulses which in Britain had set in spontaneous motion the revolution of economic growth. If India was to change, there had to be a catalyst; and this is what the British conquest came to be.

In the early nineteenth century, the first need in an India distracted by civil war and by the incursions of the

British was orderly administration. This could not be achieved without regular revenue. As Britain assumed wider responsibilities, its senior officials and its young men in the field laboured to bring the appalling confusion of land records, of arrears and indebtedness, into some kind of order. In Bengal, the decision was taken to vest the ownership of land in the Zamindars, as though they were English country gentlemen, and to fix the government's share of the crop in perpetuity. In Madras, thanks to the insight and pertinacity of the great Munro, the collectors held the responsibility of settling the share directly with the peasants. But whatever the settlement—whether with villagers, princes, or Zamindars—orderly administration returned, revenues began to flow in, and after a fifty-year interregnum of confusion and disorder, Indian society recovered a settled way of life under new rulers. In a sense, the new men were no more alien than the Moghuls had been; but the Persian conquerors had belonged to the same order of hierarchical, ritual, and static society as the peoples they subdued. The British were something quite new: children of a liberal national and developing society who, for all their determination not to change the outer customs of the alien people they now dominated, were quite incapable of suppressing their missionary ardour for the new Western ideas.

After the first period of Company recruitment, during which a man might begin as a warehouse clerk and end as a member of the Governor's Council, the authorities began to pick their officials for India on the basis of special attributes and qualifications. Haileybury was chosen as the site of a college for Indian civil servants as early as 1809; the training there was more specialized and professional than for the home service. Entrance by competitive examination, introduced in 1853, was seventeen years ahead of a similar reform in Britain. The young officials emerged, in fact, from a more rational and systematic preparation than any being given in their own country; and it is not surprising that nineteenth-century India should have been able to attract, generation after generation, recruits from some of Britain's ablest and most enlightened families. Stracheys, Macaulays, Trevelyans, Stephenses created what were almost dynasties in India, while they also led the liberal and reforming world of thought at home.

The mood of such men and of the administration that employed them reflected in great measure the rational and utilitarian movement which was at work at the same time in England. This movement abolished unpredictable casual administration and set up instead the orderly procedures of a modern civil service, working to precedent, basing itself on equity and probity, on proper records and established rules. It radically changed the framework of government. Although British rule had to be authoritarian, it was not arbitrary. Its legal limits were set by a Parliament—though it was not India's parliament—and no local official could interfere on a chance or a whim. The reorganized administration of justice reinforced the idea of a government of laws, not men. Life, property, and contracts were protected, and all branches of civil law developed. The new notion of law and legislation as instruments of rational purpose, as means of reforming society's abuses, began to encroach on the old reliance upon custom. And behind all these changes lay the often unexpressed but always potent master idea that government's main purpose must be to serve the good of the community—in short, the greatest good of the greatest number. From the earliest days in Bengal, men like Verelst or Vansittart or Warren Hastings fought against the avarice and irresponsibility of so many of their officials; and they urged the young men coming out from England to hold it their duty, in the words of Verelst:

to convince the peasant that you will stand between him and the hand of oppression; that you will be his refuge and the redresser of his wrongs . . . and finally teach him a veneration and affection for the humane maxims of our government.

In the first decades of full British rule, this tradition was amplified by men of splendid vision and responsibility —Munro and Elphinstone, Metcalfe and Malcolm; and although the Indian administration and civil service had its share of idlers and misfits and worse, the tradition of duty and devotion remained predominant and was greatly strengthened by the revival of a deep, if narrow, evangelical religion among the British middle classes.

When Bishop Heber toured North India in the 1830s, he commended the "diligence and good intentions" of the young officers and the fine quality of senior officers "who have devoted themselves for many years to the advantage of the land . . . and are looked up to, throughout considerable districts, with a degree of respectful attachment which it is not easy to believe counterfeited."

There is, of course, another side to the coin. The religion which deepens the young man's spirit of dedication also increases his sense of what he calls the paganism of the people among whom he lives; it is easy to judge them inferior as well. There are signs of an arrogant nationalism bred of Britain's growth in wealth and power. Bishop Heber speaks of the "exclusive and intolerant spirit" and "foolish surly national pride" of some of the men he met. A few years later, a French traveller, Victor Jacquemont, found the same contrast between a dedicated sense of honour and duty—the British are "always true to their word, upright and just ninety-nine times out of a hundred"—and an aloof and inescapable national pride. A Frenchman, he remarks, would feel himself first among Indians. The Englishman's pride is more disconcerting. He simply thinks himself alone.

The breach widens as British rule is prolonged. The Mutiny—the last revolt of traditional India led by the disaffected rulers of Oudh—undermined confidence on both sides. By the time the air cleared again, the Indians had begun to change. Ideals of self-rule and national independence planted by the British were beginning to spring up; and many British officials found it easier to dedicate their lives to a grateful and inarticulate peasantry than to young Indians who asked uncomfortable questions and knew the answers in Western terms. The British position had become ambiguous. From the earliest days, far-sighted officials—men with the vision of a Munro or an Elphinstone—had declared that the only justification for British rule would be to prepare Indians for self-government in the modern world. By the end of the century, the Indians began to claim that they were now trained, and that in any case nations had the inalienable right to govern or misgovern themselves. The British could not deny the principle. They could only urge that the Indians were not yet ready. Yet who could say what are the objective standards and criteria of being ready or not? No one learns to swim by demonstrations on the shore. But a child can drown if thrown into the water too soon. The British solution—a series of cautious but widening constitutional experiments in partial self-government, each designed to take India further and further into the water—met the resistance of the growing number of Indians who felt they could already swim. Nor could they be sure until 1947 whether the British seriously intended to let them take the final plunge. Under these conditions, although there did indeed remain much dedication, and, on both sides, great reserves of good will, these were shadowed by suspicion and disaffection and distrust.

Yet in spite of the ambiguities, the paradox must be allowed that British rule, authoritarian as it was, can be counted an essay in liberal education. The first reason has already been suggested: nineteenth-century Britain was increasingly liberal, and in an open society there can be no final division between ideals at home and practical action abroad. The second reason lies in the degree to which Indians were drawn into contact with the new institutions and ideas. From the earliest times they worked in subordinate positions under the British, and some of the mood of the new rational and utilitarian procedures was transmitted simply by daily work. Increasingly, as British rule developed, Indians also entered the higher levels of justice and administration. In theory they could enter the Indian Civil Service as soon as it became competitive in the 1850s; but the examinations were held only in England, a crippling handicap in a society in which Hindu tradition forbade travel overseas. A few bold spirits did make the journey and even passed the exam, but they were not thereafter very warmly welcomed in the Service. However, by the end of the century, considerably more Indians had received Western education, often in England, and they began to enter the service in greater numbers. After 1919, the examinations were held in both Britain and India; and by 1947, the number of British and Indian officials was nearly equal. A trained experienced cadre of Indian civil servants, possibly without peer in the world, proved to be one of Britain's most indispensable legacies to the new Indian Union.

And the key to it, as to every other aspect of the liberal impact, was the spread of education. In 1835, the Government of India, prompted by Macaulay, declared that "the great object of the British Government must be the promotion of European science and literature among the natives of India," and set about creating a system of education for an Indian elite who would learn modern subjects in the English tongue. Schools and colleges sprang up under government and missionary sponsorship. In 1854, under a new co-ordinated system, universities were established in Calcutta, Bombay, Madras, and Allahabad. Increasingly, as the century advanced, wealthier parents sent their sons to be educated in England. Thus began an encounter in depth between Asian and Western thought which occurred in no other Eastern community. Japan had picked over Western civilization like a bargain counter, extracting here a destroyer or there a steel mill, and leaving the goods of the spirit severely alone. China, harried for a century by Western pressure, civil war, and Japanese invasion, never had either time or tranquillity for a considered confrontation. Education, like everything else in ravaged China, seemed always to stand at panic stations. Only in India was there "world enough and time."

But all the time in the world would not have served to produce a fruitful synthesis had there been no wise, liberal, and moderate response on the Indian side. The Indian elite were, after all, confronted with an extraordinary intellectual and spiritual challenge. They had just emerged from a time of chaos and breakdown. The new ideas ran counter to much of their tradition and most of their customs and conventions. It would have been easy to go precipitately to either extreme, to reject the new polity and attempt to preserve all that was encrusted, outdated, and valueless in the old—the way chosen in other lands by reactionary conservatism; or else to jettison every value, every sacred tradition, every source of pride and comfort in the old—the route offered by the total Westernizers who, in this century, are increasingly Communist.

That India has so far followed its own route, avoiding both extremes, is due to the wisdom and resilience of its own traditions. The form that modernization might take in India was prefigured during the first days of British rule by the life of one of India's greatest reformers, Raja Ram Mohan Roy. An orthodox Hindu, born of a wealthy Brahmin family, deeply versed in Hindu thought and Islamic culture, he entered the East India Company and began to study English. To his traditional learning he now added a knowledge of Christianity, to do which he studied Hebrew and Greek. He also read widely among the rationalist writers of the European Enlightenment and followed the works of their English successors, Jeremy Bentham and the Utilitarians. His reactions proved typical of all later reformers. He did not wholly turn to Christianity; instead, he used Christian and humanist ideas to reform the depressed condition of contemporary Hindu culture. His movement of reform, the *Brahmo Samaj*, sought to recover the original purity of Indian religious inspiration, modify the superstitions of popular Hinduism, give other-worldly Hindu thought a new impulse of neighbourly love and social obligation, and fight all the legal and social incrustations of centuries —caste, the seclusion of women, suttee—which, without any basis either in the Vedantas—India's sacred books— or in natural law, masqueraded as religious rules. Thus, at the very beginning of India's close contact with the West, a way was shown of accepting Western science, Western reforms, and Western ideals without abandoning the deepest ethical insights of Indian society.

This mood, at once acquiescent and critical, made possible the speedy acceptance of the educational reforms of 1835 and the creation all over India of a small but dominant group of men educated in the liberal atmosphere of British nineteenth-century thought. Here was a revolution more profound than the building of steel mills or extensions of the cotton crop. Brahmins learned to believe that men could be born equal and free and express their free-born condition in the framework of constitutional government. Magna Carta became part of the Indian heritage; Indian boys read the thunderous speeches of Edmund Burke denouncing British tyranny in India. Kshatriyas could be taught that the pen is mightier than the sword. Youths in Delhi or Bengal or Bombay or Travancore learned in a common English idiom that they were sons of one great Indian community, united by a force new to the divided, multilingual, hierarchical India of old—the force of modern nationalism. Above all, they began to learn that they had the inalienable right to govern themselves.

At first, the effects of the new education spread only slowly. Communities with a lively intellectual tradition like the uppercaste Bengalis led the way. The Moslems lagged behind until the 1880s—a disastrous gap, for it helped to convince them that in an Indian state they would always be at the mercy of better-educated Hindus. In this gap lies one of the roots of partition. In the South for a long time, only the Brahmins and the Christians could be brought in. But in the second half of the century the tempo quickened. More schools and colleges opened in India. Hindus began to overcome the taboo on traveling overseas, and sent more of their sons to Britain for university training. A sizable educated class existed by 1900, quite large enough to provide pressure for greater

Indian participation in administration and politics—especially in politics.

Yet the pressure started so quietly that a contemporary might have been excused for missing the date. In 1884, a retired British civil servant, Allan Hume, persuaded some Indian friends to found the Indian National Congress. It was a time of some apathy in Indian life. Defeat in the Mutiny had put a damper upon Indian politics. In the next decade, economic expansion had gathered momentum and some of the most lively forces in Indian society became absorbed in the tasks of economic modernization. Men seemed more interested in new economic opportunities than in wider political rights. So Allan Hume started the National Congress to remind India's potential leaders that no country could prosper if its political life was left wholly to the discretion of foreigners.

For the next thirty years, years of growth and confidence in India, Congress leaders remained moderate, cautious men, content to petition the Government on occasion, draft memoranda, present memorials, and achieve what they could by quiet contact. But as the new century advanced, such leadership ceased to be adequate. A young and growing educated class began to feel the spur of lively nationalism and to resent its exclusion from political influence. The beginnings of a modern economy were creating new problems of mass leadership. In the industrial cities, an unsettled working class could become easy prey to the agitator. In the countryside, conditions had deteriorated and might presage rural unrest. Leaders such as Tilak began to talk the language of violent opposition. There was terrorism in Bengal. Anyone looking into the future, as the first decade of the twentieth century ended, might not unreasonably have forecast the emergence in India of opposite forms of revolutionary violence:

Communism on the left, and a backward looking, fanatical, and communal conservatism on the right, both feeding on nationalist resentment, and both destroying all moderate, liberal groups in between.

India escaped this desperate polarization—which has proved the undoing of so many developing societies—largely through the genius of three men. Gandhi, Nehru, and Vallabbahai Patel proved to be leaders in the authentic tradition of Ram Mohan Roy, reconcilers yet modernists, able to work in the Indian as well as the Western tradition, above all able to interpret India to itself at a time of dangerous and confusing transition. It is not always easy to disentangle the differences between these men, who worked so closely together and whose will and guidance dominated the Congress Party through most of the interwar years. But it can perhaps be said that Patel stood for the solid cautious men of the centre, while Gandhi reconciled, reformed—or isolated—the potential revolutionaries of the right and Nehru performed the same task with the extremists on the left. All three, in fact, commanded the loyalty of the moderate men on the right and the left.

Gandhi spoke from the depths of a profoundly Indian tradition. His leadership was a religious leadership, with the charismatic mark of austerity and holiness. He took the Congress Party to the villages by breaking its concentration on middleclass, urban affairs and compelling it to listen to the anxieties and miseries of the rural millions. His first symbolic acts of resistance to British rule concerned village needs: a refusal first to accept a reassessment of the land revenue, then to pay the salt tax. He saw India's future in terms of reviving the dying culture of village life. Salvation would lie in spinning and weaving by hand, not through "the dark satanic mills";

political health could be recovered by giving the village *panchayat* its old authority, not by building up yet more power in the vast urban conglomerates spawned by alien rule and foreign trade.

Yet the conservative was a true revolutionary. He interpreted the Hindu tradition, as Ram Mohan Roy had done, in the light of Christian love and universal ethics. He was profoundly committed to the ideal of equality, and he utterly rejected caste or communalism, class or race, or any other kind of exclusiveness in the family of man. His work in the villages centred on an unremitting effort to abolish the accumulated evils of village life, above all the hopeless plight of the untouchables on the last lowly rung of the village ladder.

His underlying political strategy remained robustly anti-imperialist. Beneath surface shifts and changes he had only one aim—to compel the British to give up their imperial control. Most revolutionary of all, however, were the reasons for his opposition to Britain and the methods he employed. He wished the British to give up the *raj* not because, like some normal coarse-fibred radical, he disliked their pretensions and wanted the power himself. He profoundly believed that Britain could not recover its own spiritual integrity while it persisted in so profound a denial of equality as to behave like a conqueror; and that India would lack wholeness of spirit until it gained equal stature and full responsibility for its own destiny. Hate did not enter into the calculation. What was at stake was the deepest need of man—to destroy the lie in the soul. For the same reason, violence, that great breeder of hate, had to be ruled out. India would conquer by the moral force of passive resistance. Britain would recognize that force and retreat.

Gandhi did not convert all the extremists. Not even his

great spirit could check the growth of communal division between Hindu and Muslim or prevent the tragedy of Partition in 1947. And he was killed by a Hindu fanatic who could not stomach his master's readiness to see a brother in every man, even the hated Moslem. Nor was he able to bring all his followers to his exalted view of non-violence. In fact, he called off one India-wide movement of nonco-operation because in one or two places violence had got out of hand. But he brought millions upon millions of simple, conservative, religious souls into a vast move-ment of mass politics without once using the slogans of hatred or pumping the bellows of angry exclusive na-tionalism. He combined the deepest inspiration of Hindu asceticism and renunciation with the most modern sense of human and national equality. He was a great saint and a shrewd politician. And therefore, conservative and radi-cal could serve him equally and he could hold together a great national movement with disciplines no more violent than his own threat to fast, if necessary to death.

Meanwhile his younger colleague had the loyalty of the modernizers and of men on the left. Jawarharlal Nehru represented the intellectual Brahmin strain in the Indian tradition, adapted to the scientific, national, modernizing side of Western thought. He respected Gandhi's religious approach, and even realized that there was no other way to the villagers' hearts. But he did not share it. For him village betterment meant a frontal attack on India's ap-palling poverty and a systematic, scientific effort to de-velop all India's resources to that end. In the crucial inter-war years, Nehru experienced at first hand the slackness and stagnation in the British economy and came to share the conviction of thousands of Westerners that the capi-talist system, operating solely on the profit motive, could not solve the problems of the world's misery. He turned to socialism and to planning as a more just, more efficient, and more scientific method of running human affairs. Yet Russia's violence repelled him. He remained a convinced believer in freedom and in the methods of democracy. His was constitutional socialism of the stamp of the British Labour Party.

All through the thirties Nehru led a group of younger men in a fluctuating battle to make socialism the declared objective of the Congress Party. The forces of conservatism proved too strong, and neither Gandhi nor Patel had any sympathy with the attempt. Yet Nehru's efforts left little place for the emergence of groups further to the left. A Communist Party had been formed in 1925, but by that time Congress had appropriated the only really mass issue in India, the issue of independence. The Communists appeared either to be trying to infiltrate Congress—which made them suspect—or to take people's minds off the struggle for independence, which was downright unpatriotic.

Then in 1941, at the height of the war, just as Congress had decided that only a strong new move against the British could ever secure Indian freedom, the Communists discovered that Hitler's attack on Russia had turned an imperialist mêlée into a people's war. They began collaborating with the British just when Congress ceased to do so, and once again they assumed an unpatriotic role. Thus, while in China the Communists gradually took over from the Kuomintang popular leadership in the nationalist struggle and thereby secured final control of China, the Indian Communists in 1947 were still a small divided group, unable to compete either with the triumphant national leadership of Gandhi or the reforming socialist energies of Nehru. At independence, India was a country in which men of moderate outlook, reforming zeal and liberal principle held the centre of the political stage.

The Congress Party had been more than a movement of nationalist protest and pressure. It had been a school of politics as well—not the strident, dogmatic politics of mass conformity, but the democratic politics of compromise and give-and-take. Lacking any monolithic unity, it turned every annual conference into a session of the keenest discussion and debate. In some degree it resembled the great political parties in America, being essentially a federation of different regional, economic, and social interests. It could hold the loyalty of the Bombay millowner and the Gandhian hand spinner, of a practical down-to-earth conservative like Vallabbahai Patel, or a visionary socialist like Jayaprakash Narayan—just as the Democrats in America include purse-conscious senators from the South and Northern liberals with ambitious programs of public spending. It is true that the main solder of the Congress Party had been the struggle for independence. Yet since 1921 some of its members had gained practical experience of government business in the successive extensions of local self-rule conceded by the British. In 1937, governments specifically based on Congress took office in some of the provinces. There was at least a chance that the vast, diffuse, ideologically various party might hold together even after the nationalist struggle had been won, simply on the typically Anglo-Saxon and pragmatic basis of "carrying on the business of government."

Thus, at the time of independence, the long years of contact with British liberal thought, the century of Western education, even the struggles with Britain to wrest self-government from an alien ruler, had all given India a framework of moderate politics unique in Asia. The new society had at least the chance of developing its political life within a decentralized, open, and pluralist society, and of preserving the methods of free elections and free consent. More than that, the vision of its own leaders had ensured that the men who came to office in 1947 were modernizers and developers, men to whom the challenges of the modern growth-economy came as an opportunity, not a disaster. At the same time, the chances that their policies would attract widespread and free support were greatly enhanced by a very considerable concensus among Indians of all political opinions that the first task of the new state must be to galvanise the Indian economy into modern ways.

Chapter Ten

British Rule and the Indian Economy

BRITAIN'S impact on the Indian economy illustrates in the clearest and most sustained way the general rule that, outside the Atlantic area, Western colonialism and Western investment launched but did not complete the processes of economic modernization; and if one reason more than any other is responsible for this phenomenon, it is that Western colonisers and Western investors throughout the crucial decades of predominant Western influence were mostly men who believed in *laissez faire*.

The system worked at home. By clearing away administrative obstructions, guaranteeing property and contract, and securing a general atmosphere of law and order, government had released an enormous flood of spontaneous economic energy which had transformed the old system with astonishing effectiveness and speed. Few people asked what might happen in a society in which the spontaneous energies were lacking—in which farmers worked only for subsistence, merchants and artisans had no sense of innovation, scientists and technicians were unknown, the leaders devoted themselves primarily to spending and display, and the whole ethics and purpose of the society were profoundly uncommercial. Such was India in the nineteenth century. It would have required heroic efforts comparable to the achievements of the Meiji reformers in Japan to have transformed the subcontinent into a modernized community. And the British could not be reformers on this scale.

For one thing, they were foreigners; and an alien government—unless it is a very ruthless one—tends to be cautious about root-and-branch reform. It may arouse more hostility than it can control. For another, the *laissez faire* of British officials in India must be considered rather an academic and specialized version of the faith. They had learned it at school and then carried it out to a vast pre-industrial economy where it was unlikely to be modified by the hard knocks of actual commercial experience. And they did not in any case feel much sympathy for whatever business groups there were, British or Indian. They had the instinctive prejudice against trade of Victorian gentlemen. They decidedly did not feel it the purpose of the British authorities in India to foster economic activities. Their task was to give law and order, administer justice, secure the land revenue, and give the mass of the people—overwhelmingly in the countryside—fair and consistent government. Where there was enterprise, such a system would not impede it and might even help—for instance, by securing internal peace, introducing modern commercial law, and ensuring orderly procedures in the courts. But where there was no enterprise, government did not intend to act as a substitute.

A wholesale application of Britain's contemporary economic philosophy to the Indian world had the result of producing a system of partial modernization. On the land, it did begin to bring more farmers into the market. Partly this reflected the British decision to collect the land revenue in cash. The peasants had to sell to lay their hands on the money, and the impact was increased by the fact that, for some time, the level of assessment was on the whole too high. But the switch to the market also meant innovation and new methods for Indian farmers once internal peace and better communications began to widen the opportunities. Cash crops for export and for local industry or consumption expanded: jute around Calcutta, cotton and groundnuts in the enterprising Gujerat, wheat in the Punjab. By 1947 a considerable number of India's farmers had entered the market in one way or another. Even so, the majority still worked mainly for subsistence.

Market influences were also extended—unconsciously —by the British in a different and less constructive sense. Applying British concepts of debt and property to Indian agriculture, they made land a salable commodity, which it had never been, allowed it to be mortgaged in return for credit, and permitted the courts to enforce foreclosure. The Indian peasant had always borrowed—to carry him over a poor harvest, to buy a new buffalo, to marry a daughter, to entertain his friends. But in the past the moneylender had no lien on his land, and by Hindu custom, interest payments beyond the sum of the principal went to reduce the debt. The situation could not get out of hand.

Under British administration, the peasant found he

could borrow more than ever. The moneylenders had every inducement to stake him to the limit, knowing that the bondage of debt, thus established, would entail either the enslavement of the peasant who would now work the year round to pay interest on an accumulating debt, or else the seizing of his land and its resale or reletting for a much higher return.

The pressures grew worse as the nineteenth century advanced. Decade after decade of internal peace brought a steady increase in India's population. There are no accurate statistics, but a rough estimate is that it may have doubled between 1780 and 1880. Thereafter it rose more rapidly—from over 200 millions in the last decades of the century to nearly 360 millions by the time of independence. More people in a still static economy meant more pressure on the land. Its market value rose, but the peasants grew poorer as their strips were subdivided. They fell more easily into debt and pledged their land more recklessly. And since its value was going up, creditors were readier to foreclose—while money lenders, richer farmers, Zamindars were all drawn into the profitable but unproductive game of rural usury and land speculation.

The whole economy suffered as a result. Agricultural productivity did not improve, and there was no growing surplus of food to transfer to urban markets. Although landlords could make large gains by usury and by speculating in land, they had little inducement to use their money for improving their farms. Nor had the wretched peasant any inducement to do so. Any surplus he might have earned by producing more efficiently for the market would have been instantly drained off to the *bania*—the moneylender—either in the shape of compound interest on past debts or else by way of current market transactions. The *banias* were usually merchants as well, buying the peasants' produce at low prices just after the harvest, since the little men could not afford to wait, and then selling him back his seed corn, his implements, and his domestic necessities at whatever price the market would bear. Between his low selling price and his high buying price the peasant's surplus vanished. This left him with no spur to greater efficiency.

Wherever such a type of self-perpetuating rural stagnation has appeared—in Japan before 1868, in China before 1949, in the latifundia of Southern Europe, or the feudal systems of Latin America—it has proved a source of dangerous immobility to the whole economy and hence a potent spur to revolutionary discontent. There were eighty-four peasant revolts in Japan in the 1860s alone. Peasant outbursts and banditry were endemic in the Chinese countryside throughout the 1920s and 1930s; and it was on peasant discontent that the Chinese Communists established the broad base of their power. In recent years Communist infiltration in the New World—in Guatemala or Cuba, for instance—has found its surest entry points among the dispossessed peasantry. And in India before the Second World War, peasant disturbances had begun in spite of a partial and belated effort on the part of the administration to protect peasants against wholesale dispossession.

To begin to break away from this type of self-perpetuating and disintegrating stagnation, there is only one sure way—decisive land reform; and whenever it has not been attempted, the prospects for either economic progress or democratic institutions must be judged very bleak. But as an alien power the British Government could not adopt such a solution in India. And its failure on the land impeded efforts of modernization in other sectors. The essence of a successful breakthrough to economic growth is that its effects should be cumulative—each sector providing stimulus to the rest, and the expansion of a growing number of concurrent activities providing external economies, markets, supplies, and opportunities to each dynamic element in the new economy. Partial modernization changes and develops sections of the economy, provides spurts of energy and growth, and increases some incomes and opportunities—but the cumulative effect is lacking. This was the pattern in British India.

In two vital sectors of the economy—the provision of the system's infrastructure of transport, power, education, and so forth, and in manufacturing—the failure of modernization in agriculture helped to keep development below the level needed for self-sustaining growth. Even if government had been less wedded to *laissez faire,* it would still have been limited in its activities by its continuing poverty. Land revenue was one of its chief sources of income, but stagnant agriculture prevented any important increase. As for the industrial sector, the rural blight impeded its growth by drawing off potential investment into usury and land speculation and by keeping peasant consumption below the level at which the villages might have become effective markets for an industrial sector producing consumer goods.

Actually the Indian government did break some new ground in the sphere of infrastructure. In nineteenth-century Britain, the economy's overheads had been largely provided by private enterprise. The greatest single element—the railways—had been built by private capital, not only in Britain but, with the help of British investment, all around the Atlantic world as well. Even education, which governments everywhere have accepted as their responsibility, was largely privately provided in

Britain until the last decades of the century. In India, in spite of the prevailing philosophy of nonintervention, government did stimulate some elements of infrastructure. It was clear that private initiative would not produce even the beginnings of a modern system of education, so this the government set out to do, concentrating, as in England, on the training of an elite at the secondary and university level. And the Indian railways were also financed on government initiative and with government guarantees, which enabled the money to be raised relatively inexpensively. In 1914, India, with 40,000 miles of track, had one of the largest systems in the world. Its principal purpose had been, in the government's eyes, to ensure Indian security—internally against the risk of disaffection, externally against possible encroachment. But its economic effect was immediate and widespread. It broke down provincial isolation and permitted the administration, after some disastrous efforts to leave the matter to the workings of the market, to evolve a proper famine code and deal effectively with the recurring crisis of failure of the monsoons. Above all, the railway system began to create a unified internal market and to stimulate the more vigorous and enterprising regions—the Punjab, Gujerat—to produce for it.

But at this point the record of the government's direct stimulus more or less ends. Nor did it try indirectly to promote growth by a better mobilization of private capital. Most banks were foreign and concerned in the main with foreign trade. Indian banking was not far removed from old-fashioned money lending. The stock exchanges in Bombay and Calcultta served a very restricted group. There was no central bank until the 1920s. Thus, even if more Indians had been interested in investment—and most were not—they would have found it hard to find the right channels. The government's attitude to the unorganized capital market was, of course, entirely in keeping with *laissez faire*. In Britain, private enterprise had created its own credit institutions. In India, the underlying enterprise was lacking, and so the system failed to take root. There was no attempt made to follow the precedent of the railways and build up by government stimulus what private enterprise could not produce itself.

Even the interventions that were made had less than their full possible effect. All the equipment for the railways was bought in Britain, and provided no stimulus to local industrialization beyond a few railway workshops—and even then the engineers were mainly British. Another potent public spur to industrial growth—a defence establishment and an arms industry—also failed to develop. After the Mutiny, only small arms were manufactured in India. Artillery, an important element in the expansion of heavy industry, was procured from Britain. India's few ordnance establishments remained too small to boost local engineering. Shipbuilding, which the Japanese government encouraged with considerable effect in the early stages of growth, was not carried on in India at all, a consequence of the Westerners' early capture of seaborne traffic and Britain's later engrossment of the Indian carrying trade. Thus India missed two or three of the main nineteenth-century boosts to growth.

These lacks should not be laid to some special and devious British desire to stunt Indian development. At that time, no one knew how vast were India's reserves of iron ore—some twenty billion tons—for the deposits lay out in the jungles of Bihar and Orissa. The raw materials for iron and steel making were not ready to hand, as they had been in Britain and America or Germany or Lorraine. Thus it seemed cheaper and more sensible to go shopping for industrial and military supplies in the developed West. However, a government really set on modernizing the economy might have done more. Japan, too, lacked iron ore and coking coal in the 1870s. But the Meiji reformers began to build up an arms industry all the same.

And, having missed some of the central nineteenth-century accelerators, India proceeded to miss the twentieth-century types as well. Roads remained inadequate and in large parts of the country quite primitive. There was no large development of electric power. Coal production, having risen from a million tons to 20 million tons a year between 1880 and the first World War, rose little further. Technical and scientific education—the essential modern pendants to the old classical training—expanded hardly at all. At independence, the number of students graduating in engineering and technology was still only about 3,000 a year.

The truth is, that in the interwar years, Britain was no longer in a position to keep up the tempo of earlier development. The twenties and the thirties brought stagnation to the British economy and there was no capital to spare for the colonies. And in India the steadily growing pressure of nationalist opposition to British rule absorbed the administration's funds and attention to the exclusion of nearly everything else. As a result, the few modest signs in the twenties and thirties of a new governmental approach—the departments to encourage industrial development, the new interest in agricultural extension work and research—never really got under way for lack of funds. In 1939, India was still essentially an economy with a nineteenth-century, not a twentieth-century framework.

In these conditions of relative stagnation, private enterprise alone could not act as a spur to sustained growth. For many years the chief investments were, inevitably, British, but they never reached a level sufficient to launch a general expansion. Before the first World War, all Britain's investments, public and private, in India amounted to not much more than 16 per cent of British overseas investment, the bulk of which had gone to the temperate lands. At independence, private investment stood at $423 millions and had been at about that level for the thirty preceding years. Thus, after more than a century of its connection with India, Britain's total private capital there was considerably less than the figure for today's capital exports in a single year.

The most usual criticism today is not, however, that foreign investment in developing countries remains too small, but that it tends to engross too large a share of the country's resources and opportunities. Why, so run the arguments, permit foreign capital to come in and develop a concession when the result is that the entire earnings are shipped overseas as payments to shareholders and creditors, as disbursements for royalties and patents, and as salaries and pensions to foreign executive and technical staff? All that remains in the host country is a small sum for wages—which will be low because workers can still be hired for subsistence pay—and perhaps some money spent on local supplies—unless all these, too, are shipped in from abroad. In these conditions the enterprise to all intents and purposes is not in the local economy at all. If, in addition, it is developing a wasting asset—a gold reef or a copper mine—the final effect will be to lose the asset and gain nothing in return. Or if the goods the company manufactures are sold locally and earn no foreign exchange, the need to repay profits and repatriate capital in foreign currency may greatly add to the problems of the country's balance of payments.

Where these conditions prevail, foreign investment clearly contributes very little to local expansion; and all around the world there are static subsistence economies co-existing with pockets of advanced technology and production run by foreigners developing resources solely for the foreign user and contributing very little to local dynamism. The cultivation system in the Dutch East Indies was an instance of this, or the early stages of rice development in Lower Burma during which the entire surplus went to British or Indian middlemen. The local peoples are not necessarily worse off—although the Javanese finally were—but they are not drawn into the functions or the rewards of new economy. Like children with their noses against the shop window, they see the sweets but they cannot go in and buy. This frustrating "demonstration effect" is, like the agrarian stagnation which often accompanies it, fine ammunition for Communist propaganda.

Few of Britain's investments in India fitted into these extreme categories. Many of the export crops—especially tea and jute—became handsome earners of foreign exchange. Between 1868 and 1928, India's exports quintupled and its imports increased eightfold. This represents a sizable contribution to national income; and since some of the crops stimulated or expanded by British enterprise —cotton, jute, groundnuts, pepper—were grown by local farmers, gains from the export trade contributed directly to their income. Around Bombay, there were even signs of a wider economic acceleration in the second half of the nineteenth century; and after 1886, when general income taxes had been introduced, earnings from foreign enterprise began to make some direct contribution to local revenue.

Admittedly more of the surplus would have remained in India if all enterprise had been Indian. But in the conditions prevailing in the early nineteenth century, this is precisely what could not happen without a jolt from outside. There were no Westernizing influences at work in India, studying and judging Western growth as the Rangakusha scholars had done in eighteenth-century Japan or the "Western Group" of Takashima and Noboru a century later. There were no influential modernizers, no prince with the enterprise of a Peter the Great to go off and learn at first hand the facts about Western development. Before the British came to demonstrate what a modern enterprise looked like, there were no indigenous patterns. Even the cloth trade of Bengal, which in the late eighteenth century exported as much as £3 millions' worth of goods to Britain in a single year, was organized by the factors of the East India Company, who harried the weavers and brought back the cloth. It is sometimes argued that if cheap textiles from Lancashire had not wiped out this export, it might have become the nucleus of a purely Indian development. But it was factory competition that destroyed the old handicraft exports; and to compete with manufactured textiles, Bengal enterprise would have needed speedy access to modern forms of power. In Lancashire, coal and the steam engine preceded the revolution in textiles. But the first Indian coal was not mined until the jute interests opened up the Raniganj colliery in 1854. What was lacking around Calcutta half a century sooner was that confluence of a wide variety of different techniques, discoveries, enterprises, and investments—of which textiles were only one—which had launched Britain on its revolution.

In the conditions of the early nineteenth century, British capital and skills brought in from outside were not

ousting local efforts. On the contrary, they were needed
to stimulate, at some point, effective local imitation. Once
the railways were built, and peace, order, and dependable
law had become habitual, Indian business did appear.
Where enterprise was strong, chiefly in the Gujarat areas
around Bombay, local cotton merchants, many of them
Parsees, established a large modern textile industry on the
basis of indigenous cotton. The most successful of them,
the Tata family, went on to launch other ventures, including the first Indian steel industry, just before the First
World War—even though, to do this, the firm had to accomplish a pioneering job at Jamshedpur, hacking the
enterprise out of virgin jungle and opening up access for
the first time to India's vast reserves of iron ore.

However, in spite of this growth of Indian enterprise,
British interests remained strongly entrenched. Much of
what was Indian business in capital and control was nevertheless managed by British firms. The system of managing agents by which a company, in return for a fee or a
percentage of the profits, provided management for other
enterprises, supplemented the shortage of Indian managers and was a convenience to British investors who
wanted to invest their money in India but did not want
to live there to supervise it themselves. Inevitably, as the
sense of India's separate political destiny increased, the
extent of British control and interest in Indian business
began to be resented. There were more Indians now who
felt they could take the British place. What had been a
spur was felt to be growing into something of an incubus.
And resentment was sharpened by the memory of some
elements of real discrimination.

In the main, it could be said that the British authorities
had not practised discrimination against Indian enterprise. They had simply failed to help everybody. But in

one local application of the rules of *laissez faire*, it must be allowed that British policy loaded the scales in Britain's favour and made a marked—and avoidable—contribution to the relative sluggishness of industrial growth in India. The Indian government was allowed to introduce tariff protection only after 1919. As a result, throughout the fifty years before the First World War, Indian enterprise always had to compete against experienced, established British firms whose products were cheaper and better known than anything a local industry could produce in its first experimental stages. That this had an inhibiting effect is confirmed by the country's experience after 1919. Between the wars, in spite of the general stagnation of the world economy, Indian enterprise managed to launch out into new lines—sugar, cement, paper—even though the procedures for procuring tariff protection were stiff and cumbersome. It is impossible to doubt that similar protection earlier would have given Indian industry a larger base. In particular, the Indian textile industry must have captured more of the internal market. But here, the interests of British industry were allowed to predominate. In fact, when for a time the government in India put a small revenue tariff on imported textiles, pressure in Britain succeeded in adding an equivalent levy on local cloth. The rationale might be argued to be one of pure free trade. The effect was protection for Lancashire.

In 1939, after a hundred years of British investment, peace, order, and modern commercial law, after nearly a century of modern railways, ports, and exports industries, after eighty years of Indian enterprise in a vast internal market of 300 million souls, India still had an industrial establishment of only 2 million workers, a steel output of less than a million tons, and a population which still depended for as much as 80 per cent of its livelihood on a static, overcrowded, agrarian economy. Not by any stretch of the imagination can this be called a record of dynamic growth. It is simply the first sketch of a first beginning. It was not therefore surprising that when the Indians achieved independence, they had one purpose above all others—to reorder their economy and catch up with the long arrears of stagnation and lost opportunity. And if there is a single definition to cover the aims of the economic plans which have since been carried through, it is to bring the Indian economy fully into the twentieth century and carry through the changes in agriculture, in infrastructure, in industrial development without which it can have no hope of achieving the dynamism of sustained growth.

Chapter Eleven

Prelude to Planning

MODERNIZATION can cover many aims: national prestige, military power, ability to throw one's weight about in the world, to become "top nation," to carry through an ideological blueprint. In India, no doubt, modernization has a number of different meanings to different groups and interests. Yet here, too, there is a concensus—the belief that the master aim of modernization must be to raise living standards and give people some hope of a better life. A genuinely democratic community can hardly have any other main purpose. The first desire of the normal citizen is likely to be a job and a home. It needs more sophisticated wisdom to tell him he really wants a slice of his neighbour's territory and the weapons to secure it. The problem of modern mass democracy is not to induce the voters to put a modest affluence first; it is to persuade them to accept some of the more uncomfortable policies needed to launch and finance it. In India, the combination of adult suffrage and one of the lowest per capita incomes in the world ensures the priority given to better standards of living. And the same combination creates some of the worst dilemmas involved in carrying the policy out.

It is hard for people in the West to imagine the scale and depth of Indian poverty. The poverty of urban slums or rural squalor in the West is confined to the margins of society. Often it reflects the inability of the lowest 10 per cent of the population in intelligence and energy to climb a social ladder which would be there if they could find and use it. But in India, it is not a sector of society but the whole of society that is poor. Only half a million pay any income tax at all. The number with incomes above £8,000 a year is about two thousand out of four hundred million. At the other end of the scale, not many slums in America or Europe equal the conditions of urban misery that exist on the fringes of Calcutta or Bombay. Only perhaps in some of the most derelict tenements of Sicily or along the poorest "tobacco roads" in the southern states of America can one still meet any Western equivalent of the extreme forms of Indian poverty. Moreover, the men at the bottom in Indian society have to bear more than extreme poverty. Most of them are untouchables and carry the stigma of social rejection as well.

But the best index of Indian poverty is not to be found among the extremes. It lies somewhere in the middle— among the reasonably prosperous farmers who make up the bulk of the population, who have a dominant influence on public opinion, and who carry enormous weight in the country's political life. A farmer with twenty-five acres of land is near the top of his village hierarchy. His neighbours respect and consult him. He probably sits on the village *panchayat* and may be a member of his caste council as well. He is courted by the local member of parliament. He must be convinced if his village is to adopt improved methods of farming or establish a co-operative or build a primary school. If he is factious and quarrelsome, the village splits into feuds and dissensions. If he has wisdom and patience, he can put his small community into the way of change and growth.

Yet his income is not much more than a British old-age pension. His house is made of mud in a village where there are neither paved alleys nor—probably—street lamps. His wardrobe may be a few shirts and dhotis with a jacket for special occasions. He is perhaps literate, but his wife certainly, and his daughters probably, cannot read. He lights his house with a dim kerosene lamp and goes to his truckle bed soon after dark to save the oil. His only link with the world is probably a rough track made impassable for months at a time by the monsoon rains. His longest journey may have been only to the nearest market town or perhaps to a more distant city of pilgrimage. He is the backbone of India, the arbiter of its destiny. But in Europe, a jobbing labourer would not put up with his standard of life.

Without drastic changes in the Indian economy, this man and his family will not only continue to be poor. They will grow poorer. The village itself has no more waste land to cultivate. He himself has split up his own acres already until his sons' strips hardly provide a living. He may be in debt for a daughter's wedding. There are no growing industrial centres nearby to absorb the labour of the grandchildren who are on the way. But they will not stop coming—eight million of them every year, mostly born in the countryside where millions are already under-employed. As the mouths increase, they eat up the margin of saving without which there cannot be more food for the new mouths to eat. Yesterday there were 362 million to feed, to-day there are nearly 430 million, by 1975 the figure may be 560 million. This, the most vicious of all the vicious circles of development, is built into the foundations of the Indian economy.

This, too, is a dilemma which Westerners can easily misunderstand, and as a result lay careless and wounding blame on Asian societies for incontinence and irresponsibility and worse. In fact, the Indian birthrate is no higher than Britain's in the early nineteenth century; and the increase in population not much greater than America's to-day. But in the West, the spurt in population kept pace with economic development, the one sparking the other. Coal and iron came before sanitation, steam engines before modern drugs. In Asia, on the contrary, the improvements in health came first, and rapid growth in population long preceded any broad industrial breakthrough. This was the consequence of living under a government which modernized law and order and introduced new measures of sanitation and public health, but which gave virtually no stimulus to economic development. The British did not plan such a disproportion; yet their actual achievement of partial modernization could hardly have proved a more explosive inheritance.

In the short run, the deadlock cannot be broken simply by working to reduce the increase in births over deaths. Much of the growth is not due to births at all, but to lengthening life. The Indian Government has started to encourage birth control—the expenditure on clinics and counselling in the Third Plan is to increase eightfold—but the policy will make an impression only when people begin to want smaller families. But before that, they must be sure that more of their children will survive and they must feel that they can give a smaller family better education and a better chance. No democratic government can force them to rear fewer children. It is a free choice which they will come to only when a certain degree of literacy and a certain experience of development have reshaped their wishes. A lower birth rate is thus as much a consequence as a condition of economic growth; and the main hope at this stage must lie in the Plan's determined frontal attack on the problem of India's too meagre resources. Once the rhythm of expansion is fully established, there is no reason to suppose that Indians, like other modernizing communities in the past—the Japanese, for instance—will not be content with smaller families.

This combination of poverty and pressure of population complicates the processes of India's democratic planning at every turn and in ways which it is often difficult for people in the West to grasp. Westerners' direct experience of general poverty is fading into a forgotten past, and the great majority never faced the dilemmas created by overpopulation at all. In Indian planning, these dilemmas have to be borne in mind at every point and they directly affect the starting point of all planning—the primary accumulation of capital.

A developing society must at some point begin to save, even though it is still poor. This is the tough early stage of growth which Marx encountered in Victorian England and unfortunately took to be permanent. It is a difficult phase in any economy—so difficult that most societies got through it by *force majeure*. India is in fact the first society to set itself on the way of growth within the framework of the free vote and adult suffrage. No one asked British labourers moving into the Manchester slums whether they wanted to save. It took time for the great uprooted mass of European emigrants to begin to exercise their rights in the new American cities. The Soviet workers who came into Sverdlovsk and Magnitogorsk from the primitive steppe had no say in the scale or the condition of their work. Nor have the Chinese in their communes to-day. It is unprecedented to ask a man to choose to submit himself to the drastic disciplines of early saving—and his most likely response will be to refuse. This is perhaps one of the chief attractions of Communism to countries caught in the vice between agrarian depression and a bursting population. The Communists break the trap violently and impose the discipline and sacrifice needed for primary accumulation. Although per capita incomes were probably about the same in India and China at the beginning of the fifties—between $50 and $55—the proportion of national income devoted to saving in China has been quickly raised to 23 per cent. One has to treat Chinese statistics with some caution; but on the basis of this forced-draught saving, they claim to have boosted steel production from one to thirteen million tons between 1952 and 1959, raised coal output from 66 million tons to 365 million tons, electricity from seven million to forty-one million kilowatt hours, and to have very nearly doubled the production of food grains. Meanwhile, per capita income in the countryside where the bulk of the work has been done—often in bursts of almost total mobilization—is still, apparently, no higher than a decade ago, and indeed may be lower. An official Chinese source recently quoted $34 as the figure for rural income. It seems clear that most of the gain from harder work and greater output has drained out of the villages to spark growth in other sectors.

In India, the villager has the vote. Nothing so drastic can be attempted. The proportion of national income devoted to investment has to rise more slowly. In 1951 it represented the normal proportion of static economies—just under 5 per cent. It has risen to 11 per cent through the first two plans (between 1951 and 1961) and should reach 14 per cent by 1966. Then, sometime in the 1970s, it should reach 17 per cent, by which time the resources available for investment ought to be comfortably above the level needed to achieve steady growth. Meanwhile, however, expansion must be slower. The figures will, inevitably, be less spectacular than those claimed by China. To give only one instance—national income—the Chinese claim to have increased theirs by more than 100 per cent between 1951 and 1961. India's increase is a more modest 42 per cent—a rise which only just permits the economy to provide for its 2 per cent annual increase in population, spare a little extra for consumption, and still devote more resources to saving. The Indian economy is dynamic—but only just. It can afford no slowing down or interruption. Its pace is almost certainly the slowest that still allows for momentum; but it may also be the fastest popular opinion will accept.

This is not the only dilemma induced by India's unique combination of national poverty and liberal politics. A great central block of the Indian electorate is made up of small businessmen. A majority of the farmers own some land. They therefore run minute independent enterprises. To them must be added artisans, small workshop owners, and the growing ranks of small-scale modern entrepreneurs. These men cannot be dragooned into rural and urban communes, told what to make, how to make it, and what they will get in return. If national income is to rise, they have to be coaxed to produce more —and coaxing implies incentives. Give up the totalitarian stick and what is chiefly left is the monetary carrot.

But in a very poor society, the provision of incentives

runs into agonizing problems of justice and "fair shares." In the domestic economy as in the great arena of the world market, the law of "to him who hath" still rules. If you want maximum output, you must give the vigorous, enterprising man his head, you must back the expanding enterprise, look out for the most profitable techniques, put more funds into the richest regions. In the long run, such policies can pay off in terms of a better life for everyone. Provided wealth is being created, some of it can be taxed away and redistributed. But the immediate effect is to accentuate and increase existing inequalities. The farmer with twenty-five acres moves further away from the farmer with five. The thrusting industrialist competes old-fashioned companies out of business. Modern enterprise wipes out village enterprise. The Punjab and Gujerat grow richer. The Eastern United Provinces slip further behind.

The choices can be cruelly difficult in any poor community, but they are enormously complicated in a federal union such as India's where not only varying degrees of wealth and poverty but deep differences in culture and language divide the sixteen member states. Under these conditions, local politics, local vested interests can become very strong indeed—as, for instance, in Assam recently where one of the factors in local unrest was the demand that the jobs in the large new centrally-financed oil refinery at Gauhati should be reserved for Assamese. At present, the fact that the Congress Party, with or without partners in coalition, is in power in the provinces, offers some counterpoise to such centrifugal forces. So do the pressures for unity inherent in so vast a common market. Even so, no province can be allowed to slip too far behind in the race for development without stirring up dangerous resentments. The task of planning is compli-

cated all the time by the need to balance the economics
of rapid growth against the politics of regional demands
and grievances.

Let us, for instance, suppose that at a certain stage in
planning there is capital available for only one more multipurpose hydro-electric scheme. Of the sixteen states of the
Indian Union, which should get it? A region where there
are lively, energetic farmers and a confident group of
artisans and small businessmen who will quickly put
water and power to good use, make the scheme a paying
proposition, and generally boost national income? Or
should it be used to end the hopeless poverty of some
backward area even though the peasants there may take
a decade or more to learn how to become wet farmers and
virtually no local entrepreneurial tradition exists at all?
If the wealthy and well-endowed states receive priority,
national income as a whole may increase more rapidly—
Gujerat, Maharashtra, the Punjab and Andhra pulling
ahead and dragging the others along behind. But, equally,
a sort of built-in lopsidedness may develop such as has
occurred in Italy, where the concentration of wealth in
the North has simply sparked the growth of further
wealth there, leaving the South of Italy and Sicily still
poorer in relative terms. Yet in Italy the chances of mi-
gration from south to north far exceed any mobility likely
in India, where the Telugu or Malayali labourer will not
be recruited for a project in the Punjab.

The same kind of problem recurs at village level. Land
has been reclaimed. Should it be added to the plots of the
four or five most efficient farmers in the district in the
certainty that it will at once be used to produce food for
the market? Or should it be allotted to the landless
labourers who, as certainly, will only feed themselves?

Industry presents similar dilemmas. The bulk of India's

workers have only recently recovered the level of real wages they earned before the war. Ought the first priority to be higher earnings for them? Or should the companies be encouraged to hold wages steady and devote their earnings to further capital formation or even to the kind of dividends which encourages the public to take its money out of gold bangles and put it in industrial equities instead? Should central taxation, some of which goes into essential welfare, be so heavy that it checks the spirit of industrial experiment and risk on which further increases in income depend? Should modern industry have to accept ceilings on production and pay levies to keep village enterprise alive? Is the gain in employment sufficient to offset the over-all loss of output and competitive efficiency? Up to a point, one of the chief elements of malaise in the first decade of the Plans—the running exchange of distrust and irritation between government and private industry—has its roots in this conflict between enterprise and fair shares.

Of the three main streams in Congress thought—the conservatism of Vallabbhai Patel, the radical anti-industrial idealism of Gandhi, and Nehru's modernizing energies—it was Patel who chiefly understood and supported the important business element which backed the Congress. Gandhi told the millowners to use their wealth as a trust; and he also built up a remarkable industrial union among the textile workers of Ahmedabad on the bases of self-help and thrift for themselves and procedures of arbitration and conciliation with the employers. But Gandhi did not see the future of India in terms of large-scale industrialization; and it is his memory more than anything else that still keeps a flickering life in the Indian Government's cooling enthusiasm for technically inefficient village crafts.

Pandit Nehru's attitude toward organized private industry is more complex. One strand of it has been mentioned already—the disgust which so many leaders of his generation felt for the stagnation and inefficiency of the capitalist economy in the 1930s. One could add, no doubt, a nationalist's distaste for an economic sector of which so large a part had been foreign-owned. There is an element, too, of the Brahmin's disdain and distrust of the trading classes, a mood shared by many Indian intellectuals and civil servants whose instinctive feeling is that servants of the State know better what is good for society and are more conscientious and objective in carrying it out. This mood in turn has been strengthened by some elements in Indian business who, coming to industry straight from trading and moneylending, brought to it instincts for the "fast buck," for cutting corners, for rigging the market, for promoting incompetent nephews, for being at times simply dishonest—all traits which in most societies seem to mark enterprise in the first stages of industrial growth. The *Marwaris*—the business clan who invariably figure in the denunciations of Indian business practices—have probably been no more contentious than a thousand other emergent entrepreneurs. But in India, clannishness and family connections are reinforced by caste differences, and thus help to underline the force and exclusiveness of commercial power.

But the deepest strand of all is the belief that in a very poor society, largely composed of small men, there is something unhealthy and socially unacceptable in allowing entrepreneurs to amass vast fortunes and capture commanding positions of economic power. India's "socialistic pattern" of society does not propose total state control. The public sector may very possibly remain no larger than the 20 per cent of the American economy dominated by government—it is not yet even 10 per cent. But the central levers of power—steel, transport, parts of heavy engineering—are to be reserved to the government so that they may not become the preserve of wealthy and possibly irresponsible men. This is the rationale of the division between the public and private sector, and fundamentally it represents the judgment that power and wealth shall be not too unequally shared, even if the price is more restraint than businessmen like and possibly some discouragement to their investment and enterprise.

There is, clearly, no one solution to these dilemmas. Most of them have to be lived with. They are not resolved. They simply change shape as the economy develops. The only reason why they do not seem to loom so large under Communism is because they are never publicly discussed. No one rocked Stalin in the seat of power because he created a labour aristocracy of Stakhanovites and let the peasants all but starve. Differences in reward between factory sweeper and factory manager, far greater than any gap in an American enterprise, were dumbly accepted for decades. In fact, a Communist society which claims to make the most of social justice can ignore it most completely in the first stages of growth. The whole emphasis can be put on expansion, for no one is allowed to dispute the cost. Only since Khrushchev's advent have some steps been taken to give the Soviet countryside a somewhat fairer share of national income, to raise the pay of the lowest ranks in Soviet industry, and to deal with really serious conditions among the aged and retired poor. Similarly in China today, after the one brief experiment of letting the flowers of criticism bloom in 1957, no one is asked whether the emphasis on work and output is not being pressed forward at too high a cost. But in India the balance has always to be struck. The dilemma is never absent.

Put too many brakes on enterprise and stagnation may undermine the Plan. Take them off too completely, do no more than repeat Louis Philippe's advice, *"Enrichissez-vous,"* and the discontent of the unsuccessful may undermine it in another way.

However, it may well prove India's strength that its political constitution, although rather cumbersome for an all-out modernization of resources, is admirably designed to work out a fluctuating concensus. A large party composed of many interests and depending on a vast variety of constituents for its re-election can be remarkably sensitive to the shifts of popular discontent, and can register with some accuracy any changes in the basic balance of forces. So long as there is a forward movement, so long as income does increase and there is each year a little more with which to reward this group or buy off that, the democratic concensus can work—an indefinable, protean force but one less brittle than the forced consent of dictators and capable of increasing its hold year by year on men and women who have acquired the habit of freedom. In India, so far, the concensus has worked, in spite of intense strain. By compromise and haggle and parliamentary debating and fixing, the dangerous corners have on the whole been turned: strikes settled, pay increases negotiated, tax administration tightened, corruption aired, public accounts examined, the states guided through the rapids of linguistic reorganization. And one underlying reason for all of the compromises that have come off and for all the failure of explosions to ignite is that, on the whole, the Plans have provided a growing national income and hence the small economic margins needed for bargains and concessions to be worked out.

Chapter Twelve

The Indian Plans

INDIAN planning can be said to have begun formally in 1952 when the Plan for 1951 to 1956 was finally published. The Second Plan is now complete and the Third under way. But in fact the various five-year periods are simply convenient yardsticks for measuring progress, charting directions, and checking any unfavourable deviations. What is happening is a process of continuous growth under broad government stimulus and guidance. The clearing house and central signal station is a Planning Commission in Delhi, under the ultimate authority of the National Development Council made up of the chief ministers in the Central and State Governments. The principal executives in the public sector are federal and state ministries with their officials, and, in increasing numbers, the officers of public corporations. In the private sector, the executive function is as

(153)

wide as Indian enterprise; it covers everything from Tata's works at Jamshedpur, producing two million tons of ingot steel a year, down to the villager selling his first *maund* of rice on the market.

One can sum up the strategy of the planning process as that of giving India the developed infrastructure, the "big push" in industry, and the modernization of agriculture without which no economy so far has achieved the momentum of sustained growth. And within this broad strategy, the scale and endowment of the Indian economy dictate two central points of emphasis: a high degree of self-sufficiency in both heavy industry and food.

The first reason for this emphasis is the relative inelasticity of India's exports. Tea, jute and cotton textiles, the three staples, are not capable of any very rapid expansion. Earnings from exports have remained steady for some time at between $11,200 million and $15,000 million a year. Other promising forms—light manufactures, for instance—imply a more industrially developed economy. Thus if India remains dependent upon foreign supplies for two such essential resources as food and capital goods, the whole economy may be held back to the relatively low level of expansion that exports are likely to achieve.

But the chief reason for concentrating on the creation of a capital goods industry is quite simply that India has the vast internal market and the abundant industrial raw materials which would make such a policy sensible, even if exports looked much more promising. Heavy industry is the greatest multiplier in any economy. Ample steel fed into a growing engineering section expands the economy's range in every direction. Behind it must be created the large-scale system of power, the transport, and the trained manpower implied in a modern industrial infrastructure. Beyond it lie the possibilities of mechanization and modernization in every sector: the whole range of organized machine-making and machine-using industries, electrification in the villages and on the farms, modern power and machinery for small-scale enterprise, bicycles and sewing machines—the first consumers' durables—for the mass consumer. If one step more than any other creates the essential interlocking of effort and enterprise by which each sector provides stimulus, external economies, resources, or markets for the rest, it is to launch out into heavy industrial production. This is the basic reason why railways and wars have been such potent modernizers: they drag the rest of the industrial economy into being in their wake.

The only condition under which steel mills and machine tool plants do not represent the height of economic wisdom is when there are no local raw materials or power for a steel industry, and no potential market. India has no such handicaps. A market of rising 500 million people waits to be developed. Inevitably the pattern will resemble that of the continental United States rather than the early stages of smaller trading communities such as Britain or Japan. And the physical resources needed for industrialization are abundant: the largest iron ore reserves in the world, manganese, bauxite, enough coal—though coking coal is deficient—a still very largely untapped reservoir of hydroelectric power—perhaps 8 per cent has been developed—and the materials for nuclear power. It is thus an entirely rational decision on the part of the Indian authorities to put food and heavy industry at the core of their plans. Indeed, the chief criticism one can make is that they have not pursued the two objectives wholeheartedly enough. Food production has so far been blurred by wider aims of rural renewal. Steel plants, the core of heavy industry, could with advantage have been initiated earlier in the planning process. Agreements with foreign interests—with a German and Austrian group at Rourkela in 1953, with the Russians at Bhilai in 1955, and with a British consortium at Durgapur in 1956—were not concluded in time to give India much steel during the Second Plan. The Third Plan starts at a level not much above 2 million tons of ingot steel a year. Moreover, the target of 10 million tons of ingot steel by 1966 may prove too ambitious. The managerial and technical skills demanded in the staffing of three vast plants simultaneously —not to mention the doubling of India's two private steel plants—have been underestimated and technical expertise seems now to be the industry's chief bottleneck. It is not yet fully available in India. It is scarce abroad. Yet without it, even the most modern plants will not work to capacity.

The details of the plans can be expressed in either financial or physical terms. Table I below gives the broad financial outline of the Plans; the chief physical targets are outlined in tables attached to the three following sections—infrastructure, industry, and agriculture. There is, however, one preliminary point to notice. It is a matter of perspective. The total investment, public and private, under the three Plans should amount by 1966 to some $42,000 millions for an economy which by then will number at least 480 millions and of this, over $18,000 millions is to come from private investors. But American private enterprise, for an economy of some 180 millions, usually invests above $30,000 millions each year—nearly twice as much as Indian enterprise expects to spend for an economy of nearly 500 millions over the full fifteen years of the present Plans. The contrast simply registers the fact that America is immensely wealthy while the Indian economy is still desperately poor—one of the poorest in

TABLE I PUBLIC AND PRIVATE EXPENDITURE IN THE
SECOND AND THIRD PLANS
(*In Millions of U.S. Dollars*)

| | Second Plan | | | | Third Plan | | |
| | Public Sector | | Private Investment | | Public Sector | | Private Investment |
	Outlay	%	Original Estimates	Revised Estimates	Outlay	%	
Agriculture and minor irrigation	672	6.9	577	1,417	1,312	8.6	1,784
Community development	441	4.6	—	—	839	5.5	—
Major irrigation	944	9.8	—	—	1,364	9.0	—
Power	860	8.9	84	84	1,941	12.8	105
Village and small industries	378	3.9	210	472	525	3.4	682
Industry and minerals	1,847	19.1	1,207	1,469	3,148	20.7	2,204
Transport and communications	2,707	28.1	178	283	3,043	20.0	420
Social services, inc. housing	1,805	18.7	1,941	2,099	2,623	17.2	2,360
Inventories			839	1,102	420	2.8	1,259
Total	9,654		5,036	6,926	15,215		8,814

the world. The Indian effort of investment means that, with a very great effort and strain, a little dent is beginning to be made in the monumental scale of national need. By Western standards these are very small Plans; and by Western standard, too, their results will be very modest for decades to come.

INFRASTRUCTURE

Although the physical and social overheads of the economy are in a sense secondary to the central tasks of agricultural and industrial production, they absorb a very high share of savings in a developing economy. They must do so, since, without its infrastructure, an economy does not function at all. In the first two Plans, overheads have taken over half the Plan's expenditure. In the Third Plan, the share is a little less—49 per cent instead of the 55.6 per cent of the Second. This reflects the amount of construction already completed, especially on the railways. But in every category, spending is to be higher than in the last five years: the investment on power rising from $860 millions to $1,900 millions, on transport and communications from $2,700 millions to $3,040 millions, on the social services from $1,800 millions to $2,600 millions.

The physical overheads—power, fuel, transport—should not create exceptional problems for the planners. It is not too difficult to estimate what increases in power and transport will be needed; the services themselves are technically not too difficult to provide and they can pay their way as they go. In India, however, the task is proving more complicated. For one thing, so much of the normal twentieth-century infrastructure had still to be provided after 1947, and the old services—railways, ports—emerged from the war in a considerable state of dilapidation. Much of the expenditure in the first two Plans simply aimed at getting the railway system back into normal running repair. But the chief problem faced by the planners at this stage of India's development lies in the degree to which the central blast of government investment has fanned the processes of growth on every side, particularly in the private sector. The demand for more transport, for more fuel, for more power is becoming steadily more urgent and since most of the basic services are in the public sector, the pressures exerted on them are transmitted directly to the ministries and the public

TABLE II SOME TARGETS FOR INFRASTRUCTURE

Item	Unit	1950–51	1955–56	1960–61 (estimates)	1965–66 (targets)	Increase in 1960/61 over 1950/5 (%)	Increase in 1965/66 over 1960/61 (%)
ENERGY							
Electricity generated	mill. kwh	6,575	11,000	20,700	42,250	215	104
Towns and villages electrified	thousands	3.7	7.4	19.0	34.0	414	79
Coal	mill. tons	32.0	38.0	53.0	97.0	66	83
TRANSPORT							
Passenger train miles	million	95	109	124	143	31	15
Freight carried	mill. tons	91	114	162	235	78	45
Surfaced roads	thou. miles	97.5	122.0	144.0	164.0	48	14
Shipping	mill. GRT	0.4	0.5	0.9	1.1	125	22
EDUCATION							
Students in school	million	23.5	31.5	41.1	64.8	75	58
Students in engineering & technology:							
degree level (intake)	number	4,119	5,888	13,165	185,000	220	41
diploma level (intake)	number	5,903	10,484	24,020	34,000	307	42
Students in agriculture:							
degree level (intake)	number	1,060	1,989	4,510	6,000	325	33

corporations and indirectly back to the Planning Commission. Yet in most of these bodies the tradition of speedy decision-making and swift executive action is not yet very highly developed. The tough breaking of bottlenecks does not come easily to the civil servant trained in the British tradition. He prefers to defer action while all the alternatives are weighed—or simply pass on the file. Cumulatively these delays are creating pressures in the core of the Plan, on its vital infrastructure, which, unremedied, could slow down the whole decided tempo of Indian advance. Each sector is rather behind. In each sector, crucial decisions have to be taken—and taken soon —to reverse the trend.

On the whole, the railways have kept pace; but undoubtedly they have been helped by the unexpected liveliness of road transport in the private sector which has flourished in spite of high taxation and vexatious licensing regulations on interstate traffic. Yet road building still does not receive the priority it deserves in the Third Plan. Expenditure on the railways is still to be five times larger than on the roads. This reflects in part the greater cheapness of road construction. But its cheapness should also be its attraction. And road building has the particular merit at this time of opening up the villages to outside stimulus.

It is a law of life of developing economies that there is never enough power. India is no exception. Although energy generated has risen from 6,575 kwh in 1951 to 20,700 kwh in 1961, and is to reach 42,250 kwh by 1966, demand continues to forge ahead. As with roads, one of the most important contributions the development of power could make to the economy would be to bring new stimulus to the villages. A man who has power for his tube-well and an all-weather road begins to feel quite differently about the chances of change and progress. The difficulty lies in the expense of rural electrification, the length of the transmission lines, the small demand waiting at the end of them.

Three-quarters of India's power comes from thermal stations; this proportion is not likely to change. The big hydroelectric schemes, in spite of their attractive provision of other benefits—irrigation, flood control—are becoming more expensive as the easier and more accessible sites are used up. Of the other alternatives, nuclear power, for which two plants are to be built, is also much more expensive than thermal power. Oil-fired stations must wait upon larger discoveries of oil inside India.

So far, the country produces only 6 to 7 million tons of petroleum products a year from its domestic oil fields and must import annually another 6 million tons. Production in Assam is going up, however, and there is evidence that 400,000 square miles in other areas may be oil-bearing. To speed up the discovery of additional reserves, the Indian government has now invited foreign oil firms to join with it in specific programs for leases and exploration, thus opening up to private participation a sector hitherto reserved to the Government's Oil and National Gas Commission. But no one yet knows what the oil potential may be or how much the new fields will contribute to India's needs which are expected to reach 14 million tons of crude oil by 1965.

All this throws greater responsibility on the coal industry; and here has arisen one of the few really clear instances of direct damage caused by the Government's preference for public enterprise. Coal output has lagged far behind its targets; the chief reasons are that public collieries have not increased their output sufficiently and that private industry has been hampered by a prohibi-

tion on opening new pits anywhere save in the immediate
area of existing concessions. The coal target for the Second Plan had been set at 60 million tons. The 1961 figure
is 7 millions below it. Yet the target for 1966 is now 97
million tons. It seems certain that some relaxation of the
limits on private activity will be essential if anything like
that figure is to be achieved.

All these physical services begin sooner or later to pay
their way; then, if they are efficiently run, they become
revenue earners for the government. The railways provided over $280 millions for public investment during the
Second Plan, over and above their own reserves for de-
preciation and renewal. Surpluses from public corporations are to be one of the staple sources of investment in
the future. But the social overheads of an economy cannot give so immediate or measurable a return. In such
categories as cheap housing or public health, where people are not prepared to pay very much or feel they should
not pay anything at all, the needs are no doubt almost
limitless; but what can be afforded is limited by the surplus the economy can spare from immediate revenue-
earning investment. In most developing economies, housing comes low on the priority list. It absorbs considerable
resources and gives a very meagre return. In Communist
countries where social justice tends to be sacrificed to
expansion, housing receives almost no priority at all.
Urban dwellings are still Mr. Khrushchev's largest piece
of unfinished business, and *Pravda* even publishes letters
saying: "Sputnik is all very well, but what I really want
is a new apartment." In India, narrowness of resources,
not indifference to needs, has dictated a low figure for
public housing development in the Third Plan: only $250
millions. Expenditure on health, which includes sanitation and water supplies, does a little better, with $620

millions. But the largest category is inevitably education, which is to receive $1,200 millions. The reason is simple. At this stage of development, India is as short of trained minds as it is of railways, roads, steel, or power. Indeed, the need is even more urgent; for not one sector of a modern economy can work efficiently without men and women trained in modern methods, and here there is a vast leeway to make up.

The simplest way of expressing India's plan for education is to give the figures of pupils enrolled for school and the proportion they represent of all Indian children:

TABLE III ENROLLMENT OF INDIAN PUPILS

year	enrollment (in hundreds of thousands)			percentage		
	6–11 age-group	11–14 age-group	14–17 age-group	6–11 age-group	11–14 age-group	14–17 age-group
1950–51	192	31	12	43.1	12.9	5.4
1955–56	252	43	20	51.0	16.3	8.1
1960–61 (est.)	330	61	30	60.0	22.6	12.0
1965–66 (target)	504	100	44	80.0	30.0	15.0

This in itself gives some measure of the vast expansion entailed in premises, in equipment, above all in trained teachers—of whom 400,000 more will be needed in the next five years alone. To this must be added an expansion in the numbers of university students, from some 420,000 in 1951 to 900,000 today.

But sheer scale is not the end of the problem. In 1947, India inherited a system of education still profoundly weighted on the side of the arts and the classics. It is not only the quantity of education that has had to be changed, it is the content as well; more practical technical training at the primary and elementary level, more science teaching in the secondary schools, a wholly new emphasis on science and technology in the universities. At present only 270,000 college students out of the 900,000 study science. The aim is to increase the number to about 460,000 by 1966. Such a shift requires new types of teachers and teacher training; and in colleges preparing for degrees the teaching staff in technical subjects is over 30 per cent below strength. It also involves the introduction of costly educational aids in the shape of new textbooks, equipment, and laboratories. In addition, it requires the establishment of wholly new academic institutions. Four institutes of technology have already been built. More are planned.

Inevitably, the effects of an educational revolution on this scale are uneven. More pupils crowding into existing classrooms and taught by a still inadequate and often undertrained staff encounter a lot of unsatisfactory teaching. The relatively poor rates of pay for teachers mean that some of them supplement their salaries with outside work and cannot give their best attention to their pupils. Such problems are not unknown in other far wealthier and more developed countries; but India struggles with them against a background of far smaller educational and financial reserves. The unfortunate result of so many interlocking shortages can be seen in unsatisfactory final results. Perhaps less than 50 per cent of the students graduate successfully, whereas the percentage of success for the master's and doctor's degree is just under 80 per cent.

As a result, there is inevitably a certain amount of frustration among the young. Unemployment is specially prevalent among young people who have completed their secondary or junior college education. The discontent shows itself at times in considerable turbulence among university students and it reaches a special pitch in West Bengal, where a whole extra Hindu middle class from East Pakistan has had to be absorbed, and in Kerala, where high rates of literacy coincide with rather modest prospects of economic expansion. Significantly, these are two areas where Communism has a hold on educated opinion.

But these danger signals should not be exaggerated. A general increase in the numbers receiving a modern education affects the community favourably in two ways. It trains a much larger range of people to accept what one might call the preconceptions of modern living: belief in the possibility and desirability of progress, interest in self-betterment, some understanding of what modern development and modern production demand in such simple but fundamental needs as punctuality, orderly records, continuity, and sustained effort. The spread of education also greatly enlarges the number of jobs which are being done by skilled people. If, before the war, the salesman in a firm was a matriculate and is now a graduate, the chances are that he does his job better, and that the whole level of competence in the firm has risen.

At the same time, the very great expansion in the economy is constantly creating more skilled jobs. For every university student who does not find a place at once, there are four or five who can set to work with the prospect of steady employment, reasonable promotion, and an income on which to found a home. The cements of Indian society remain very strong: the influence of the family, a pervasive ethical tradition, the sense of belonging to a proud and ancient civilization which has now, by the vicissitudes of modern politics, become a proud

and self-reliant nation-state engaged in the monumental
process of modernizing itself. Nor do external politics
make for the old clear-cut dogmatisms. The "imperialists"
—Britain, America, the West—are generally peaceful and
have not only retreated from empire but given considerable support to developing nations, including India. The
Communists—at least in their Chinese incarnation—combine denunciations of aggression with a ruthless war of
extinction in Tibet and an unashamed grab of thousands
of square miles of Indian territory. There are enough restraints, contradictions and divergent interests here to
put a brake on extremist politics. Only if the economic
experiment were to falter and a majority of students found
themselves facing the overeducated, underemployed dilemmas of Calcutta and Kerala would student extrem-
ism or anarchy or nihilism be likely to take the place of
the present hardworking, somewhat self-absorbed, and
relatively acquiescent mood of Indian youth. And for-
tunately for graduate prospects, the crucial industrial
sector of the Indian economy is doing rather well.

INDUSTRY

Even if the expansion of Indian industry does not equal
the "great leaps" claimed by China, it compares favourably
with the most rapid expansion achieved anywhere else in
the free world. In eight years, between 1951 and 1959,
the general index of industrial production rose by over 50
per cent; and the process is gathering momentum. By the
end of 1961, the industrial increase for the decade should
be nearer 120 per cent. Moreover, this general figure masks
some important distinctions. Expansion in the older industries—textiles, coal, the plantations—has been relatively slow; in cotton textiles, for instance, not more than
11 per cent over the eight years. But the newer categories

have grown with much greater impetus—iron and steel by 63 per cent, chemicals by 114 per cent, machinery by as much as 324 per cent.

These advances register more than growth. They show diversification as well. The Indian economy is ceasing to be an economy of a few relatively isolated industrial lines. Not only the final products but the machinery and the machine tools to make them are beginning to be manufactured. Indian industry can now produce virtually all the components of entire sugar mills. It can undertake the complete planning of a fertilizer factory, and provide over 50 per cent of its components, whereas when the plant at Sindri was built at the beginning of the First Plan, blueprints, materials, and technicians all had to be imported. By value, 90 per cent of the components of Tata's diesel trucks are of Indian origin. Industrial boilers, milling machines, diesel road rollers, newsprint, DDT, sulpha drugs—these are just a few of the new products introduced for the first time in the last decade.

Another index of diversification is the rapid growth of small-scale industry. It is, after all, always possible to order a whole industrial complex abroad and set it down in a country, or allow a foreign enterprise to provide and construct it. But if it remains an isolated monument to would-be industrialization, it contributes little to economic growth. One of the indices of a spreading energy of modernization lies in the number of new entrepreneurs whom the opportunities of growth draw into the effort— and their emergence is by no means certain. Some societies simply do not breed men who want to plan and risk and create.

There has, however, long been excellent evidence that Indians, given the opportunity, have the entrepreneurial gift. Indian migrants in Africa, in the West Indies, in the

Pacific have created economic opportunities for themselves, even though commercial activities predominate. Now in India the impetus given by central investment to the whole economy is creating local opportunities; and there are men to seize them. Statistics are difficult to come by in the small, relatively unorganized sectors of industry. "Small enterprises," which employ twelve million people, also include village handicrafts of a premodern type. But the new model of small enterprise, employing power and modern techniques on the Japanese pattern, is undoubtedly on the increase; and its liveliness is confirmed by the eager response to the Government's efforts to help small men—through State Bank loans, through the sixty new industrial estates in various parts of the country, through the Service Institutes that have been set up in each state, and through the imaginative plan under the National Small Industries Corporation, which allows small entrepreneurs to procure the machinery they need under a system of time payments.

This expansion among the smallest units in private industry reflects a general liveliness throughout the private sector. Its grievances and difficulties will be examined later. Here the point needs to be underlined that in India, as elsewhere in the non-Communist world, a vigorous government stimulus to investment—whether through an arms program, basic development, or large-scale foreign assistance—is proving the most effective spur to private development as well. India is repeating the experience of France under the Monnet Plan. Never has private enterprise expanded or diversified so quickly as in the last decade. Its investment in all sectors, including agriculture, almost doubled between the first and second plans—to nearly $7,000 millions between 1956 and 1961. The estimate for the Third Plan goes up again—to $8,400 millions.

And this is almost certainly an underestimate; for one of the features of the last ten years has been a tendency to underestimate the possible performance of the private sector. During the first plan, it invested $450 millions more than the forecast, in the Second Plan the excess was nearly $1,500 millions.

Public enterprise, in keeping with government philosophy, is in charge of the commanding heights of the economy: steel-making, power, important sections of transport and heavy industry. The bulk of the public investment in the next plan is to go to half a dozen major essays into heavy engineering. Since they all represent crucial and expensive sectors in a developing economy, the public share of new investment is moving upward, even while it still represents a relatively small proportion of the whole. The division of total investment between public and private enterprise in the Third Plan represents a ratio of about 60:40. If to public investment is added current outlay * on the plans, the ratio is nearer 67:33; and many critics feel that such a proportion may represent too high a public claim on savings which tend, in India, to flow more readily into private channels. There is no set level or quantum of savings which can be switched at will from private to public investment, from equities to government securities. A promising industrial issue is almost sure to be oversubscribed, and has the chance of tempting out savings that might otherwise remain hoarded. Put too much emphasis on public borrowing, and saving as such may slow down and compel the authorities to resort to deficit

---

* *Investment* is expenditure on the creation of physical assets (e.g., buildings and plant and equipment), including expenditure on personnel required for putting up these assets. The expression corresponds broadly to expenditure on capital account. *Current outlay* corresponds to expenditure on revenue account on plan schemes; it is expenditure other than that classified as "investment."

financing and secure by inflation what they have been unable to tempt out of the people's pockets.

The argument remains rather inconclusive. The main limit to private investment in recent years has proved again and again to be not lack of savings, but a shortage of crucial foreign exchange. Nor has the government had any difficulty in covering its public issues. But the critics have a real point when they ask how the government can hope to find an adequate number of managers and technical staff for its vast new enterprises when resources of trained manpower are already strained to the limit by the existing scale of the public sector. It may be that official second thoughts on this score have allowed private investment a rather larger part in the Third Plan than was forecast a few years ago.

Regardless of such divisions between public and private responsibility, all forms of enterprise together make up a powerful break from the *immobilisme* of the past, and offer very fair hopes of sustained expansion; and, as is so often the case when the spirals in an economy begin to move in a beneficent upward direction, expansion in one sector helps toward the solution of obstacles in others. A sharp rate of industrial advance goes some way to reduce the pressure of India's spurt in population. Six-and-a-half million new jobs outside agriculture have been created in the first decade of planning, a further ten-and-a-half million are forecast for the next Plan, together with three-and-a-half million in agriculture. Unfortunately, this increase does not fully cover the expected need. There are over a million jobs too few in industry now and the surplus may have risen to three million by 1966. This is perhaps the chief reason why the Indian programs cannot, on any standard of judgment, be called too ambitious. They are barely ambitious enough. They have, even at their present level, to accept for a time the possibility of increasing unemployment. If they were reduced further, the whole liberal framework and open politics of Indian society could be jeopardized by a growing undercurrent of worklessness and despair.

The labour force is growing. It is also gradually changing its character. The early stages of building an industrial labour force are never easy. Raw recruits come in from the villages. They know nothing of the disciplines of factory life. Bad as their living conditions may have been in the underemployed countryside, they lived in a community they understood and could rely on some family solidarity to help them in their needs. But in the city, the worker's way of life is no more comfortable—and it is alien as well. He has to learn how to be a settled worker in conditions which give him little chance of learning anything at all. His instinct is not to settle finally, to keep his links with the village, to remain, mentally, and in some degree physically, in a half world between urban and rural life. Absenteeism remains very high, skills are not fully learned or passed on to children. The factories have to cope with a group who are in spirit nearer to migrants than to a settled labour force. With a few exceptions— notably in Ahmedabad, where Gandhi's influence had been strong—the Indian worker in 1947 was still ignorant, unsettled, exploited, sometimes violent, and as a result not always even cheap.

Yet he can be skilled and stable in the right conditions. Most foreign firms, with their standards of comparison drawn from other countries, testify that the Indian worker is just as intelligent and adaptable as labour in more developed countries and wants very much the same things: a steady job, decent wages, chances of promotion, reasonable living conditions. His skills can be quickly developed, and this is what the general industrial expansion, with its special emphasis on engineering, is helping to bring about. In the Hindustan Machine Tools plant in 1955, for instance, four Indians were needed to do the work of one Swiss worker: to-day, three Indians can equal the output of two Swiss. At Jamshedpur in 1954 it took six of Tata's workers to equal one German's output on similar work for Mercedes at Stuttgart: now the ratio is 6:5. When the Integral Coach factory at Perambur began to produce railway carriages in 1954, it took 19,648 Indian man-hours to finish one carriage, compared with the Swiss figure of 6,500. To-day the Indian figure is 8,519 hours, and is still falling. These improvements mean that with comparable productivity the Indian worker's lower wages give Indian industry a competitive edge. Indian railway coaches are now 20 per cent less than their ex-works cost in Switzerland. Similar evidence can be drawn from many new engineering plants; and they represent the real growing points of India's future industrial expansion.

It is among the older industries, particularly in textiles where a measure of rationalization and reorganization is long overdue, that all too many firms and factories can be found in which productivity remains low, where workers are restless and occasionally violent, and where they resist any scheme to increase their output by a more concentrated use of machinery—an attitude which exposes Indian textiles in the export market to dangerous competition both from the highly specialized and rationalized Japanese factories and from the totally disciplined Chinese.

On the other hand, the new plants, with their modern layouts, their good design and lighting and their amenities help, almost by simply existing, to produce a new type of labour force. And their modernizing impact can be greatly enhanced by the activities of unions, government, and, above all, management. The unions, it is true, have not so far made too much of a contribution toward building a stable, well-trained, self-reliant, and independent working force, although the part they could play has been demonstrated by such bodies as the Ahmedabad Textile Labour Association. This union received its shape and spirit from Gandhi, and to-day, some forty years after its formation, it not only acts as a responsible wage-negotiating agency for its members but also provides hostels, cultural centres, reading rooms, twenty-eight housing societies, and ten consumers' societies. It also runs a co-operative bank with a working capital of nearly half-a-million dollars. But Indian unions in general are too evanescent and poverty-stricken to develop either welfare services or a philosophy of operation. Even the best organized—the railwaymen, for instance, or the workers in defence industries—have almost no funds.

A further weakness lies in the division of the movement as a whole between rival political factions. One Congress federation (the Indian Trade Union Congress), one Communist federation (the All-India Trade Union Congress), and two socialist federations all claim to organize the whole of Indian labour and compete confusingly for support in trades, factories, and industrial areas. The Communists are, inevitably, as political as they dare be, preaching class war, extolling Russia, and, more mutedly, China, and pressing for wage increases that are calculated to encourage inflation. They cannot, of course, afford to neglect the ordinary day-to-day needs of the workers, and in many plants, seem no more difficult to deal with than any other group. But they are hardly a body working to consolidate the status and independence of Indian labour.

The INTUC, too, has a complicated path to follow, for, as a Congress body enjoying official support, it must in some measure back the government's economic policies. But these policies inevitably include some veto on strikes and some element of wage restraint in a time of rapid growth and a degree of inflation. In public industry, government is the employer; the union would be reduced to a labour front on totalitarian lines if it simply acted as the government's agent to the workers. And so long as rival federations compete with it for support, it cannot afford to become the government's stooge. But the number of different directions in which it has to look all at once weaken the effective leadership it might otherwise provide.

Much more, then, has to be done by government and management. The government certainly does not reject or underestimate the task. The workers are an important element in the electorate and in some areas hold the balance of power. Moreover, they are foremost among the mass of small men for whom the government wishes to provide greater welfare and status. Yet its policies run into some formidable dilemmas. It wants the industrial workers to secure a larger share of the country's wealth. It tends to distrust the willingness of employers to play fair or to improve conditions, and has therefore passed legislation to regulate codes of discipline and behaviour, working hours and conditions, insurance, the assessment of bonuses, the appointment of labour officers—to name only a few. It believes in the Gandhian principle of settling wage issues by agreement, not strikes or lockouts, and has set up an elaborate system of compulsory arbitration. It believes, with special emphasis, in providing more opportunities for skill and training. In the Third Plan, for instance, the number of training institutes for industry is to increase from 59 to 250. All in all, the government intervenes in virtually every aspect of industrial life.

But then the contradictions appear. Exert too much influence on the side of welfare or higher pay, and industry is burdened with charges which make its goods uncompetitive while the risk of inflation in the economy rises sharply. Up to a point, the government can lessen the risk by compelling the worker to pay for quite a large share of his welfare systems himself through compulsory provident funds and insurance schemes. But there are limits to which these and other more direct and obvious restraints can be imposed. If government authority is used to hold down wages, put up hours of work, stop strikes, and squeeze savings out of the workers—as it is in Communist countries, with ruthless effect—society loses its essential stamp of liberty and elbowroom and the more extreme leaders take over the unions. This is simply one more specific instance of the general fact that a massive mobilization of resources for economic advance offers problems to free governments which totalitarian states can cope with by brute force. Liberal administrations such as India's have to pursue a fluctuating, experimental line, giving way to pressure here, stiffening discipline there, attempting to combine maximum effectiveness with maximum agreement. It is a method more in keeping with the varieties and inconsistencies and vitalities of human existence. It does not necessarily release massive resources for investment and growth.

These inhibitions on union and government influence throw all the more responsibility on management; and one of the most significant by-products of rapid industrial advance in the most modern sectors of the Indian economy is a very great strengthening of the new managerial class in India. Numbers have increased at least tenfold since 1947 and are going steadily up. The managers bring a new professionalism to their work and are the spearhead of changing attitudes throughout industry. India, like

(175)

every other economy in the early stages of industrialization, needs these new patterns. The merchant turned businessman, avid for the last rupee of profit, treats his labour
force like a raw material; and since, in India, labour was
abundant and cheap, it was treated wastefully, like any
other cheap and abundant resource. The system of managing agencies—although it fulfilled an indispensable function in supplementing the quite insufficient cadre of managers—did not encourage very careful techniques, since
one firm or family might be running a score of businesses
and the local manager had often no more authority than
a hired hand. At the bottom of the scale, jobbers recruited
labour from the villages for a commission and provided
what organization and welfare there was. Naturally, these
were negligible.

Even so, the shape of better things to come could be
found in some areas at quite an early stage. Some leaders
in the Ahmedabad Mill-Owners Association carried on
relations with the unions in something of the spirit of
Gandhi, caring for the workers' welfare, attending to
labour-management relations in the factories, and trying
to put consultation in place of the old giving and taking of
orders. In Bombay, the Bombay Mill-Owners Association
tried as a group to introduce new attitudes. More recently,
the Jute Mills Association in Bengal began to move in the
same directions; and Tata's did a pioneering job, trying to
create stable conditions in the remote centre of Jamshedpur. In fact, in almost every region, one or two firms,
often foreign-owned and managed, have stood out as pace-
setters for more productivity, a better trained labour
force, more welfare, and effective and responsible relations between management and labour.

The impact of the Plans has speeded up the process.
More of the sons of Marwari managing agents are taking

degrees in technology instead of sitting at a desk in uncle's office to pick up the rudiments of the business. More sons of educated families look to industry, not government, as a career; and some, incidentally, are beginning to interest themselves particularly in welfare and labour relations. The staffs of foreign firms are being steadily Indianized. There are more openings for managerial education, more programs for training within industry, more conferences bringing managers together to discuss their problems. Management associations have been formed in all the big cities. The oldfashioned entrepreneur who orders subordinates about, insists on rigid control of his workers, promotes caste relatives, however incompetent, and cuts every possible corner in pursuit of a quick profit is giving ground rapidly to a more sober and professional body of responsible managers; and their emergence affects far more than the efficiency of enterprise. It leads to new attitudes in labour-management relations. It creates a new image of business on the public mind. It is even tending to increase the areas of understanding in the troubled relations between government and business enterprise.

In the last decade, prejudice and suspicion have coloured much of the government's legislation, utterances, and policies with regard to private enterprise. But its attitudes have been inherited from a past in which, on the one hand, a large part of Indian business was foreign-owned or else managed by the rawest local type of new merchant-turned-industrialist; and on the other, government, in the shape either of Congress party members or of senior Civil Servants, had no first-hand experience of business problems.

The very great expansion of modern business in the last decade has begun to alter this. Government itself is now an entrepreneur. Profits look less discreditable when one has to earn them oneself—and this public enterprises must do, if they are to contribute resources to further expansion. The notion that large enterprises should be run as public services on a no-profit, no-loss basis has vanished. So has the idea that so long as a large scheme is useful and needed, it hardly matters when it begins to pay its way. In the Third Plan, for instance, there is less emphasis on large multipurpose schemes which may perhaps pay 2 per cent on their capital by 1980, and more on smaller schemes—tanks, tubewells—which can give a return within five years. At the other end of the scale, enthusiasm has cooled for peasant crafts which need to be subsidised to keep them competitive. Village textiles receive a fairly small increase in the capital allocations of the Third Plan. But the share of small-scale industries and industrial estates—the workshops and small factories using power and machinery—is nearly doubled.

This sense of the need to secure a return on what is undertaken may not yet amount to the rigorous cost analysis and market forecasting of a really modern firm. Nor have planning authorities and public corporations yet acquired that capacity for foresight and decision without which plants may get built and then, all too frequently, run at a loss. An entrepreneurial revolution is what the public sector chiefly needs.

Yet a Government which is in business itself has a better chance of understanding the grievances of private enterprise. Some of these are already less acute than they were. No one now expects wholesale nationalization to follow the earlier taking over of airlines, life insurance, and the Imperial Bank. Sections of the economy formerly closed to private enterprise—oil exploration, for instance, or the manufacture of aluminium and fertilizer—have been opened to private business. Even while it plans the expansion of its own activities, the government speaks of the "complementary character" of private enterprise, and in fact fosters it—not only by the vast stimulus given indirectly through the public investment program, but also by more immediate methods. Public capital is put at the disposal of business through such new financial institutions as the Indian Finance and Credit Corporation. New enterprises are encouraged by large rebates on taxation in the first years of growth. Government licensing, for all its irritations, also gives a direct stimulus. Since 1957, virtually all imports of consumer goods have ceased. This gives the Indian producer a completely protected market. The license he needs to import materials may be a nuisance to secure—undoubtedly it is; but the fact that he and not another producer secures it gives him something of a monopoly.

There are even signs of greater flexibility in what is undoubtedly the business community's greatest and most justified grounds for complaint—the draconian regulations which the government passes to control every aspect of enterprise, down to the last rupee of pay and expense account for the directors and the last percentage that may be paid to a managing agent. These regulations reinforce the rigours of the licensing system, which tells businessmen whether or not they may issue a new product or change a brand, and which controls the availability of currency, scarce materials, power, and industrial sites for current use and future expansion. Industrialists speak of the "seventy hurdles" they have to clear before they can expand an old enterprise or start a new one, and they protest with especial bitterness about the attitude of the officials on whom falls the responsibility of issuing licences. These men, trained in the Indian Civil Service's tradition of probity, equity, control, and careful verification, cannot realize that the businessman's opportunity may have faded while he sits about in the outer office waiting for a decision. And lower down, even the probity may be lost. If the license-seeker is a small man, he probably waits longer than the others and still only sees—and pays—a junior clerk.

The government has taken some notice of these grievances. Steps have been taken to simplify and streamline the whole business of licensing. Plans which involve less than a hundred employees and fixed assets of less than about $200,000 now need no licenses; and the government is to publish from time to time lists of industries in which licenses can be easily obtained and those in which they will be granted only with difficulty. As steel and power and cement become more abundant, licensing will presumably be abolished in these categories—and some businessmen believe that affairs would be smoother if state governments were not so paternally determined to do the work of finding the entrepreneur's site and labour force for him.

But in one area, licensing must continue: for the provision of foreign exchange. This lack, probably more than any other, has disrupted and delayed industrial development so far. In 1957–58 the run on the Indian reserves caused a sharp crisis in Indian growth, cutting back public expenditure and pulling private enterprise back on its hind legs like a horse too suddenly reined in. With foreign exchange for private use reduced to a trickle, the hopeful boom of 1955 to 1957 ended abruptly. In 1958, industrial expansion fell below one per cent. And although foreign assistance, austerity in imports, and some revival of exports have eased the position since, inadequate currency reserves remain as a continuous threat, month in, month out, to the whole Indian industrial experiment.

AGRICULTURE

In spite of some difficulties and disappointments, the Indian record in both infrastructure and industry is one of substantial advance on a broad front, amounting to something very like the "big push" needed to achieve sustained growth. But so far it has not been supported by a comparable advance in agriculture. The difference is not really surprising. In farming we come to the oldest, most deeply traditional, most profoundly entrenched of India's—or indeed of any developing nation's—activities. It is here that the winds of change blow most fitfully, that men are most firmly attached to the ways of their forefathers, that all the encrusted customs, traditions, and superstitions—of caste, of ritual observance, such as the prohibition of cow slaughter—survive most tenaciously. It is also in the villages that the dilemmas of development in a poor and overpopulated society take on their most forbidding and inescapable form.

The fundamental aim is to grow more food. Otherwise the new urban and industrial sectors of the economy cannot expand, and the growing numbers on the land will not be fed. Food grains have increased from 52 million tons to about 75 millions in the first ten years of the Plans. The minimum target for 1966 is 100 to 110 million tons, but the present rate of advance offers no hope of securing it. But equally, development must be designed to bring a somewhat better life to the millions who live on the land. They still make up nearly 80 per cent of the population. If their lives do not improve a little, how can a democratic government be said to be fulfilling its mandate? Unfortunately for smooth planning and easy advance, the aims of more food and greater productivity on the one hand and a better rural life for the majority on

TABLE IV SOME TARGETS FOR AGRICULTURE

Item	Unit	1950–51	1955–56	1960–61 (estimates)	1965–66 (targets)	Increase in 1960–61 over 1950–51 (%)	Increase in 1965–66 over 1960–61 (%)
AGRICULTURAL PRODUCTION:							
Foodgrains	mill. tons	52.2	65.8	75.0	100–105	44	33–40
Cotton	mill. bales	2.9	4.0	5.4	7.2	86	33
Sugar cane-gur	mill. tons	5.6	6.0	7.2	9–9.2	29	25–28
Oil seeds	mill. tons	5.1	5.6	7.2	9.2–9.5	41	28–32
Jute	mill. bales	3.3	4.2	5.5	6.5	67	18
Tea	mill. lbs	613	678	725	850	18	17
AGRICULTURAL SERVICES:							
Area irrigated	mill. acres	51.5	56.2	70.0	90.0	36	29
Consumption:							
Nitrogenous fertilizers	000 tons of N	55	105	360	1,000	555	178
Phosphatic fertilizers	000 tons of P_2O_5	7	13	67	400–500	857	497–646
Community development							
Blocks	number	—	1,064	3,112	5,217	—	68
Villages covered	thousands	—	150	400	550	—	38
Population served	millions	—	78	200	374	—	87

the other do not always coincide—at least in the short run. The dilemma of expansion versus equity, of rapid growth versus social justice, reappears in the village perhaps more acutely than in any other area of Indian life.

The starting point must be to secure more food; and this means, in effect, to persuade farmers to produce more of their food for the market. Yet the market itself has been a source of uncertainty and discouragement to the farmer. The markets for industrial corps—for groundnuts, for cotton, for tobacco and tea—have worked reasonably well, in spite of worldwide fluctuations. It is the food market that has been most unsteady. Part of the reason is India's pattern of rainfall. The monsoon deposits the whole year's supply of rain between June and September. This supply is uncertain, sometimes failing in one district, sometimes in another; and lack of storage or shortages of transport complicate the problem of distributing grain smoothly from deficit to surplus areas. The last great famine—in Bengal in 1943—was greatly aggravated by the fact that the Army had pre-empted the transport system.

Such uncertainties naturally give rise to intense speculation, merchants holding grain for a rise when a shortage threatens and clearing out stocks in neighbouring areas which suddenly and unexpectedly find themselves going short. Hitherto the Indian government seems to have made the uncertainties rather worse by imposing price control and zonal restrictions, without having sufficient reserves or authority to make the system work. The result has been to provide new opportunities for hoarding. For the same reason, its own direct entry into grain trading only increased market pressure on prices.

Now, however, the government has the means to make its controls more effective. There should soon be enough storage space to create a large decentralized grain reserve;

and an imaginative act on the part of the American government promises to ensure that the reserve is full. The United States has released 600 million bushels of wheat and 22 million bags of rice from its food surpluses over the next four years at a price—in rupees—of $1,276 millions. This new, solidly supported reserve needs another half-a-million tons of rice to be fully secure. Then the government should be able to negotiate fixed prices for food grains—say, for two years in advance—which will cover the farmers' costs and be kept stable by public buying of surpluses if harvests are too abundant, and by selling from the reserve if there are crop failures.

Given a more stable market, the next step is to encourage the farmer to produce a bigger surplus for it. The prospect is not impossible for the primary reason that Indian productivity is still very low. Japan probably produces three times as much per acre. The problem is to persuade the Indian farmer to be as productive as the Japanese. Part of the government's policy to this end consists in the provision of massive irrigation. Since 1951, the acreage under permanent irrigation has grown from 51.5 million acres to 70 millions, and the target for 1966 is 20 millions more. But the full value of the water can be secured only if the farmer is ready to complete all the subsidiary channel-building which the schemes entail—on an average, one million irrigated acres require 2,500 miles of government canals and 10,000 miles of private channels built by the villagers—and also to use water in combination with new methods, better seeds, and a large increase in fertilizers. These are not changes that come naturally to all India's farmers; and for this reason the government has provided the farmer with a vast, all-embracing, hopefully guiding, gently prodding, super-extension service in the shape of the Community Development movement, which already covers over half India's villages and should have reached the remainder by the end of the Third Plan.

The network created by Community Development brings together blocks of a hundred villages under a Project Officer who can call on various specialist services —agricultural, veterinary, educational, co-operative—to assist him in his work. In the administrative hierarchy he reports directly to the head of the district—the old centre-piece of Indian administration, the collector—and in the villages the last link in the administrative chain is the village-level worker, through whom advice and assistance are made available directly to the farmers. The Project Officer's responsibility to the Collector puts the whole prestige of government behind the project, and symbolizes the change from a "law and order" state in which collect-ing the revenue was the administrator's main responsi-bility to the "development and welfare" state in which the village school, the local clinic, the all-weather road, better seed, more fertilizer, plots for demonstration, and rural credit are all first charges on the officials' time and energy.

The change in attitude toward village problems is as sweeping. The old system accepted the conservatism of the countryside. Now the villagers are encouraged to look for a better life by being shown models of what it could be like. Formerly the administration gave the orders, and the villagers looked on it as "father and mother" and gave an unquestioning obedience. Now the aim is to discover what villagers themselves want to accomplish and then help them do it. There is more in this than a democratic desire not to prolong authoritarian attitudes at the very roots of Indian life. The reckoning is that the farmers will not pay for improvements they have not sought themselves nor maintain them once they are built.

If the village wants a school and the project officer insists on a road, the people will begrudge the work and leave the track unrepaired if the next monsoon washes it out.

But perhaps the dominant idea behind the projects is the belief that rural change can never be achieved by picking at a problem here and a problem there, by making a series of partial adjustments—since what is needed is a universal change in attitudes. It is no use proposing a school or a clinic unless the farmers' income is increasing enough to build it. Income will not rise without more literacy and better health—which takes one back to the school and the clinic. A developing village is rather like an economy trying to achieve an economic breakthrough. One or two changes do not produce momentum. The advance has to be general, each innovation strengthening and reinforcing the rest.

The Community Development projects have now been in existence for a decade. The first enthusiasm in which they were seen as instant instruments of rural renewal has given way—at least in some quarters—to an almost equal pessimism about their chance of ever securing any real change at all. The small increase in foodgrains, the continuing mass of rural underemployment, the slow take-up of irrigation water are cited as evidence of an inertia that nothing as gentle as persuasion can dispel. Short of this extreme view, there is very general agreement that the outcome has been uneven, the good projects giving very satisfactory results, the poor projects lapsing back into the old ways.

Why have the differences been so great? On the side of the administration, there have been local breakdowns in the supply of such essential instruments of development as improved seed and fertilizers. The output of these vital products has not kept pace with the spread of the Community Development movement. Farmers whose interest was caught by the evidence of better yields on a demonstration plot found that no improved strains were available when planting time came round. One of the most encouraging features of the last ten years has been the farmers' steadily increasing demand for fertilizer. It has tripled since 1955. But local production was limited by rather unambitious targets for fertilizer in the first two Plans; and the government seems to have decided that there simply was not enough foreign exchange available for a big increase in imports. Yet nothing dampens down fresh enthusiasm for new methods so quickly as to discover that necessary supplies are intermittent or not available at all.

At times, the holdups have been due not to absolute shortages, but to clogged or confused channels of delivery. The fertilizer or the seed did not turn up when the time to use it had come. And this type of delay points to a wider problem, the fact that the agricultural services in India do not get their fair share of India's best brains. In all underdeveloped areas, farming tends to be a stepchild. Agriculture, so long neglected under colonial governments, still lacks prestige and glamour. The lad who thinks nothing of lying under a car covering himself with axle grease does not want to dirty his hands with soil or manure. Only industrial dirt is "progressive"—partly, of course, because industry pays better.

The mood can be found at all levels. The Ministry of Agriculture is only a stepping-stone to a more glorious post in Finance or Foreign Affairs. Mr. Nehru has, it seems, urged the State Premiers to take over the portfolio of agriculture as well as their own—with no result. The keenest young officials make for revenue or, now, for industry. The agricultural colleges attract too few of the better students.

The government is attempting to change this, to improve pay and prospects and secure agriculture its share of able people. Yet it is a disturbing fact that, alone among India's university faculties, agriculture produced fewer doctorates in 1956 than in 1951.

For this reason, one discovers again and again that the biggest contribution government can make to Community Development is to provide competent officials. Where the Collector and his Project Officer are keen, interested, knowledgeable, able to use their experts, and both delegate responsibility and follow up results, the project is usually a success. But there are not enough such officers; and unless attitudes change toward agriculture and rural needs generally, it does not seem likely that there will be enough for years to come.

When one turns to the farmers, the reasons are more diverse. To give a comprehensive answer one would need to peer into each of the village units, and be able to understand the balance of forces inside the community, caste differences and caste leadership, the crops produced, the distance to market, the availability of water, and a thousand other details. Yet a few judgments can be risked. Villages produce better when they are linked to the market by reliable roads. Community Development's greatest contribution so far may well be that it built 80,000 miles of new roads and improved 100,000 miles more in the first eight years of the Plans. Anyone who has watched the stream of bicyclists with tins of milk strapped on their handlebars heading for Delhi market in the smoky dawn has seen at first hand what the combination of road and market can do for even the smallest entrepreneur. The siting of new industrial centres, such as the steel towns of Bhilai and Rourkela, in open country will activate in time a thousand villages round about. Decentralized industry is thus a way to stimulate agriculture as well.

Much depends upon the question of whether local cultivators have a business tradition. The Punjabi loves change and the good life, the farmers of Gujarat are as hardheaded as any *bania*. Both, too, have supplies of water—the Punjabi from the canals, the Gujarati from a reasonably reliable rainfall. They have long produced for the market—Punjab's wheat, Saurashtra's groundnuts and cotton, Gujarat's tobacco—and are now avid users of all the fertilizer and better seed and water that come their way. In Eastern Uttar Pradesh, on the contrary, the villages are hierarchical and caste-ridden. They barely produce for the market at all.

The same differences can be remarked between village and village in the same area. If the dominant families are sensible, enterprising, and just, they can carry a whole village with them into new patterns of production and marketing. If caste feuds divide the leaders, or the richest farmers are selfish money grubbers, the village falls apart in bitterness and apathy.

At this point we meet the second objective of government policy—a better life for the villagers—and all the challenges and complications which it entails. The dilemmas are rooted in over a century of agrarian history. Although wartime inflation did very greatly reduce the inherited load of peasant debt, it was still true that in the agricultural system India inherited in 1947 there were a great many reasons why the small farmer never had much chance of earning any surplus. The revenue-collecting intermediaries—the Zamindars and the Jagirdars—took their share, and the farmer's dependence upon the local *bania*-merchant probably took the rest. If he went into debt, he was reduced to a species of tenant-at-will. If he

(189)

sank still further, he became landless and dropped to the bottom of the village scale.

It is the prevalence of these stagnant hopeless conditions in countries of low productivity and high population that tempts governments into drastic methods of breaking out of the vicious closed circle of rural poverty breeding ever more poverty. Fuse the tiny plots into single working units on an economic scale, turn the peasants into farm labourers paid in the equivalent of labour days, organize them into gangs for sewing, harvesting, draining, bunding, and building irrigation channels, control the supplies of fertilizers and improved seed through central channels, put in an efficient farm technician to manage the unit, introduce mechanization, remove as much of the surplus as possible to other sectors of the economy, carry out the whole technique with the ruthlessness of the Communists in China—and the result does seem to solve all the interlocking problems of rural stagnation in one mighty act of mobilization.

Politically, the cost is enormous. Peasants pay for the change in sweat and tears and blood. Even economically, the long-term results are still uncertain. No country in Asia approaches the productivity achieved in Japan, where agriculture is based on very small peasant proprietors using the most modern farming techniques, backed by a full range of co-operative services. But for the first big push in agriculture, the Chinese claim to be achieving startling results; and many Asians, looking with desperation at the stagnant, crowded villages and shrinking farm plots, cannot wait for the longer calculus. They simply want results now. Even in India, some Congress members have suggested that villagers might fuse their plots in co-operative farms; and the saintly leader, Acharya Vinobe Bhave, has persuaded some villages to pledge themselves to *gramdan,* the pooling of their lands for joint operation. But such a solution would have to demonstrate its effectiveness very clearly in hard economic terms before it would appeal to farmers for whom land ownership is still the touchstone of security. Nor, meanwhile, can a liberal government dependent upon the peasant vote impose it by force. Reform has to proceed cautiously, not outstripping the readiness of the majority of the rural voters to follow.

The first step has been generally accepted and concluded—the abolition of the Zamindars and the Jagirdars. Like Japan's Daimyo and Samurai, they have gone their —compensated—way. But the next step is not so clear. The great cultivating castes have moved to the top of the village hierarchy. They are substantial men with sizable farms by Indian standards. Ought they, too, to be subject to land reform and be made to give up part of their holdings to the landless men? On the basis of "fair shares," one can advance such an argument. But the answer does not add up in market terms. It is the bigger farms that now produce a surplus; and it is precisely the multiplication of tiny plots that impedes greater output and actually extends the area of subsistence farming.

There is no easy way round the dilemma. The Planning Commission recommends an upper limit equal to three times the land that can be worked by an average family. Some states are considering a limit based on income— for instance, $756 a year—others a maximum acreage of 30 acres. In Uttar Pradesh, land above 30 acres is subject to a heavy progressive tax. The Ford Foundation, which has played a pioneering role in every aspect of recent rural development, suggests that a temporary ceiling be fixed now so as to end uncertainty and encourage farmers to invest, while leaving the possibility open of setting higher limits later on, when industrial openings in the towns will have reduced the pitiable pressure of men without any land at all. The experience of Japan, however, suggests that industrialization is more likely to take care of the births to come rather than to reduce in any decisive way the numbers in agriculture. There are still almost as many people on the land in Japan as there were in the 1870s. But there are over 60 million more people elsewhere.

The answer almost certainly is—as it must be in any non-Utopian society—that there is no single solution; the hope is that many proximate answers will add up to a policy which, if not perfect, at least will allow people to live with each other without too much discontent. Better methods of farming, especially when combined with irrigation, will give larger incomes from smaller plots. More intensive agriculture will provide labourers with more work locally. Rural industries will provide more opportunities in the village; and the towns will steadily drain off the future surplus. And the best of the more inclusive answers lies in the development of the movement for co-operative credit, processing, and marketing which will allow farms, large and small, to achieve—as in Japan—important economies of scale by working together. The government encourages co-operation strongly—through the Community Development Movement, through the State Bank, by the establishment of special co-operative banks backed by public funds, by training an expanding staff of co-operative officials and advisers. As a result, the number of farmers' co-operatives has increased from five to twelve million since 1951. Annual advances have risen from $56 million to $250 million; and co-operative credit now covers 10 per cent of rural borrowing, compared with only 3 per cent at the time of Independence.

This figure, however, shows how much credit is still secured from traditional sources; and there is evidence to suggest that only the wealthier families in the villages can give the co-operatives the security they require for loans. The little man is likely to be in debt, if not to the *bania*, then to a wealthier neighbour; and the danger remains that the more prosperous farmers in the village may come to dominate and exploit rural society as the old Zamindars and moneylenders used to do. Success in all the various forms of attack on rural poverty will mitigate this risk. So will the good sense and good will of the wealthier farmers themselves—the lead they give in the *panchayat*, or the caste council, or the co-operative. So, too, will the fact that small villagers have the vote and they are the majority. But the crucial question remains whether rural income and well-being as a whole will go up steadily enough to take the sting out of differences in caste and income and provide sufficient margins of welfare to soften the possible emergence of a sharp class cleavage between the wealthier families—the "kulaks"—in the village and the rest.

To this question, a decisive answer cannot yet be given. Rural poverty remains acute and widespread. Food production is rising only slowly. Progress and improvement are patchy. Most agricultural experts are dissatisfied with the progress made so far. In fact, to speed matters up and give a new impetus to the Third Plan, the Indian authorities have taken up a suggestion first put forward by the Ford Foundation to set aside a special development district in each state where an intensified effort of community development is to be tried out, using all techniques to the maximum and demonstrating what a really concentrated effort can achieve. The government has also allotted a larger proportion of its funds to farming in the Third Plan than in the Second, and has given a higher priority to such crucial needs as fertilizers and improved agricultural implements. There is thus evidence of greater energy and purpose in current farming plans. But agriculture still remains the most vulnerable sector on the Indian scene.

Chapter Thirteen

Resources for the Plan

I N THEIR forecast of re-
sources for public investment in the Third Plan—given
in Table V—the Indian authorities expect a small contribution of $735 million from revenue levied at the present
levels of taxation. Otherwise the whole effort, $15,215
million, will have to be based on resources raised outside
the regular budget. This is in line with experience under
the Second Plan; and even the small contribution from
current revenue is in doubt, for nobody yet knows how
much extra defence spending will be forced on India by
Chinese pressure along the Himalayas. It is perhaps safer
to assume that the whole figure for public investment will
be over and above current revenue.

Private enterprise is to be left to find its own funds and
on past experience should have no difficulty in doing so—
provided buoyancy and growth are maintained. During

the Second Plan, every category of private investment has proved higher than was expected. The trend will probably continue. Much of the investment for very small-scale enterprise cannot be estimated accurately, since it represents work and direct saving on the part of the owner and his family. According to some estimates, villagers often save upwards of 10 per cent of their income. There is thus quite a large margin here for productive investment, provided villagers can be persuaded to put it into a tubewell and not an expensive funeral.

The pattern of public investment outlined in Table V is also perfectly achievable in a lively atmosphere of economic expansion. But it entails real sacrifices and includes some elements of great uncertainty. India's direct taxation is among the highest in the world. If more taxes were added to the income tax, super-tax, expenditure tax, and wealth tax that the richer classes already pay, and if, in addition, company taxation were to be increased—at present, either directly or through the tax on distributed dividends it takes over 50 per cent of the profits—the relatively small sums gained by the exchequer might hardly offset the disincentives to organized private industry which has to raise $8,395 millions in its own right.

The argument is sometimes advanced that since incomes below $7,280 a year are less heavily taxed in India than in Britain, Japan, or Germany, some increase in the lower rates would be possible. Yet the small Indian middle class has borne the brunt of the inflation; and unlike the middle income groups in the West, it receives little back from the state in the shape of welfare. It also provides most of the men and women in public and private life on whose enthusiasm and drive the success of the Plan depends. The added revenue might be a high price to pay for their discouragement.

The poor man already pays quite sizable taxes through the excise taxes levied by the central government and the sales taxes of the states. Half the federal revenue is raised in this way, and most articles in common use are taxed

TABLE V ESTIMATED FINANCIAL RESOURCES FOR THE PLAN
(*In Millions of U.S. Dollars*)

	Second Plan	Third Plan
Balance from revenues on the basis of existing taxation	—210	735
Contribution from Railways on existing basis	315	315
Surpluses from other public enterprises on existing basis	—	923
Loans from the public	1,679	1,784
Small savings	797	1,154
Provident funds, betterment levies, and so on	447	1,070
Additional taxation, including increased surpluses from public enterprises	2,099	3,463
Budgetary receipts corresponding to external assistance	2,061	4,617
Deficit financing	2,466	1,154
Total	9,654	15,215

except salt, which has been made sacrosanct by Gandhi's refusal to pay the salt tax. Kerosene could certainly carry a higher tax. The workers in organized industry also pay what is in some measure a tax by their contributions to compulsory provident funds and insurance schemes. The whole community, rich and poor alike, will pay more for their goods as the government marks up the price of products from public enterprises in order to create a surplus out of their profits for further investment.

From all these sources—direct and indirect taxation, compulsory saving and insurance, and surpluses of public enterprise—the government hopes to raise $8,709 millions over the five years. Even with national income rising by 5 per cent a year, this is a sizable sum and entails real sacrifices of possible consumption. Even so, some critics, looking at the amount of deficit financing during the Second Plan and the sharp increase in prices that has followed argue that India's tax policy is not tough enough. A determined effort should be made to increase all categories of taxation. Least of all can the government be content to raise more income and company taxes simply by improving tax administration and checking tax evasions. But at this point, there are no facts, only judgments. How far can larger amounts be squeezed out of private funds in an economy which is still so very largely private? If higher taxation were to check industrial investment, if it lessened the public's readiness to lend to the government, if small savers continued to make a rather unsatisfactory response, the government would simply lose on the roundabouts of borrowing what it had gained on the swings of taxation. True, the forecast for borrowing must always be in some measure a gesture of hope. But it is based on a good response hitherto. No one can estimate exactly at what point the propensity to lend might be checked by the compulsion to pay more tax. But in a liberal society, the government naturally inclines to give the private citizen the benefit of the doubt and to persuade rather than dragoon him. But it is a risk; and if the calculation is wrong and deficit financing has to fill in the short-fall in resources, inflation may use its blind bludgeon to extort funds not made available through more orderly and socially desirable procedures.

The Government believes that deficit financing of the order of $1,154 millions—which is only half the level reached during the Second Plan—can safely be attempted. Production is rising; the American release of wheat and rice will stabilize food prices; inflationary trends have a reasonable chance of being controlled. But not even the most accurate planning can counter the risks of inflation endemic in a society subject to the major uncertainties of the monsoons. A bad harvest lowers incomes and checks savings throughout the economy. Poor monsoons in the 1957–58 season had disastrous repercussions, reducing government revenue, reducing the public response to government loans, sending food prices up and industrial activity down. The economy still suffers from excessive liquidity caused by the amount of deficit finance which the Government felt obliged to undertake at that time in order to keep essential developmental work moving forward. Another really bad harvest could once again upset all the calculations. India simply has not sufficient reserves to take such major upheavals in an even stride of growth.

Nor do the monsoons end the influences over which the Indian Government has little or no control. There is no mistaking the extreme dependence of the whole effort of planning upon the scale of foreign assistance. In the first place, a large part—nearly 30 per cent—of the internal finances earmarked for the Third Plan represent the equivalent in rupees of funds received from abroad. Without such assistance, the whole internal programme of austerity would have to be nearly one-third as great again —and it is almost at the limit of what can be secured by persuasion already.

But this is not the only nor even the most dangerous aspect of India's dependence on foreign funds. Without command of $5,456 millions in foreign exchange, some of the essential elements in the Third Plan cannot be secured at all. This figure is arrived at by first adding together India's expected receipts from its exports and invisible earnings between 1961 and 1966—$7,492 millions. These together would just cover the expected level of imports needed to keep the economy working at current levels— also estimated at $7,492 millions—were it not for the fact that in the next Plan period, repayments on earlier loans quite offset new private capital and will amount to $1,049 millions. Thus, even before thinking of new investment and further expansion, the Indian economy faces an annual deficit of $210 millions. The whole foreign exchange component of the new Plan must therefore be raised from new funds. The need is estimated to be $3,897 millions for capital goods, and $420 millions for materials, components and so forth to set them to work. If the $1,049 millions deficit in the current balance is added, the total requirements are $5,366 millions * over the five years.

It should be underlined at once that there is nothing strange or unnatural about India's present dependence upon outside supplies. It is still caught fast in the typical dilemma of early development. An economy first leaving the static stage must, by definition, be very short of all the capital goods needed for more rapid advance. The machines, the tools, the technical knowledge and expert manpower have to be procured abroad, but the economy is not yet productive enough to pay for them—one reason why in so many previous breakthroughs to modernization,

---

* To this sum should be added about $1,276 millions already secured from America for the Third Plan from the latest release from the food surpluses.

the development of materials for export or massive foreign lending has played a decisive part. The growth of cereals in North American and Russia, timber exports from Sweden, British investment in American railways, European investment in Czarist Russia, British capital in Australia since 1945—all are examples of a crucial advantage gained by trading with and borrowing from abroad. But in the circumstances of the 1960s, nothing like such an outside stimulus can be looked for in India. Exports are likely to move up only slowly. Each of the staples faces special obstacles: jute, the alternative methods of packaging that have been developed; tea and coffee, the imposition of heavy excise duties in the West, especially in Europe; cotton textiles, the upper limit of quotas imposed by the advanced nations. It is true that Britain has made remarkable efforts of adaptation in Lancashire, abandoning the cheaper cloths, concentrating and rationalizing the industry, and transferring workers to a growing engineering sector in the same area. Britain buys about a fifth of India's exports of cotton textiles and has in some measure allowed cheap Indian manufactures to do to Lancashire what Lancashire once did to Bengal. Yet the advanced countries, generally, fix an upper limit for textile imports and beyond that point give their own higher-cost textile industries complete protection.

India will develop other exports. A promising line has been opened up in the bulk sale of iron ore to Japan. Manganese exports are picking up again. The engineering industries are certain to increase their range as they expand; but there seems little doubt that the whole environment for the exports of developing economies is not so favourable now as it was a century ago—when, incidentally, most of the theories about the beneficent and automatic workings of world-wide trade were first devised.

It is not simply a question of fluctuating world prices for raw materials, although India, like all other primary producers, has suffered from the instability in primary prices particularly since the end of the Korean War boom. One cause of the 1957–58 crisis was an unfavourable movement of about ten points in India's terms of trade—the amount of exports needed to procure a given amount of exports. But there are wider difficulties.

A general change in the climate of international trade has recurred in the last fifty years. In the nineteenth century, the world market was dominated by Britain, a tiny island with few resources and an unquenchable appetite for overseas supplies. Its demands sparked investment and trade abroad and led to reciprocal growth between the developed and the undeveloped lands. In this century, America has become the central economy, and it is an exporter of both goods and raw materials. At the same time, modern chemical and synthetic industries have expanded to such a pitch that they create a constant possibility of substituting home-produced materials for the supplies that once could only be secured abroad. Scientific research elaborates new synthetic fibres, transforms domestic low grade ores, increases efficiency in recovering industrial scrap. The old compulsions to look overseas diminish; and the vast expansion of the postwar mass economy in the West has simply failed to transmit any comparable impetus to Asia.

Of course, some increase in trade can be forecast. The growing market of the Soviet bloc offers large though uncertain prospects; and both Russia and its satellites are ready to provide trade credits, some of them repayable in rupees. Trade with Japan should increase steadily as that country's national income goes up. If India's chief trading partners—the United States, Britain, and Western Europe

—more or less double the scale of their economies by 1980, estimates suggest that their demand for primary materials ought to rise on the average by as much as 70 per cent above the levels of 1957–58. Unhappily, India's staple exports—cotton, jute, tea—belong to the very slow-growing categories, with an average rate of increase of less than 30 per cent above the 1957–58 base year. Yet if India is to cover its present need for imports, a rise of more than 30 per cent in its exports should be achieved, not by 1980, but in the next five years.

The other traditional way out of the dilemma—that of massive investment from abroad—is also ruled out for India by this same change of atmosphere in the international economy. Nineteenth-century capital used to go out from the Atlantic area to discover and develop new raw materials. To-day, the growth of Western self-sufficiency checks this impetus. In fact, were it not for petroleum, the underdeveloped areas would have had only a very small part in postwar private investment which has gone overwhelmingly either to other developed countries or to oil-producing states. India has received a higher share than its neighbours because of the scale of British investment. Eighty per cent of India's foreign capital of $1,120 millions is British; and British investment doubled between 1948 and 1959. Yet the whole $1,120 millions represents only about one year of India's current need for extra foreign resources, and in 1958 fresh investment fell as low as $21 millions.

Today, it is true, the Indian government shows a more encouraging face to private investors. The insistence on Indian majority control and ownership has been dropped in cases of investment which the government particularly wishes to encourage. Joint ventures between Indian and foreign firms are welcomed. Double income tax agreements are being negotiated—although, by an extraordinary oversight, not with London. All the tax rebates offered for new industry are available to foreign enterprise, and the government has an impeccable record in allowing the repatriation of capital and profits. In addition, the constitution gives guarantees against expropriation without compensation. These safeguards and incentives will, it is hoped, in some measure offset the risk foreign enterprise faces in investing abroad at all, as well as the particular disadvantage created by India's high taxes once the first stage of development has come to an end.

Yet the government's own estimate of new private investment does not go beyond $211 millions for the whole of the Third Plan. The gap of about $5,000 to $5,600 millions remains, and India is left with two alternatives: either to look abroad for help or to introduce a quite new campaign of mobilization and austerity at home. The former is beyond the government's control. But so, in fact, is the latter as well.

It is not that patterns of total mobilization are unknown. On the contrary, the techniques are all too familiar. The Government could stop all foreign trade on private account and virtually abolish the consumer goods industries. It could institute a series of forced loans as a strict percentage of everyone's income. It could mobilize the half-employed and unemployed into forced labour brigades working sixteen hours a day on a subsistence diet. It could fix food prices at the lowest level compatible with the farmers' continuing to live and work, transfer the food to the towns by forced deliveries, and allow rising costs for manufactured goods to drain off what was left of the rural surplus; inflation, in general, would ruin the middle classes, destroy private savings, and channel resources into industrial profits which, in an increasingly nationalized economy, would be the equivalent of handing them over to the state. All these policies and variants of them have been practised in totalitarian countries in the last forty years; and there can be no doubt about their success in placing resources at the disposal of the central authorities. China's economic drive is only the most far-reaching and ruthless example of total state mobilization —a mobilization which all states practice in time of war, and which the Communists carry on for the purposes of their version of peace.

But to do this India would have to become a completely different kind of country. Today it is a voluntary society from the Cabinet at the centre down to the smallest village *panchayat*. The two mainstreams in Indian political thought—the constitutionalism of liberal Europe, and the religious and social inspiration of Mahatma Gandhi—may not fuse very comfortably in some aspects of the nation's life. Between central industrial planning and hand-spinning in the village, economic policy has had to pursue a somewhat wavering line. In the matter of party structure and representative institutions, a Gandhian socialist of the type of Jayaprakash Narayan prefers far more decentralization, far more emphasis on the primary village unit, than do India's socialist planners for whom centralized authority and decision-making is a precondition for a successful Indian take-off into sustained growth. But in their attitudes to the ultimate purpose of society, in their belief in the rights and dignity of ordinary citizens and the subordinate role of government as servant, not master of the people, in their deep dedication to persuasion and conciliation and nonviolence as the only legitimate means of politics, the two traditions fuse and support each other. The synthesis of the Western rule of law and Eastern metaphysics, of European rights and

Indian values continues to produce the fullest Asian version of an open, plural, mixed society.

Congress, the continent-wide coalition of different groups and interests, is committed to compromise fully as much by its internal constitution as by its political outlook. Even if it wanted to be a totalitarian party, it could not be so with its splits between policies and personalities, its regional distinctions, its broad appeal. In fact, some critics doubt, especially in view of its present divisions, whether it has even enough drive to carry through the existing degree of mobilization. The smaller parties—Socialists to the Left, Swatantra to the Right—are even less monolithic in tendency and inspiration. The communal Hindu parties exercise little but local influence. Only the Communists are committed to total organization and total control. But just because Congress is a party of coalitions and compromises, it demands a little elbowroom to act effectively. So long as disciplines are not too rigid, so long as income is edging up and there is a little more each year with which to bargain with friends and buy off opponents, so long, in short, as the mass of the people feel they are making some progress, even if it is slow, Congress can act and organize—if not brilliantly, at least well enough to enable the government to be carried on. And in non-Utopian societies, nobody wants it to do very much more.

But if the margins were to contract, if the whole effort were to bog down in a morass of contradictions and impossibilities, with capital short for lack of saving, saving short for lack of income, income short for lack of work, work short for lack of capital—the whole series of vicious interlocking spirals of a stagnant economy in which only population goes up—in that kind of economy, politics by persuasion would vanish. Either the government itself would need to introduce draconian austerity, and for this, the Communist model in China—the new Communism of the poor—is as effective as any; or discontent would drive out the moderate men and put the extremists in with the mandate to lift the economy off the ocean bed by effective measures, however violent. These are the only alternatives once the economic experiment of developing in freedom begins to fail. Even the setback caused by the poor monsoon in 1957 greatly increased political bitterness. Where extreme degrees of stagnation and aspiration are combined, as in Kerala, the Communist vote has already risen to—and stayed at—40 per cent of the electorate, a warning of the consequences of failure, a portent of possible things to come.

In short, the two versions of society which have divided the West in the last hundred years—the Utopian version of total mobilization and total control and the moderate version of choice, persuasion, and privacy—now divide Asia as well: China dedicated to the one, India upholding the other. But the Indian experiment is approaching a crucial test. Through a decade of independence and economic development, it has proceeded by the techniques of freedom. The result has been a modest but promising success. Now, however, even the minimum rates of further advance depend upon temporary but important assistance from outside. On its mobilization the political as well as the economic future of India—and indeed of all Asia—depend.

PART

3

••••••••••

After China's Attack

Chapter Fourteen

The Immediate Crisis

THE Third Plan was barely two years old when the drama between totalitarian and liberal society in Asia flared up into border war. But was it more than a border foray? Was it a prelude to all-out war? Or pressure designed to bring India back to the negotiating table in a more compliant frame of mind? Or opportunism, part of a long process of probing here and probing there, weakening the independence of border states, undermining India's status and self-respect and reducing the Himalayas from a secure frontier to a threatened no-man's land? Having no direct insight into Mao Tse-tung's thinking, we can only guess and the most informed guesses these days seem to conclude that India is faced with one of the most unpleasant and most difficult kinds of conflict a nation can be compelled to face—a sort of "on-again, off-again Flanagan" conflict, in which the

(211)

enemy never gives its opponents for any length of time, the brisk, invigorating sense of open struggle, but continuously saps away at the foundations of their essential interests and of their long-term defense.

What happened in October–November, 1962, certainly fits into this picture. Indian troops, the Chinese alleged, were probing forward in Ladakh, part of which the Chinese are determined to keep. Now, the Chinese could, in these conditions, have responded solely in Ladakh, delivering a very strong attack there to bring their frontier within sight of Chusul. What did they do? They chose instead by a surprise attack in North Eastern Frontier Agency to deal a devastating blow at the Indian Army and hence at Indian prestige. Here was the demonstration that, when it comes to *power*, there is at this moment only one effective power system inside Asia—the Chinese system.

It served notice on the Indian people that their frontiers are very largely defenseless. And it reminded them of how vulnerable the lands behind the Himalayan frontier really are. Aggression in Ladakh could hardly have illustrated this point so clearly since the loss of Ladakh would not open the great river plains of India to direct attack. Of course, the Ladakh aggression cannot be simply swallowed. India's reaction has been entirely sane since nothing is more dangerous than that any great nation should acquire the sense that it can take what it likes from its neighbours' territory. This attitude is one to be discouraged from an early stage in any dispute. But in NEFA, the issue is more than one of discouraging aggression. Look at Assam, study the map of that corner of India and you will see that it is the intersecting point of half a dozen states, all vulnerable, some at odds with each other, most of them open to Chinese pressure. And behind NEFA, any renewed drive could carry the enemy into the tea gardens of Assam and with their loss would go nearly 20 per cent of India's foreign exchange earnings—already grossly inadequate to the tasks facing the Indian economy.

In short, the Chinese, by striking in NEFA, have certainly exposed much more immediate and crucial interests than any at issue in Ladakh. Ladakh touches, of course, on national prestige. When, however, the issue at stake is an essential element of a nation's economy and beyond that, the survival in security of vital, developed industrial regions—one thinks of the vulnerability of West Bengal and Bihar—then clearly the Chinese have served notice on India that its vital interests are at the moment wholly unprotected. Whether the Chinese have withdrawn for good, or only for a time, the grim fact remains that, so long as the present Indian defensive posture remains unchanged, India is undefended.

The fact that the Chinese have made the demonstration so brutally could turn out to be their gravest error. If a nation intends a long spell of expansion, it would be well advised to go about it quietly at the start. Of course, the Chinese consider power a perfectly legitimate weapon for dealing with people with less power. But their neighbours were perhaps not fully aware of the fact. Now, the violent warning they have given cannot be disregarded and perhaps it could not have been hammered home in any less brutal way. Was this a lesson they really wanted to teach so soon?

The openness of the aggression is the first reason for supposing that Chinese aggressiveness cannot be simply wished away by appealing to "Panch Sheel" or Asian solidarity. Nor do Chinese withdrawals point in a different direction. It is a well-known trick in jujitsu to give your opponent a blow, brace yourself to receive his counter-blow, then when he launches it, fall back and allow his own weight to bring him down. The basic fact remains that the Chinese have the power to come and go as they choose.

What they will choose is locked in the minds of China's leaders. But we have some ominous pointers which should not be ignored. To restore the sovereignty of Peking over lands once owing it allegiance is a recurrent aim of new Chinese dynasties—and the Communists are in a real sense a reincarnation of the old dynasties thrown up by popular despair and led by peasants. Such an aim involves very extensive potential enlargement of Chinese control.

Quite apart from states such as Viet Nam which were once part of the Chinese system, a further vague penumbra of states could be included. Often, in times gone by, when harmless ambassadors arrived in Peking and, as was the custom of the time, gave his celestial majesty a present, his celestial majesty, with his profound contempt for everyone outside the "Middle Kingdom," simply assumed that, as "barbarians," they were naturally paying tribute and accepting vassal status. On this interpretation, Burma, Nepal, Bhutan, possibly Assam and even states as remote as Indonesia, could be reckoned part of the Chinese area of predominance. Now, if all these states come, as it were, to be "gathered in," India would be confronted with an overwhelming concentration of power and one which would have altered the balance of power in the world in a formidable sense.

It is these larger ambitions and possibilities which make it impossible for India simply to accept the current Chinese withdrawal as equivalent to the removal of danger. The Chinese have gone. They can come back. They have historical and imperial reasons for doing so. Therefore, the only sane thing for India to do is to buy time. The mistake must not be made, as was made by Mr. Chamberlain at Munich, of believing that, because something turned out to be not quite so bad as he had feared, he had bought peace. Actually, the British did do something with that bit of time between 1938 and 1939; they "bought" Spitfires. But in general one can say that during that year, from Munich to the outbreak of war, we did not buy enough. Today India may be going to be given time. The essential thing is to concentrate on "buying" a frontier that is defensible and a military system that can defend it.

Let us look first at the military side—the problem of mounting an effective defense force capable of seeing that, the next time the Chinese try a probe in NEFA, it is they who get the shock. There does seem to be a certain concurrence of military opinion that to restore a proper posture of effective defense on the northern frontiers India would need to envisage a doubling of the present defense establishment and a considerable modernization of arms and equipment. And equally there seems to be broad agreement that such an effort would not cost less than from $945 million to $1.05 billion in the initial phase.

If we accept this as a reasonable estimate, we can begin to measure its impact on the Indian economy. And there is no disguising the fact that the emergency overcame India at a time of very considerable economic strain. Let us look at the position as it was in August 1962. At that time, it was already clear that the Third Plan was running into some very real difficulties. In the course of 1961 and 1962, the general growth of the Indian economy had been disappointing. To reach the targets of the Third Plan, an annual rate of growth in national income of the order of at least 5 per cent had been forecast. Instead of that, growth barely reached 3 per cent and, with a population increase of about 2 per cent, there was clearly very little margin left for further investment or rise in consumption —and very little margin for satisfaction either. To find India's rate of growth among the lowest in Asia—a fact brought out in a recent UN Report—was an unpleasant shock.

The various reasons for this slow-down point to some of the pressures that were at work on the Plan even before the emergency arose. First of all, we must look at the disappointing performance in agriculture. The hope had been to secure an annual rise of 6 per cent in farm production; instead, in 1961–62 the level was just under 2 per cent. This relatively unsatisfactory performance had something to do, as usual, with the weather. But it had more to do with the fact that reform and reorganization in agriculture were proving slower and more complicated than the planners had hoped. Existing channels still fail to get to the farmer, either in sufficient quantity or on time, the fertilizer, the improved seed, the insecticide and so forth that he needs. One particularly critical aspect of this widespread failure to meet farming targets can be seen in the field of irrigation. Here, after all, is the chance to achieve complete independence of the weather. The target for increased irrigation—both major and minor—in the Third Plan is something like 26 million acres. Yet, in 1961–62, only about 3 million acres of fresh land were brought under irrigation. If this figure were projected, it would mean that not much more than half of the Plan's final target would be achieved. Nor are agricultural delays significant only for farming. Industry, too, has been affected by the fall in cotton production from 5.4 million bales to 4.5 million and the failure of oil seeds to grow in any significant way. Table VI gives some of the key figures.

(216)

TABLE VI

	1960–61	1961–62	Target 1965–66
Cereals (mill. tons)	67.5	67.2	83
Oilseeds (mill. tons)	6.5	6.8	9.8
Sugar cane (mill. tons)	10.4	9.7	10
Cotton (mill. bales)	5.4	4.5	7
Jute (mill. bales)	4.0	6.3	6.2

Source: *Official Statistics.*

In fact, one must go further and underline the degree to which, in an economy still so near the edge of subsistence, agriculture tends to condition the whole performance of the economy. The fact is not surprising. Some 70 per cent of India's peoples live on the land. Nearly 80 per cent of its crucial export earnings depend, directly or indirectly, upon the countryside. Above all, in any time of inflationary strain, it is the country's food supplies that will determine whether or not the strain can be carried without catastrophe. People living near the margin will always spend almost the whole of any increase in income on food. Between 1958 and 1961 the output of food grains grew by about 12 per cent. But the number of people grew by about the same percentage. Releases of American food reserves have helped to offset sudden fluctuations. Yet the upward pressure on prices has not ceased. In 1962, the increase in the wholesale price of food was as much as 11 per cent. Even before the emergency, the margins looked very narrow.

However, before we turn to the industrial record, this is the point at which to underline one fact. Any criticism, any pointing to shortcomings must be placed in the proper context—and in India, this context *is* one of sustained growth. The growth may not be as high as the planners would wish but, before the advent of the Plans, India's economy had been either stationary or regressive for at least twenty or thirty years. The spurts of industrial growth of both world wars had been offset by political confusion or economic stagnation or both. In agriculture, the failure was worse for, in 1947, India inherited a farming system which, caught between rising population, rigid landowning and tenancy systems, growing fragmentation and lowered productivity, led, decade after decade, to a fall in per capita consumption. Independent India inherited the typical framework of a post-colonial economy—the processes of modernization largely centred on the export sectors, a relatively small educated élite, little industrial development and stagnant agriculture—and although it was better than the norm in some cases, for instance, in education, administrative talents, a railway network and some lively indigenous business groups, it was worse off in the pressure of population on the land and the long stagnation of agriculture.

Given this background, it has been a Herculean task to swing the whole vast system out of its stationary mold and into the ways of growth—growth in every sector, growth which is ahead of the population and growth which, it is not unreasonable to hope, can lead, at last, to settled growth which sustains itself without exceptional, outside assistance. Therefore, when the critics pick out things that are not going as they would wish, it is not to say that there is not, underlying the whole of the economy, a new surge of growth.

It would be equally unwise not to look at the areas of pressure. In 1961–62, the industrial record, apart from textiles, was not too far behind the 8–10 per cent average of the earlier Plans, but it was pulled down by a bad year in cotton to about 5 per cent. Here we meet straightaway the essential interdependence of farming and industry and this is a point that one has to underline over and over again. In all developing countries, the health of the land determines almost everything else. This is not to say that industrial growth is secondary. On the contrary, it is the way ahead—but the launching pad is agriculture. No sane man questions India's need of industry—including heavy industry. In a country with the resources possessed by India, with massive supplies of iron ore, with reasonably good supplies of coking coal and a fine potential in hydro-electricity, it makes every kind of sense to have a steel industry. One must not be misled by starry-eyed back-to-the-landers who tell you that any developing country which wants a steel mill is behaving in an irrational way. The emphasis here is simply designed to counter any tendency to obsession with steel mills to the exclusion of other essential things.

Every now and then when people turn with gleaming eyes to look at a steel mill, they forget that steel is just one small part of an advance in the whole industrial sector; in point of fact, at this stage they ought to look with eyes that gleam no less at any really perfectly cultivated field of cotton or jute or groundnuts. A smoking factory chimney should not be more of a status-symbol than the efficient seed farm by which Indian standards of productivity can begin to reach world levels. It is a fact that Indian cotton output is, on the average, only about 90 lbs. an acre. Yet it is 540 lbs. an acre in Egypt, and even in Pakistan the average has gone up to 230 lbs. India's low productivity menaces its industrial as well as its agricultural growth. So let us keep the balance of our enthusiasm and let us not only look at steel mills as the "cathedrals of the future" but also remember that a great deal of proper devotion should be dedicated to the economy's more modest performers and that a fine fertile field of cotton is one of the great supports of rapid industrial growth.

This absolute dependence of industry and, indeed, the whole economy, upon a vital, growing, well-organized and fruitful agricultural sector is something which all developing countries, and India in particular, have to bear in mind. There must be no snobbism in favour of industry, and no idea that some forms of output are more "chic" than others. The only really "chic" form of economic activity is the one that will give you a steady return of 10 per cent on your investment. If farming, industry and services are all reaching that level, savings will appear, further investment will be possible and more growth will result.

Other elements in the slow-down are, of course, quite familiar. They amount to a series of interlocking bottlenecks at the base of the economy. Steel has been slow to expand. Coal production was stagnant for some years before it began to grow in 1963. Then there are transport problems. The wagon-dispatching system has not proved adequate to keep the coal moving to the power plants and the steel mills. Nor has it kept the end products moving away steadily from the plants. And, although the evidence likely to be given on the subject by a steel man may be different from that of a railway man, there is a general belief that the turn-round time in the marshalling yards could certainly be shortened.

And all these interlocking difficulties hit back to the crucial element of power. Certainly, power production is increasing in India. During the Second Plan, power capacity nearly doubled—to 5.7 million kilowatts. It is to double again by 1965. Yet it is apparently a law of life in economies that, once a projection of power demand has been made, it should be increased by at least one-third; and even then shortages are likely, because a growing economy is so voracious of power that it is practically impossible to over-estimate the need for it. You may get local pockets of over-production of power when you plan, for example, a power station with a particular purpose, say, to serve a local aluminium plant, and the aluminium plant is not ready on time. But in general, even the best conceived power system is bound to be under strain in periods of growth. But in India severe interruptions in the supply of coal have added to the strain and have led to widespread dislocations and even shut-downs in industry.

Yet internal difficulties are not the most serious of the shortages plaguing the Indian economy—the worst is the shortage of foreign exchange. It is not entirely new. In 1957–58 there was a similar crisis in foreign exchange because, in both Plans, there seems to have been a similar difficulty in forecasting the scale of foreign exchange likely to be demanded by an economy which is growing steadily along a wide front. In 1958, the shortages led first to severe cuts in the core of the Plan. Some of them —notably in coal washeries and power capacity—have been a disturbing element ever since. Yet the crisis did lead to the forming of the Aid-India Consortium of Western nations which has been on the job ever since and contrived between 1958 and 1961 to make available about $2 billion in outside aid.

Now, however, in spite of commitments to the Third Plan amounting to a billion dollars a year, new stresses have appeared. The scale of the crisis is not entirely clear. At the moment, Indian exports seem to stick fast at a level of about $1.26 billion while imports remain above $1.89 billion. Exports barely increased in 1962—but the various policies induced to increase exports have not yet had much effect. Perhaps they were introduced too recently to expect any very big result. Nor is the climate for exports in the international market all that it should be. There is an element here quite certainly beyond India's control. The steady decline, relatively speaking, in the prices of primary materials, the competitiveness of Asian manufactured exports, the great uncertainty introduced by the Common Market negotiations—all these have a depressing effect upon any developing country's ability to earn large increases in foreign exchange.

Most of these difficulties lie outside the control of the Indian government. But there is one point over which both India's planners and the members of the Consortium have perhaps not been sufficiently clear-sighted. Have they sufficiently measured the amount of foreign exchange, in terms of maintenance imports and of raw materials, which a functioning economy inevitably requires? So much of the planning of projects and the general expansion of capacity appears almost to have assumed that the foreign exchange needed for running the projects would follow from the general development of the economy. In point of fact, what does emerge—and at once—is a steadily growing strain on foreign exchange. By the middle of 1962—as in 1957—it was quite apparent that some of the calculations of the Plan would have to be very drastically revised. Between 1960 and the middle of 1962, the revision of foreign exchange requirements uncovered by exports or foreign investment has gone steadily upwards from about $4.2 billion up to some $6.3 billion. At this point, it became apparent that, although the Aid-India Consortium was probably likely to maintain its aid at the level of about a billion dollars a year—or 5 billions over the five years of the Plan—the revisions were leading to requirements that would be nearer $7.5 billion. Of such an increase, there was absolutely no sign at all.

So, in the course of the summer of 1962, the need came to be more and more keenly felt to re-tailor the Plan to the flow of foreign exchange that would be likely to be available. While, however, this whole re-consideration of the Plan was going on, the emergency supervened and all the planning and reckoning had to begin again from a new starting point—the impact of the emergency.

Such, then, was the condition of stress and strain in the Indian economy when, in October 1962, the Chinese launched their attack and put the Indian people on notice that nothing less than the most rapid and radical expansion of their defenses could give them any hope of preserving even a semblance of security on their northern frontiers. This expansion appears to entail an addition of at least $950,000,000 to defense expenditure. What will its impact be? Will it worsen existing strains? Will it retard the Plan? Or is it conceivable that its shock and discipline could help India to overcome the failures and bottlenecks which have so drastically held down its rate of growth?

The first consequence of extra spending on defense is likely to be increased purchasing power in the community. The new expenditure will be for defense goods, in other words, for goods which will not enter the market for sale and hence help to mop up the purchasing power made available by the salaries and wages earned in producing the defense goods. Unless this extra, unbalanced purchasing power is in some measure kept off the market, India risks inflation. Prices are already on the rise, the first two budgets of the Third Plan have already exceeded the "safe" limit of deficit financing—set at $210 million a year, food production cannot be very quickly expanded. True, new American releases of cotton and grain under Public Law 480 were announced at the end of 1962. But they cannot fill the whole potential gap. If the defense effort is not to be financed by inflation—which risks catastrophic pressures on food prices and is socially the most unjust and irresponsible way of going about the task—taxation and savings have to take up the slack.

In theory, there is still a margin for increased taxes and savings in India. Both are still under 10 per cent of national income and many economists argue that a government cannot really be held to be serious about development until 20 per cent of national income is secured for taxes. And a 15 per cent level of saving is often claimed to be the minimum compatible with "take-off" into self-sustaining growth. The difficulty is, of course, the extreme poverty of India. Not to consume an important percentage of income would be the equivalent among many groups of slipping fatally below the level of subsistence. Taxes have in any case been going up. They were increased in both the most recent budgets—$178,500,000 in 1961–62, by $143,220,000 in 1962–63. The States, too, have increased their levies. The figure was $29,400,000 in 1961–62 and the new proposals for 1962–63 should bring in an extra $149,100,000 a year. Is there scope for more?

Middle class tax rates in India are rather lower than in Japan, agricultural incomes largely escape income tax, indirect taxes on such necessities as kerosene would help in the rationing process, business firms may benefit from the extra stimulus defense gives to the economy and could be expected to relinquish the extra profits, in spite of a 5 per cent increase in company taxation in the last budget. There are thus opportunities, but all of them present difficulties. More taxes on the poor could weaken national unity. More taxes on the middle class hit people most sorely beset by inflation. Business taxation can lessen essential capital formation. The choices before the Finance Minister, Morarji Desai, are not enviable. But a clear choice is better than the confused sacrifices and inequities of further inflation. His decision in the 1963–64 budget to raise $577,500,000 in further taxation is clearly correct.* But it does not cover the full sum of extra expenditure. Some purchasing power remains to be mopped up.

Could savings do more? The margin is there and the Finance Minister has called for an immediate increase in the savings rate from 8 to 15 per cent of national income. But, in fact, the habit of saving—as opposed to hoarding—has still to be learned. Small savings consistently fell behind their target in the First and Second Plans and the response to patriotic appeals for higher saving since the emergency has been very uneven. By January 1962 the National Defense Fund had only received some $56,700,000 against expected receipts of $344,400,000. Nor has there been much more success with the effort to tempt gold out of private hoards—where as much as $4.2 billion may be hidden away. In November 1962 Mr. Desai offered to buy gold at the international price ($35 an ounce) in return for 15-year bonds at the very attractive rate of 6½ per cent and free of the wealth and the capital gains tax. No questions would be asked, either, about the provenance of the gold. But by January 1963 subscriptions were still below $56,700,000—$210 million had been hoped for—and it remains to be seen whether the new measures making non-ornamental gold hoards illegal will encourage a greater flow. The truth probably is that the distrust of government and the fear of inflation which lead men to hoard in the first place have not been so dissipated by China's aggression as to modify the uncertainties and uneasiness of a lifetime.

One is left with the likelihood that not all the extra pur-

---

* One may, however, criticise some aspects of the taxation on business enterprise since, by hitting hardest firms which have accumulated large reserves for further development, it threatens to undermine India's greatest need—the need for growth.

chasing power can be mopped up by fiscal means. This possibility makes all the more urgent an effective and rapid physical mobilization of resources.

At this point, one thing has to be made clear. There is no essential, total contradiction between the kind of mobilization needed for an effective war effort and the kind of mobilization which India needs to ensure the success of its Plan for development. In fact, one can safely say that quite a high percentage—we can guess and put it as high as 70 to 80 per cent—does not contradict the long-term aim of strengthening the Indian economy. The defense effort can speed up the development of power, the fulfilling of the steel target, a raising of the level of coal output, the turn-round of wagons and deliveries to factories and power plants. The expansion of certain forms of mechanical engineering, even though it takes place in ordnance factories, creates no insoluble problems of conversion against a happier day. Certainly the skills which are rapidly expanded in times of war for a bigger defense establishment are skills which are not lost. In fact, an expansion of the whole industrial working class can go forward; and, in the modern army, there is an added chance of a further dispersion of special skills. In short, the emergency, far from contradicting the Plan, could be an immense spur to its more rapid development. It is a fact that, again and again in human history, war efforts have been part of a decisive breakthrough to industrialization, and there is no reason why, if the emergency is wisely handled, the same should not hold good for India.

With this possibility in mind, let us look at the various sectors and bottlenecks and try to assess the likely effect of the defense effort on them.

To begin with a general point, it seems essential that the need for an effective centre of authority capable of

deciding priorities should be urgently stressed. A cabinet
of 50 members is not such a body. A lasting division of
function between the Prime Minister's office, Finance,
Defense, Economic Affairs and the Planning Commission
could lead to prolonged confusion. This problem of decision plagues every country in time of emergency and
one cannot say that any ideal solution has been worked
out. But a small inner War Cabinet was found necessary
in Britain, served by a coordinating staff. There are special
reasons in India for hoping that a greater concentration
of decision-making will come about. Hitherto, Indian planning has seemed somewhat weak on the side of follow-
ing-up speedily the decisions that are taken. Delays that
are awkward in development become downright dangerous in defense. Clearer lines of responsibility could help
to lessen the risk. Then the emergency demands closer
co-ordination of the tasks of all the State governments.
Sixteen separate governments reporting back to a body
of 50 ministers hardly suggests speed and clarity. Above
all, priorities cannot be weighed in a free-for-all between
ministries. There must be some firm arbitration to decide
not only on the priorities defense should enjoy but also
on the points at which its claims should be overridden in
the interest of other vital, supporting sectors. It is no use,
for instance, permitting defense factories to engross so
many extra scientists and engineers that transport or
power development begins to falter.

To turn now to particular sectors, the impact of the
emergency on agriculture may not, in direct terms, be
very great—the amount of food that needs to be diverted
from civilian consumption to an enlarged military establishment is relatively small. But the indirect effects could
be great, either way. If farming is seriously down-graded
in terms of essential capital, able administration, skilled

(227)

staff and ministerial preoccupation, the emergency could worsen what is already a grave feature in agriculture—its relative failure, in spite of much rhetoric, to attract the men and the attention which really effective administration demands. The government's preoccupation with the weapons and tools of a defense effort in camp and factory carries with it a certain unconscious down-grading of farm and field with possibly disastrous longer-term results.

There is, however, an opposite chance that the emergency can jerk the governments—at the Centre and in the States—into a new sense of opportunity on the land. Nothing, apparently, took India's leaders more by surprise than the response throughout India of ordinary men and women, the great majority of them country-dwellers, to the fact of aggression. Before the autumn of 1962, the picture given to outsiders of the state of the Indian Union seemed to be darkened on every side by communal divisions, linguistic differences and a growing break between North and South. In a trice, the Chinese abolished the feuds and set in their place a profound response to a sense of common Indian nationhood and destiny. The villagers gave in their jewellery, queued to be blood donors, besieged recruiting offices, all in an immense upsurge of a patriotism as profound as it was unforced.

This fact faces the Indian government with a risk and an opportunity. The risk is that, if a long indecisive period of "no-war, no-peace" ensues, the stimulus and fervour will die down but the bangles and the savings will have been irretrievably lost. The opportunity is to canalize the evident energies into works of rural construction which, in India, have been so often discussed and as often laid aside. A movement of National Defense Work, which could include the new Home Guards and village savings groups, might enable the government to get started all over India on such work as bunding, levelling, road-building and, above all, the completion of thousands of miles of minor irrigation channels. Some States have not yet passed the necessary legislation and the obstinacy of a single farmer can still prevent the final channels from being built. The central government has now sent out an urgent request for the legislation and a big effort on this front might permit India to finish by 1964 the 13 million acres of minor irrigation forecast in the Plan for 1965–66. Few policies could contribute so directly to that sharp rise in food output needed to counter the risks of inflation.

But one should, perhaps, enter a proviso here. The organizing and sustaining of such a nation-wide effort—central backing, co-ordination with State governments, action by the Collectors, co-operation with Community Development officers would seem to require some innovations in leadership. Possibly an Office of Civilian Mobilization working as the executive agent of the central ministries concerned would offer a possible solution.

Let us look now at the industrial side. The first point to underline is how much better equipped to deal with an emergency Indian industry has become as a result of ten years of uninterrupted growth and diversification. A glance at Table VII will illustrate the range and variety of expansion that has taken place—the list has been chosen from categories essential to defense.

If there are reserves that can be drawn into the industrial economic system, then the strain on the productive capacity of the economy is clearly less. One of the factors which undoubtedly helped mobilization in Britain, and then again in America, was the existence of unused industrial capacity and of trained unemployed industrial labour. In 1939, Britain still had a large pool of unemployed; it may, in fact, have been, at that time, the

TABLE VII INDUSTRIAL PRODUCTION FOR DEFENSE

	1950–51	1955–56	1960–61	Capacity Working %
Machine tools (mill. $)	.7	1.64	15.2	125
Copper (thou. tons)	6.6	7.5	8.8	118
Automobiles (thou. tons)	17.4	189.3	387	98
Steel ingots (mill. tons)	1.4	1.7	3.3	80–90
Steel castings & forgings (thou. tons)	—	15	69	80–90
Cement (mill. tons)	2.7	4.6	7.8	85
Finished steel (mill. tons)	0.98	1.3	3.3	75–80
Railway wagons (nos.)	2,924	8,393	13,826	50

Source: *Indian Institute of Public Opinion.*

equivalent of 7 or 8 per cent of the labour force.

There is some possibility of setting unused capacity to work again in India. One of the factors revealed in the foreign exchange crisis of the summer of 1962 was a disturbing amount of working at less than full capacity. In fact, in some industries probably not more than 60 per cent of the plant was being utilized. The collapse of the Stock Exchange in the autumn and the investors' extreme reserve also encouraged working at less than full capacity. And one should also mention a sort of psychological under-working—the slack which occurs when labour is disaffected and management discouraged.

Table VII attempts a quantitative estimate to all this. In some key industries—machine tools, for instance—there is capacity working and two to three shifts. Some others reach 80 per cent. Very few fall as low as railway wagon production at 50 per cent. But the emergency does seem to have contributed at once to a lessening of the psychological difficulties. Everywhere there have been reports of workers offering no-strike pledges and asking to work overtime at normal rates. If management can canalize and maintain the enthusiasm, extra-shift working and more output per man hour could, in theory, provide a large part of the needed extra production.

But this possibility depends in turn on the bottlenecks—coal, steel, power, transport, foreign exchange. How does the emergency affect them?

Once again, in theory, it could help. Industrial regulations have been modified to permit three-shift working in the coal mines, at least for the time being. Under these conditions, coal output could be speeded up and the 97 million ton target for 1965–66 look a little less unrealistic. But more coal must be moved and here tighter management and more willing labour might cut some days off the turn-round of wagons. This in turn would enable coal to reach the power stations in a timely fashion—and since three-quarters of India's industry depends upon thermal stations, steady provision of power could immediately enhance production by cutting out the old uncertainties and shut-downs.

Nonetheless the amount of spare capacity that can be set to work does not depend wholly upon Indian efforts. One quickly comes up against the overwhelming problem—the shortage of foreign exchange. Although the extra steel is indigenous, though the extra coal is indigenous, the fact remains that the more a mine tries for accelerated coal production, the more it is up against the need for explosives and other maintenance materials which are still purchased from abroad. Although virtually all consumer goods industries are having their allotments slashed, and the whole of the available foreign exchange is being diverted to essential sectors, the diversions cannot fill the gap. One has to remember that in the summer of 1962 all import licenses had already been halved and at least 80 per cent of India's imports are for essential goods in any case.

On what scale will the new demands for foreign exchange need to be financed? Nothing specific has been published so far. At present economic aid is running at the level of about a billion dollars a year. If we estimate that arms aid will come directly from military aid and defense support, then the sums needed for special steels and alloys, for petrol and wool and other vital supporting materials, might, at a guess, amount to another 200–300 million dollars a year.

The immediate position could, perhaps, be eased by transferring some existing aid from its link with future projects over to free exchange which can be spent rapidly on raw materials and maintenance imports. Yet the step is not easy. For instance, out of the 500 million dollars America makes available each year, over 100 million dollars are already provided in free exchange and, if one examines the composition of the rest of this sum, one finds that it is mainly earmarked for tools and machines which help in the further development of transportation and power. Nonetheless, in the immediate emergency, it might be possible to achieve some kind of switch from project aid for future factories to more aid for imports of spares and raw materials designed to maintain capacity production in already functioning factories.

Of course, the Western Powers might decide that this whole aspect of defense support should be dealt with on the basis of lend-lease, offshore purchases and all the other devices for burden-sharing which were worked out in the last war. The analogy is not irrelevant. In resisting crude aggression, India inevitably identifies its cause with the national freedom of the rest of the world. Holding the Chinese in check not only serves India's security but that of everybody else as well. Surely the lessons of past aggression are that every nation has a profound interest in seeing that those who want to use force do not get the idea that they can do so without fear or cost. India's security is in a real sense the security of its neighbours and friends as well.

It is doubtful, however, whether this view of India's crisis is yet fully accepted. Until it is, the financing of extra military aid presents considerable difficulties. The American defense support program for 1962 amounted to about 1.6 billion dollars. The figure covers every part of the world and no one will be surprised to learn that there are a great many claimants for that support—some of them illegitimate, no doubt. Nonetheless, the pressures are there. India, with its new and utterly legitimate need to be supported against an unscrupulous aggressor, has to take its place in something of a queue. The issue is not simply that of putting India's claims at the top of the list. The sum itself available for defense support is not adequate to cover new claims. Moreover, the Kennedy Administration, with immense persistence and hard work, persuaded Congress to accept a limited shift from direct defense support to economic aid. It is an ironic thought that one reason why the shift was made was because of the feeling that, within the non-aligned and neutral world, the change would be seen as a sign of good faith; now non-aligned India has rather different needs than seemed to be the case only a year ago. The American administration must in some measure reverse itself if it goes to Congress to ask for more military support for India. And go it must for there are no spare funds.

What is likely to be the Western response to the need for an accelerated and sustained effort to help Indian defense? In point of fact, one cannot really assess what the internal strain and the pressure are going to be unless the scale of economic assistance from outside can be roughly assessed. Let us begin by saying that some of the supposed obstacles in the way of a greater Western effort are not obstacles at all. There was a furor in the middle of 1962 over the question whether India would receive its billion dollars a year in Western aid if it insisted on buying MIGs from Russia. In the event, after some angry senatorial comment, the year's allotment of economic assistance to India went forward smoothly.

The Kennedy Administration had been moving quietly for some time towards the position that nothing must be done which would risk a deterioration in relations between Russia and the West. The change had little directly to do with ideology. Insofar as Soviet Russia continues to look to the disappearance of every other form of society, the gulf between philosophies must continue. Insofar as it actively encourages such an outcome, hostility will remain. But two facts have modified the bleak confrontation.

At the time of the Cuban crisis, both sides stood at—and retreated from—the hideous brink of atomic destruction. Mr. Khrushchev proved his preference for survival, at whatever cost to his ideological purity. And this choice has become the chief issue between him and the more radical Chinese who denounce his caution as "bourgeois revisionism."

The rift between the Communist contenders has coloured their reactions to the Indian crisis—Mr. Khrushchev continuing his aid to India and pleading for a "peaceful settlement," the Chinese bitterly attacking his lack of Communist solidarity. In these conditions, the West need not regard Russian support for India as any sort of obstacle to Western assistance. One may even say that to this extent America itself is now "non-aligned." The suggestion that the West hesitates to give aid because India wants to go on being non-aligned is regarded with a sort of humorous fraternal indulgence. On the contrary, since non-alignment helps to prevent Russia aligning itself automatically with China and keeps open the possibility of a Russo-Western *détente*, both London and Washington support non-alignment and are utterly opposed to the idea that India should spoil it by asking for formal military treaty relations with the West.

The Russian question is not decisive. But there is another question which is infinitely more difficult for India and it, unhappily, is absolutely crucial. No friend of India should disguise the fact that the scale of assistance to India in the emergency will be greatly influenced by its relations with Pakistan. This does not spring from *parti pris;* it does not spring from favouring one side or the other; it does not even spring from any kind of judgment about the rights and wrongs of the Kashmir case, which seem to most people to be infinitely involved. It does spring from something quite different, yet absolutely basic —a shrewd military look at the northern frontier. Such a look inevitably instills the belief—which it would be hard to eradicate from the minds of Western chiefs-of-staff —that one cannot in the long run mount and maintain a credible defense against the Chinese on the northern frontiers if a strong, profound internal quarrel is continuing on this side of them.

There are a number of reasons for this belief, first and foremost the arguments of history. Nearly always, a suc-

cessful invasion has been able to exploit an internal struggle—by "internal" in this case, *this* side of the Himalayan
barrier is meant. The last time England was conquered
—by the Normans in 1066—King Harold was away fighting the Scots; so what happened? England was taken over.
If one wants to go to another continent, what happened
to Montezuma? How was it that Cortez, almost unarmed,
reached the court of the Aztecs? The answer is not in
doubt. When Cortez landed, Montezuma was caught up
in a fight between his tribes and the tribes on the coast.
The coastal tribes simply took Cortez through the high
passes, seeing in him the enemy of their enemy.

If one must include analogies which come nearer home,
one can ask whether the British would have gained control of India if the Moghul Empire had not been at the
point of collapse and the Marathas had not been busy
fighting the Muslims. In fact, it is quite likely that the
Marathas would have triumphed over the British had they
not had their minds on other things. It is, in fact, the
unanimous judgment of history that an internal struggle
continuing at a time of external aggression fatally weakens
the ability of any nation to withstand onslaught from outside.

Strategy tells the same story. The Ladakh front may
not entail a fatal exposure of India's weakness. But in
NEFA the blow could be lethal. Behind NEFA lies Assam,
beyond and below Assam, access to India's essential industrial strength. Yet look at the map. Look at the frontiers of
East Pakistan. Look at the Silliguri gap, only 30 miles
wide and often flooded. Consider the possibility—*without*
some kind of working understanding with Pakistan—of
defending the eastern frontiers at all. The question of
Pakistan is thus crucial to any long-term question of sustained defense, aimed at building up these frontiers so

that the Indian experiment in peaceful economic growth can go forward uninterrupted by casual hammer blows from power-hungry neighbours.

India's friends outside cannot ignore these historical and strategic facts. They must in all honesty say that the outlook for effective defense is grim indeed without some kind of co-ordination with the Pakistanis and perhaps with the Burmese. The idea has, in fact, been put forward by such distinguished Indian leaders as the late Mr. K. M. Pannikar, who wrote of the possibility of a defense community designed to safeguard the integrity of the whole northern frontier.

Some Indians tend at this point to protest that after Pakistan's recent readiness to work with the Chinese, no co-operation is possible. Yet the reaction of the Pakistanis to the Chinese aggression, though regrettable, illustrates precisely the point India's friends are trying to make—that if a nation tolerates an agonizing, embittered and venomous quarrel inside its frontier, an external aggressor need not confine himself to direct pressure. He can play one side off against the other. The emotional levers are put into his hands. He can play upon the temper, the violence, the distrust of the disputants just as contemptuously as Rosencrantz and Guildenstern tried to play on Hamlet's emotions. In other words, the aggressors treat the quarrellers as malleable instruments, as emotional raw material for their own plans. The fact that the Pakistanis have reacted in precisely this way makes it, in one sense, much more difficult to reach a settlement. But in another it only underlines with increased intensity the need to see that a settlement is reached.

Successful negotiation of an envenomed issue means compromise and "give and take," and a number of compromises are, of course, under discussion. What any out-

sider thinks about the possible compromises is wholly
unimportant; the issue is to find one acceptable to the
parties concerned. But it may be helpful to outline one or
two that are under discussion now. One lies in a fairly
drastic reorganization of the cease-fire line, which would
give the Pakistanis some of the upper waters of the
Chenab and a larger part of the upper Indus valley. This
might have been negotiated two years ago. It is doubtful
whether Pakistan would accept it now; still, it is one of the
possibilities. Secondly, there is the possibility of trying to
get a West Irian type of solution. The disputed area, in
this case the Valley of Kashmir, is put under U.N. trustee-
ship, with the eventual choice of independence. This
would have the advantage that it does, as it were, with-
draw the centre of the dispute from the claim of rival
sovereignty. Another possibility would lie in trying to do
in Kashmir what the French and the Germans achieved
in a sense in the Saar. One does not solve the problem in
terms of itself, but one makes changes in context within
which an ultimate reconciliation can take place. In other
words, if over the next 10 to 15 years, the Indians and the
Pakistanis determine to form a defense community and
an economic community with an increasing degree of economic mobility and interdependence, the outcome might
be an environment into which an autonomous Kashmir
might fit—as a sort of Asian Andorra.

The only way in which a compromise solution is likely
to be found over Kashmir is for both Indians and Pakistanis
to come to feel profoundly that the threat beyond the
northern frontier is greater than any of their internal differences, that this running sore is now affecting their
ability to survive as independent countries and that the
highest priority of all has to be given to finding a solution for this ultimately fratricidal struggle *within* the

northern frontier.

It is difficult at this stage for India's friends in the West to know quite how to handle this problem. If they say, "Well, long-term assistance to be effective must depend upon a settlement," they look like blackmailers trying to force out of India when it is weak the concessions it would not make when it was strong. The question whether the nation was sensible when it was strong is not raised at this point. On the other hand, Indians have to try to realize the implications of the fact that the question of defense support to India has got to go back to Congress and to Parliament, that very substantial sums of other people's tax money are at stake, that the arguments for added assistance have to sound reasonably convincing to a large and not always well-informed electorate. There is some difficulty in arguing for generous and effective long-term defense support so long as the dispute with Pakistan creates such vulnerability along the Himalayas and allows critics of ill will to suggest that the arms could be used against Pakistan. This is not a question of taking sides. It is a problem of finding convincing arguments to persuade suspicious Congressmen and harassed Conservative M.P.s that their electors will think it reasonable to be taxed for such an uncertain venture.

This is the fundamental political problem. Soviet Russia's support of India presents no difficulty to the West. The West would be absolutely delighted if Mr. Khrushchev's dispatch of MIGs to India meant that Mr. Khrushchev had some more rude words to call "the Albanians." But the issue of Pakistan confronts the Western world with profound dilemmas of political and parliamentary persuasion and as such it cannot just be wished away or brushed aside or dismissed. It could affect the whole nature of India's defense relationships. It could af-

fect the whole tempo at which outside assistance flows in
—or does not flow in—to meet India's intensified needs.
And since, in the long run as well as the short, access to
foreign exchange remains one of the chief keys both to India's defense and to its development plans, the question-
mark over Indian-Pakistani relations is a question-mark
over the country's whole prospects of effective survival
and growth.

Chapter Fifteen

Planning: the Next Phase

THE immediate emergency, thrust upon India by Chinese aggression, has underlined two major difficulties. The first is the disappointing performance of a number of key sectors in the economy—in other words, the economy's slow rate of growth. The second is the biting shortage of foreign exchange which places further curbs on expansion. The emergency has underlined them. But they were there before it and could outlast it unless the extra urgency and energy it breeds can lead both India and India's friends abroad to take a fresh look at the difficulties.

The First Plan ended in 1956 in an atmosphere of some euphoria. By setting under-used, war-developed capacity to work fully and by completing schemes started soon after independence, industry achieved a very favourable capital-output ratio. The weather was kind and gave such

(241)

bumper harvests in 1953–54 that many people erroneously attributed the rise in output to irrigation, better methods and the success of Community Development. Above all, foreign exchange faced little or no stringency. India's sterling balances were not exhausted and all its primary exports earned record returns in the post-Korean boom.

The spectre of slow growth and low reserves began to appear in 1957 and, since that time, the Indian economy, in spite of steady growth, has always run behind its targets. Perhaps the simplest fashion of illustrating the shortfall is once again through a table (Table VIII). Similarly

TABLE VIII SOME SECOND PLAN RESULTS
(*In Millions of U.S. Dollars at 1952–53 Prices*)

	Target 1956–1961	Actual Achievement	Difference %
Plan outlay	10.1	8.6	−14.6
Investment	13.0	12.6	−3.2
Savings	10.9	8.6	−21.1
Money supply	7.6	6.1	—
External payments deficit	2.1	4.4	+110.0
Food imports	.5	1.7	+229.2
Estimated foreign assistance *	1.7	3.2	+87.5
Withdrawal of reserves *	.4	1.3	+200

Growth rate 1956–61 per cent

National income	25	18–19	−24
Industrial output	64	42	−34
Mining	50	22	−56
Agriculture	18	19	+5

* At 1960–61 prices.
Source: The Economist Intelligence Unit.

in the first two years of the Third Plan, output has been disappointing. Nearly all the indices for agricultural production in 1961–62 were static or falling and industry's rate of advance has been held back as a result.

In all this, one factor of growth has, however, surpassed all expectations. The Second Plan had estimated that in 1961 India's population would have grown to 408 millions. In fact, it reached 438 millions—an annual rate of increase of 2 per cent. With growth in national income not exceeding 3.5 per cent, the margins for rising consumption and investment were thus exceedingly narrow.

Therefore, something should be said about the problems posed by the pressure of growing population on India's still-limited resources. Westerners should feel a certain modesty in lecturing other people on the critical issue of what they should do about their population. It is an immensely popular pursuit among many distinguished Western leaders and one can respect their sense of purpose and dedication. Yet this is a subject on which countries must make their own decisions without too much exhortation from outside.

There is, however, one issue that should be stressed. Over and over again one encounters the belief—often stated with the dogmatism of a proven fact—that without population control there can be no economic growth. It is not unknown in the Western world to hear the statement that it is absolutely no use helping a country whose population is still increasing at the rate prevailing in India. Now, this is a radical misconception. Far from a slower rate of growth in population determining economic growth, economic growth determines the trend towards smaller families. It is economic development, in fact, that gives people the incentives to want smaller families. We are not, presumably, postulating a World Population

Council which will say: "Now, Mrs. Smith, you have 2.3 children and this is .3 too many; what are you going to do about it?" We are thinking in terms of what parents actually want. It is really only when economic growth begins in earnest that enough parents see it to be in the profound interest of their family, their own children and, indirectly, of their community to bring up only that size of family which they can provide with food, health, education and reasonable opportunity.

This has, in fact, proved the pattern of population in cultures as different as those of Western Europe and of Japan. The last two hundred years have proved that when people *want,* for a whole variety of economic and social reasons, to have smaller families, they do, in fact, have smaller families. The number of children begins to diminish when the inducements to concentrate upon the well-being of children begin to increase—when child labour comes to an end, and reliable children are no longer the greatest single asset of old age, when epidemics are brought under control, and parents no longer feel they have to produce twelve children if they hope to raise three, when skilled and educated labour, not numbers and brawn, begin to determine the labour market. The trend can be observed in Japan; it can be observed in Western Europe; in fact, the only country where the trend has been once more reversed back towards greater numbers is in the affluent United States: one may even wonder whether the time will come for some very serious-minded Indian delegations to go to America and preach the doctrine of fewer Americans.

Given the historical evidence available, it is wrong and, indeed, dangerous, to suggest that economic development and economic aid given to that development must depend upon a reduction in the birth-rate. It is an especially inappropriate connection at a time when, as in India, increasing population is partly due to the lengthening of life. The only certain way of lowering the birth-rate is to hasten the processes of economic growth and the assistance which accelerates them. This does not mean that aid-givers may not stress the degree to which population pressure nullifies growth. It does not mean that every effort should not be made through better research to find acceptable means of controlling fertility. But what is inadmissible is the remark so often made in the West: "Well, you cannot help those people because they have so many children." If one had used this argument about Japan 80 years ago, one would have foreseen continued stagnation. Yet Japan now is a classic example of a population which, after reaching the highest rates of growth, reverted towards stability.

It is, in fact, sobering to remember that 80 years ago the Malthusian argument that the poor always bred too fast was used to counter all the early efforts at social welfare. Yet both the case of Japan and of working-class Europe reinforce the point that when the processes of economic growth, social change, and the education of women go forward, families fall to the level at which parents can raise them with reasonable elbow room—which, surely, is the fundamental meaning of parental responsibility. There will, no doubt, continue to be a vital moral debate about the means of birth control but there can surely be no debate over the injustice and cruelty of bringing into the world children who will be barely able to eat, who will be crippled with disease and after a brief life of pain and deprivation will be snuffed out before they reach their teens. The profound miseries of millions of the world's children will end only when economic development has been successfully pushed forward with every possible means of economic assistance from the outside world and by every possible means of internal economic mobilization.

Let us turn now to the problems raised by India's relative slow rate of economic growth. We can usefully start where the outlines of the future Indian economy are being shaped—in the planning process itself. One should say straight away that anything advanced on the difficulties and delays that have been encountered must be put in the context of the overwhelming, the really titanic scale of the tasks which planners and administrators have to face. No government has ever before tried to administer with freedom and decentralized authority a nation of 450 million people, dispersed in sixteen states and speaking half a dozen major languages. To achieve civic order and legal government is in itself a formidable achievement—one, certainly, that has escaped Latin America with one-half as many people and one-third of the languages. To administer in addition a dynamic economy planned for welfare and development implies a range of responsibilities of an even more taxing kind. The most totally literate and educationally advanced community would find the task formidable. Given the size of India's educated cadre at Independence—about 400,000 students graduating each year in a population of nearly 400 million—and given the fact that British rule was "law-and-order" rule, only indirectly related to welfare and wholly unrelated to economic growth, then one has to admit that the achievement is the vital thing, not the shortcomings which have sometimes seemed to overshadow it.

However, it is by facing the weaknesses that even better results can be secured. Let us look at the planning process itself. In many ways it has steadily improved. The First Plan was little more than an assemblage of desirable projects, some of them already launched. It was not until the Second Plan that a real attempt at forecasting was made—with the facts on national income, on saving, on industrial and agricultural possibilities and performance assembled in an orderly way. The background to the Third Plan again demonstrates greater sophistication— more detailed in-put, out-put analysis, more specific calculation of future needs, clearer efforts to see that the various sectoral plans complement each other and make up a coherent whole. Indeed, it can be said that Indian planning has become the model of planning all round the world in all mixed, developing economies. Yet the rate of growth still lags. Why?

One should concentrate at this point on two of the major difficulties. The first concerns administration, the second, technique or approach. It is not unfair to say that from the beginning Indian planning has been stronger on formulation than on implementation—or, less pompously put, on thinking things out rather than getting things done. The bias springs in part from inheritance. Delhi was molded on the Whitehall model and, as Britain discovered between 1945 and 1950, men trained in the tradition of equity and precedent do not always take kindly to the short-cuts and quick decisions of an effective follow-up. For a long time there seemed to be no specific point in the structure of government at which active and, if necessary, angry officials asked why decisions reached months ago had not been put into effect.

In the last few years, the Planning Commission itself, with its evaluation teams and its contacts with the State governments, has attempted to fill the gap. But the degree to which one government department can effectively prod another is limited—and the Planning Commission has tended to grow into one. This issue is so urgent, the risk of delay so great, the loss of development through loss of time so dangerous that one wonders whether a sub-committee of the cabinet or some other high-level body reporting directly to the Prime Minister should not undertake the responsibility of seeing, month by month, that planned development is going forward at a coherent pace and that the various schemes and sectors hang together. *Could* the bottlenecks in basic industries have developed so far if a strong cabinet body had been breathing down the neck of the Minister responsible for coal mines and demanding why, month after month, his figures were below target?

Possibly the emergency will help here. If a small War Cabinet or committee of the Cabinet oversees the rapid expansion of the defense effort it could acquire the taste for results as well as programs. Then it would have the experience needed to ensure, after the emergency, that urgency and speed do not fade from the direction of the economy.

A speedy and effective checking on performance would be needed in any system of planning. But in India's mixed economy where Delhi's oversight over the whole system makes every sector, public or private, subject to the decisions that are taken at the Centre, the need for speedier decisions and greater concentration on action and results is overwhelming. Over a whole range of issues, effective administration may demand the abandonment of direct controls. Once the emergency is passed, it is arguable that enterprises, private and public, should be left to struggle for themselves to secure cement and steel and power and building sites. There would be inequities, no doubt, and some wrong decisions. But they cannot equal in devastating effect the infinite delays of referring priorities to Delhi, there to be worked out by officials who, all too often, have no more sense of priority than the man requesting the license. They may, in fact, have less. He at least has a vital interest—to make a profit and keep in business, whether he is the director of Hindustan Machine Tools in the public sector or head of a private steel works. But the official in Delhi has chiefly to avoid making a mistake. This is not a spur to decision-making. Delay—which may be the greatest mistake of all—will not appear as a blot on his record.

True, the limiting case of intensely scarce foreign exchange cannot be dismissed. Some licensing has to continue. But it is surely not necessary—as has been the practice hitherto—to license each particular element in an allocation as well as the allocation itself. Is there not a case, too, for forming industrial groups and giving them a block issue of foreign exchange to work out between them? No doubt, some firms may profit unduly. But is that more damaging than that delay should prevent them all from making a profit and hence cut back their possibilities of further investment?

Now let us turn to another factor in planning. It is not enough in estimating future needs to establish the physical components of what is to be produced—to make sure that there is enough steel for the railways, coal for the power stations and power for everything. These physical availabilities are immensely important and some of them—transport and power above all—condition everything else. But combining them in such a way as to achieve maximum growth involves more than physical calculations. The combination must release the greatest amount of resources for further investment. Otherwise, a great deal of physical resources can be used up and actually produce *dis-investment*—the absorption of precious materials into undertakings which earn no surplus themselves, yet deprive enterprises that might have done so from starting up.

So a calculation of the cost of projects and of the likely release of further resources that can be looked for as a result of incurring the cost is an essential part of planning. The profitability of an undertaking is more vital to growth than even a correct calculation of the materials going into it. To take an extreme case, the amount of bricks and mortar going into a museum or a powerhouse may be equivalent. The difference in their immediate earning power decides which of them a poor community ought to aim to have first.

All this is very obvious but it is surprising how often, in the planning process, cost—and profit—consciousness seem to be lacking. Let us look at some instances. Because there is a certain prejudice against the idea of capitalists making a lot of money, it is often thought that the rate of return on capital ought to be low. But interest is the *price* of capital and if you put the price low, it is the equivalent, for planning, of saying that capital is cheap. But capital is, on the contrary, the scarcest commodity in any poor, developing country, and, since it is scarce and precious, it should be dear. If the price—interest—is kept too low, this scarce, indispensable resource will be used carelessly. It will go into enterprises giving little return. It will not be available for enterprises that could have brought in much more. Since the early stages of development do entail large expenditures on projects with very little prospect of quick direct returns—schools, health centres, urban housing—it is all the more vital that planning should concentrate in other fields on the projects which earn high rates and turn the capital over in the shortest space of time.

In fact, one should allow interest rates to rise sharply —one can always tax the bankers—in order to reflect capital's scarcity and the planners might well adopt as an essential yardstick the rule that, save in exceptional circumstances, the green light should be given only to enterprises that earn 10 per cent on their capital and amortize themselves in a decade. With such a rule, a plan will not end up with too many high dams earning 2 per cent over 80 years, too many factories designed for making factories, too many public buildings earning almost nothing, too many public services—again power and transport—charging less than the going rate to cover interest and obsolescence on the grounds that, as public services, they should be run at cost. Much of the success in Japan's early planning was due to the degree to which the planners concentrated on agricultural productivity and on small industry with high returns. The larger enterprises—steel, armaments, machine-building—were introduced more slowly. It is in Russia, with its vast supplies of coal and iron ore, that heavy industry received such an overriding priority. It may be that the Japanese pattern is sounder.

So far, it does not seem to have attracted as much attention. The planners' temptation is always to leave the big things in the Plan. The political leaders like them. They have a prestige value. Often they are in the public sector. In any case, if during a plan period, something has to be abandoned, it is difficult to cut the big projects. Half a dam is not just half as efficient. It contributes nothing. So the cuts always land on the little projects further down the list—the medium irrigation, the local tannery, the extra industrial estate. Yet it is precisely the multiplicity of smaller enterprises, using little capital and earning good returns, that provides the profits and hence the capital for the next phase of advance.

It is just because the vital role of profits—in the public

as in the private sector—has been neglected in the world's various "socialistic patterns" that growth has often been slow—as in parts of Eastern Europe—or living standards have remained so relatively low—as in the Soviet Union. Why is Mr. Khrushchev now turning to the idea of "the firm" as a basic economic unit and urging that the firm be profitable? It is because the statistics of Russia's *physical* expansion have disguised appalling waste and misuse of resources. Steel output can go up and up but if the factories into which it goes produce shoes with two left feet or coats which the Soviet consumer now refuses to buy, the physical statistics are misleading. They suggest genuine growth and hence rising standards. But a bad shoe is not a productive fact. It is waste and you cannot improve the economy's performance or the people's living standards by accepting waste. So Mr. Khrushchev is feeling his way back to the stern discipline of profits. Only thus can the genuine contribution of factories to real growth be measured—whether they are state enterprises or private firms.

The risk to effective planning of accepting wrong yardsticks of real cost can be illustrated in another way. Twice Indian estimates of needed foreign exchange have proved to be grievously wrong—in 1957–58 and again in 1962–63. Two years after the beginning of each Plan period, it is discovered that far more foreign exchange is being absorbed than was estimated in the Plan itself. Some factors we will discuss later—the weakness in world primary prices, the tendency of imported manufactures to rise in price, the lack of "free exchange" in the available aid. But there is another factor: the rupee is almost certainly overvalued and in calculating their need for imports, public and private managers may well be encouraged to treat imports as "cheap" and to neglect the strenuous search for and development of indigenous resources. If I may illustrate this point from my own experience, I recently visited a rayon mill; it looked magnificent; it had just been built with all the lastest technologies from Japan; the gleaming, electronic looms stretched on and on; it was going to give work to all of thirty people. So I said: "Will this fine mill produce for the export market?" They said: "A little, yes, but mainly for the domestic market." Then I said: "How about the raw materials?" "Oh! they are all imported," they said. "India has no indigenous pulp industry at present." Yet, the day before, I had been taken up into the mountainous, forested part of the State, and heard officials complain about the difficulty of providing extra income for their forest-dwelling tribals. In the forests, no pulp industry; at the port, a plant costing millions, giving virtually no fresh employment, serving only the domestic market and relying on imports of pulp for its raw materials. It would be hard to picture a more complete contradiction of India's true needs and it is doubtful whether such a perversion of true planning could have occurred in an economy in which foreign exchange was valued—as it should be—"above rubies."

The answer is not devaluation. India's opportunities of increasing its exports are so meagre that the rupee would hardly benefit from a cut in its earning capacity. But might not an "accounting price" be fixed in the planning process which would give the rupee a truer exchange value? In other words, in making the estimates, could not all imports be calculated as costing more? And might not a tax on import licenses, or possibly the auctioning of import licenses, compel the industrialist to use his imports more carefully? Once again, distrust of business people and fear that a few big firms would engross all the licenses make the government reject the idea of auctioning, and it is true that the import duties introduced in the 1963 budget may help in this respect. But will they go far enough? Might auctioning supplement their effect? Business men do not bid for licenses they cannot use profitably and the more profitably they are used, the more capital accumulates for further investment. The government can tax distributed profits more heavily. It can increase, if need be, expenditure taxes and duties on luxury goods—although, once again, the new budget leaves little margin—but it should not prevent the profits being made in the first place. This should be the first law of a developing economy— yet the latest budget seems once again to underestimate this fact.

Now let us try to trace these two difficulties—administrative and managerial shortcomings and inattention to profitability—through the agricultural and industrial sectors. Once again, the right context for these criticisms needs to be repeated. To bring change, radical change, to 500,000 villages cannot be done overnight. Nor can it be accomplished without a vast increase in the number of competent technicians modernized agriculture demands. To achieve a 40 per cent increase in food output over the last 12 years is a very considerable success, especially when we remember that this growth follows decades of stagnation and even regression. Nevertheless, agriculture is handicapped by administrative shortcomings and by some lack of appreciation of the profit motive or, if you like, of incentives. In fact, many of the particular problems can be only understood in the light of these two wider issues.

Most of the theoretical solutions to low agricultural productivity are now well known. They have been known for ten years. Irrigation, the right fertilizer, improved seed, better cultivation and better implements can double and treble output. Better storage can prevent the loss of 10 to 15 per cent of the crop. Adequate credit can break the peasants' dependence on the usurer—who is still said to provide 80 per cent of India's rural lending. Cooperatives take the peasant out of reach of the middlemen. Roads bring him to market. There is no secret about this essential core of any effective program of agricultural reform. The trouble lies in its patchy implementation and, if any one reason more than any other lies behind the patchiness, it is the lack of administrative concentration and skill. On the technical side, it is doubtful whether the universities are producing enough young agronomists—agriculture was the only school to experience a fall in graduates between 1950 and 1956. They are probably not being sufficiently persuaded to work actually in the countryside. Village level workers often know no more than the farmers, who do not respect someone who cannot in fact advise. The block officer may know more but his availability is restricted by the number of villages he has to cover and his difficulties with transport.

On the side of administration proper, from the highest level downwards, agriculture gets priority in rhetoric but rarely in fact. No Chief Minister in a State has taken over the portfolio of agriculture. The bright entrants to the civil service head for the old levers of power—finance—or for the new prestige areas like industry. No young collector is likely to feel that his promotion will depend absolutely on raising productivity per acre in his district. The urgency and interest are simply not there. So the known solutions do not receive that charge of administrative drive and follow-through which would help them to get off the ground.

This phenomenon can be seen in agriculture all round the world. The Cinderella of the colonial services, it has entered Independence in a depressed state and has not yet recovered. The better methods may be known but the men to carry them out are lacking. The result is all too often a tolerant acceptance in agriculture of slacknesses and inefficiencies which on the railways, in public works, in industry would lead to courts of enquiry.

Let us take a concrete illustration. All through India and Pakistan, you will encounter the phenomenon of dams that are finished and feeder channels that are not. When the corps of engineers or the contractors who are going to build a dam set to work, what happens? They put the on-site roads in first; if cement is lying about before the monsoon, they cover it because otherwise they know it will be useless. In any case, they have seen to it that it has arrived on time. A trained labour force has been assembled, or one at least within the limits set by the desperate shortage of skills. Housing has been provided for the workers. In other words, the project has been prepared and laid out in a systematic way.

When we turn to the village, there is little of this orderly procedure. The channels have not been dug because Mohan Lal refuses his permission. The "on-site" roads may be built but, just as regularly as clock-work, they are cut off for three months during the monsoon. The degree to which the fertilizer does not arrive before the harvest has become a sort of wry joke from one end of the country to the other. When it does, it lies about in rotting sacks and coagulates. Improved seed farms are allowed to run down and, when the seed appears, it is found to be very unimproved. One could continue the list. The sort of disproportion between the aims of policy and what is actually done would not occur if farming were approached with the professional competence apparent in, say, building dams. And it seems all too likely that the lack of professionalism is due to the low actual priority suffered by agriculture both in technical recruitment and political interest. If a "project area" were approached in the spirit of a big public works project—with the same business and professional skills—India's food problems could be solved in short order.

Nor can one use the alibi that the farmers resist change. In many districts this is no longer true. They are positively harrying the officials to get more support and better results. The farmer is often ready to pay black market prices for fertilizer if he can get his hands on it; he is prepared to put up the work and money for the local road, if somebody will come and give it a tarmac top. In area after area, local energy is not lacking. What *is* lacking is the effective entrepreneurial, professional and administrative background into which this local enterprise can fit.

Greater emphasis on making farming pay would also accelerate necessary changes. Building up the farmers' income has negative aspects—ending his dependence on the *bania* and the middleman. It has positive aspects— enlarging by at least a third the flow of credit to the farmer, moving seriously to give him support prices, which make extra work and fertilizer worth while. Perhaps, too many people have seen Community Development not as a way in which the farmer can be helped to make money but, rather, as a way to persuade him to lead a purer, better life. Now, while wanting this outcome, one can still suspect *he* will decide whether he will or not. But one thing is sure. He needs a larger income if he is to enjoy any of the possibilities of a larger life.

Once again, a concrete example may better illustrate my meaning. One of the most lively centres of village expansion is to be found at Anand in Gujerat. The starting point was the link between a first-class dairy under highly

skilled direction, the large milk market of Bombay and
the farmers of Kaira District with their buffaloes. By making the dairy the core of a co-operative and collecting the
milk daily from the farmers for cash payment, the scheme
has drawn the whole district into a creative and stimulating relationship with the market.

As a result of this experience, the farmer has acquired
more than a better income; he is beginning to ask the
right things about what he should do with his income.
Today, for instance, he says: "Wouldn't I be much better
off if my cow gave twice as much milk?" Now, you can
spend ten years telling him this—rushing in on a motor-
bicycle and saying: "What you need is a better cow," and
rushing out again—but the farmer will do nothing about
it. It is only when he has in fact been assured of a steady
market for his milk, and thus the incentive to produce it,
that the blinding insight strikes him—with a better cow
he could do twice as well.

What does he do at this point? Being a shrewd man, he
decides to put some of the co-operative's earnings into an
artificial insemination centre and into a cattle-feed factory.
Incidentally, on the side, he puts in a lime-crushing plant
too to provide a little subsidiary income and keep his limes
from glutting the urban market. In other words, out of the
right kind of structure flow the right kind of inducements
to the farmer and the right kind of growth. His increased
capital inputs have been earned already by his ability to
make a profit on his milk. The original base of the operation—the daily collection of milk from a score of villages
by a milk co-operative in whose profit they share—may
seem small. But, launched on the right lines, the nucleus
creates further growth. Today, Anand is a big profitable
enterprise with an annual turnover of $1,050,000 and it is
providing its own capital for further expansion. Surely it

is a most striking example of what market incentives, properly used, can achieve.

This realistic, and, if you like, hardheaded approach to agriculture might help in one of India's unique obstacles to rising productivity—the problem of the cow. Now the Indians do not need outsiders to lecture them about their cultural patterns. But the problem must be mentioned because it is vital to the farming revolution India needs and because so many Indians have said: "The cow slaughter that we have—which is to leave animals to die of starvation—is the most cruel kind of cow slaughter imaginable. Cannot something be done about it?" One could suggest that something *can* be done within the context of what the farmer has an economic interest in doing.

One of the possibilities lies in the building of modern abattoirs where the beasts can be painlessly slaughtered and the by-products used. Yet, for sensitive people, this method is perhaps too perilously close to direct cow slaughter. Another possibility has therefore been put forward—the building of desiccating plants for fallen animals. A desiccating plant tries to use what is usable in the hide and in the carcass of the cow, for exports of hides and for bone-meal and fertilizer. This method does not take up any direct position on the issue of cow slaughter. It simply tries to avoid waste once the animal is dead. The farmer is thus offered an incentive to think about alternatives to simply allowing the animals to starve.

There are perhaps 80 million surplus cows in a country very near the limit even for human feeding. The choice between better, healthier children and the continuance of useless cows is hardly one that can be evaded. In one sense, perhaps, the problem of the cow is not unique to India. In Africa, where cows are still reckoned not as an investment but as a status symbol, or as a bride price, there is a cultural problem to be resolved. Of course, since it *is* a cultural problem, many devout and sincere Indians will make nothing of the economic argument. If it is sinful to kill a cow, no amount of explanation about the value of hides for export will make any difference. We do not kill our grandparents for their gold teeth. But perhaps the issue may be mentioned not simply because of its immense economic significance, but because the cultural argument itself seems faulty. From what one gathers in rural areas, the cows do appear to get the very worst of the bargain— dying in a slow misery of starvation—and this surely is a very odd outcome for a doctrine which was clearly designed to ensure the loving care and up-keep of the cow. There is here a certain disproportion which perhaps an outsider may mention without appearing to intervene gratuitously and discourteously in other people's cultural patterns. Nor from an economic point of view can it be denied that the load useless cows represent upon the Indian economy is almost insupportable.

There is one further point to be made before we move on to industrial questions. A clearer view on profitability might encourage an approach to agriculture more clearly based on the concept of the *best* use of land. Self-sufficiency in food can certainly be attained since Indian yields are still so low and the gap between present and needed levels is relatively small. But self-sufficiency is not a final answer. If much of Indian land can earn more through cotton, groundnuts, spices, fruit, soya or any other commercial crop, it is certainly not against the interests of the economy to use the sales of commercial crops to buy food abroad. The important point is optimum land use and this implies a concept of profitability. It is only when agriculture is seen as a flexible, varied, expandable source of all manner of supplies—industrial supplies fully as much as food supplies—that it can play its full role in Indian development. Indeed, harking back for one moment to the example of the rayon mill, one could underline the country's interest in seeing the land play its full part as an *industrial* provider. It may be that the spectre of a foreign exchange shortage which keeps factories working at 40 per cent below capacity cannot be wholly exorcised in orthodox terms of increasing exports. We will look at this possibility later on. But if it is the case, then indigenous industrial supplies become infinitely more important.

Here is the point, perhaps, to make a small digression on the role of wood in developing economies. The rayon mill's lack of pulp is a good instance. Now that wood can be treated against ants, it could be a much more widely used and attractive building material. It has an essential protective part to play. In the Damodar Valley over the last ten years the organization of the dams, of irrigation, of flood control, have all gone ahead dramatically. The Valley has become one of the great industrial power-houses of the country. Industry is developing on every side, above all the big steel giants at Burnpur and Durgapur. Yet, during a recent visit, one official echoed the concern often expressed in 1952. "You know," he said, "it is very worrying; we still really haven't got on to the conservation problem in the water-sheds"; and one or two of the experts said: "If we are not careful and quick, these dams will have silted up in 30 years." In other words, just for the planting of a few trees, one risks losing the whole power complex based upon the dams. Why is the connection not made? Because trees have no glamour. Dams have glamour; steel has glamour; but, when it comes to the honest little aspen that you plant up in the water-shed, nobody behaves as though it were worth thinking about. Yet good afforestation is within the reach of any developing economy. There must be some way of giving it glamour—not a great *tamasha* during which, on one day a year, everyone plants a tree (for the goats to eat)—but a full-scale, nation-wide drive for reafforestation. It would include a separate Ministry of Forestry. It would make trees an essential part of community development and respect for trees a part of rural education. Why not train the little boys to control the goats? Why not, as in Cyprus, plant fruit trees between villages and plantations so that the villagers, not wishing to lose the fruit, keep the goats tethered?

Once the sense of the trees' vital importance grows in the countryside, one can think of further vital contributions. Given the expense of electrification on a nation-wide basis, it is doubtful whether village electricity from any general grid system will be possible in this century. Why not try the experiment made in some parts of Africa—that of basing a village generator on a small village plantation, on a sustained yield basis and perhaps reinforced by solar energy? Too much of our thinking about development is conditioned by the experience of Russia and North America—continents with such vast supplies of coal and iron ore that massive thermal electrification and a quick advance to the heaviest of heavy industry made perfect economic sense. But India resembles the other developing continents—Africa, Latin America—in being comparatively short of major supplies of energy and lacking a whole range of essential minerals. May it not be a more sensible pattern of growth to look to the land for a great mass of renewable materials and to attempt a more decentralized, small-scale Japanese type of advance? Today, when interruptions to the regular supply of raw materials has become a major factor in India's slow rate of growth, when factories working below capacity are in some measure the chief symbol of what has gone wrong, it may be that a fresh look at the whole pattern of industrialization needs to be given and a quite new priority and urgency given to the possibilities of wood and oilseeds and cotton and fibres.

Such a reconsideration might incidentally help more directly in India's daunting problem of unemployment. Like the rayon mill, the heaviest forms of industry swallow down capital and provide only marginal new employment. A refinery costing $33,600,000 employs 350 people. The early Japanese pattern of artisans, cottage industries and small enterprises—more like a Milky Way than five or six large planets—may be a better model at this stage.

Thus insensibly we have moved from agriculture to industry—and this is right, since in fact they are the Janus heads of a single productive process, indispensable to each other, each determining what the other can effectively do. So now let us look at the twin problems of administration and profitability in the industrial sector.

Indian planning began, not unnaturally, with many of the moods and reactions of British opinion after the war. There was the same desire to make a fresh start, the same sense that, after the collapse of the thirties, the market could not be relied on, the same widespread hunger for "fair shares"—indeed, a much deeper hunger in India where the extremes of wealth and poverty are so much greater; a considerable confidence—after the experience of a war economy—in government as a stimulator and director and, among many people, an equal lack of confidence in business decisions and business motives. A rawer, rougher, newer industrial leadership in India made the suspicions all the more acute.

If one were to try to define the changes of mood which have occurred in Britain since then, as a result of post-war experience, one would find three to be most widespread —the realization that a large centralized government bureaucracy may not be the best managerial answer; that profitability and efficiency are often allied, not opposed; and that the ideal of "fair shares" is even better if there is something to share. Managerial efficiency, profitability, productivity are a new trinity. To a considerable extent, they cut across the old public versus private controversy. Public enterprises need decentralized decision-making. Public enterprises and services must pay their way— which means earning a large enough profit to cover realistic rates of interest and rapid amortization. All enterprises must press output with all the skill and ingenuity they possess.

This change of mood is appearing in India, although it is held back by ideology, by continuing prejudice, by a lot of misunderstanding and by frequent abuses. Nonetheless, it represents the climate of growth and should be fostered, not impeded. It is perhaps the most important single change needed in the entire industrial structure.

A few illustrations will make the point clearer. There is much more general realization that Delhi cannot make all the decisions. The attempt has been made to give bodies like the Damodar Valley Authority more genuine autonomy. Decisions are being decentralized in the public steel industry. At the same time, there seems to be much more awareness of what good management entails. The belief that a retired permanent secretary can run anything from a fertilizer plant to a pencillin factory has given place to the recognition of skilled management as a scarce and invaluable resource. In any developing economy, manning and managing three giant steel works simultaneously—with private expansion going ahead as well— would have virtually drained the managerial and technical

(264)

pool. Having discovered this fact the hard way, the Indian government has very sensibly gone about finding more skilled men from outside—from private industry, from abroad if need be.

Profits are perhaps ceasing to be a "dirty word" and their essential economic function of providing the surplus for further expansion is much more widely recognized. If Hindustan Machine Tools does so well that it can finance a doubling of its plant out of profits, the result is a "gift to the nation"; if Mr. Mahindra makes profits on the same scale and reinvests them, there will still tend to be murmurs of capitalist exploitation. But at least public corporations are no longer expected to run virtually as charitable agencies, subsidizing everyone else.

Yet it is doubtful whether the change of mood has gone far enough or that government yet recognizes the extreme scarcity and preciousness of really good entrepreneurial talent capable of reaching targets and earning handsome surpluses for reinvestment along the way. In fact, the business world before the emergency seemed more discouraged than at any previous time—more convinced of government hostility, more fearful of being squeezed out, more convinced that no productive achievements on their side could ever change the ideological bias at the Centre.

One must hope that some abatement of the ill will can be achieved out of the emergency, out of the experience of further growth. The atmosphere of distrust and discouragement can become a singular dis-incentive to further growth. Few if any Indians dispute the "socialistic pattern" or the government's desire to control "the commanding heights of the economy." But many of the men actively engaged in the private sector wish that the value of their work could be less grudgingly assessed. It is a fact that throughout the Plans, private investment has exceeded its target; public investment has fallen short. And in one crucial sector—fuel—government bias has undoubtedly led to absolute shortage.

In the case of the oil industry, a country as short of capital as India might well have left a lot of costly exploration to private companies. There has been nothing but loss to the economy in the delays imposed on the expansion of existing private refineries or of the utilization of their by-products. With farming in mind, one thinks with particular regret of the fertilizer plant that never got built at Bombay.

The coal record is disastrous—simply because coal enters into everything. The private sector, hampered until recently by unrealistic prices and by prohibitions on any expansion beyond contiguous areas, has nonetheless fulfilled its Plan target. The entire shortfall—of over seven million tons in 1960–61—has occurred in the public sector.

TABLE IX COAL OUTPUT
(*Million Tons*)

	Target 1960	1960–61	1961–62
Private Sector	44	44.39	45.62
Public Sector	16	10.45	8.73
Total	60	54.8	54.3

Yet, in the Third Plan, this faltering public sector is allotted the bigger rate of increase and a larger share of capital with which to achieve it. In 1963, coal output, having received at last a good deal of concentrated attention, has begun to pick up—an encouraging sign that effective action occurs when the needs knock on the door. But until this spurt, the Indian economy had been slowed down for nearly five years by the coal shortage.

To recognize realities, to encourage the sectors that are meeting their targets, to applaud the earning and reinvesting of profits, to reward efficiency wherever it appears, and castigate it when—as in the big Delhi power breakdown of 1961—it most manifestly does not: all this entails no sacrifice of justice and fair shares. It is perfectly compatible with all sorts of measures to ensure greater equity —by income taxes, wealth taxes, inheritance taxes. In fact, firms might well be fiscally encouraged to make wider experiments in profit sharing and in giving more "fringe benefits"—pensions, in particular—which would give better living conditions without risking inflationary wage increases. Nor does greater recognition of the function and value of efficiency, profitability and productivity wherever they appear affect the socialistic pattern. The "commanding heights" will be largely controlled by government for it alone can provide the needed capital. But a few private groups competitively scaling some of the slopes will strengthen the structure and, perhaps more often than is comfortable, provide a yardstick for measuring the effectiveness of public performance. This is all to the good. What India needs to avoid at all cost is an economy in which neither incentives nor sanctions work. A stagnant economy may achieve fair shares but sharing scarcity is hardly an adequate goal—least of all for a country in which national income is still no more than $70 a head.

Chapter Sixteen

The Foreign Exchange Crisis

WHEREVER one starts in the effort to disentangle India's difficulties, the thread leads back sooner or later to the shortage of foreign exchange which, in both 1961 and 1962, led to a deficit of the order of $630 million and, at the beginning of 1963, reduced India's reserves to $450,660,000—or the equivalent of 2½ months' imports. Each of the three ways of securing foreign exchange—foreign aid, foreign investment, or exports—presents problems and none is strictly adequate. This may seem an extreme statement with regard to aid since the Aid-India Consortium of Western Nations under the chairmanship of the World Bank have guaranteed more than $2 billion in aid during the first two years of the Plan.

But we have to remember, once again, the question of

TABLE X WESTERN AID TO THE THIRD PLAN
(*Million Dollars*)

	1961–62	1962–63	Total
Canada	28	33	61
France	15	45	60
Germany	225	139	364
Japan	50	55	105
United Kingdom	182	84	266
United States	545	455	1,000
World Bank International Development Assoc.	250	200	450
Austria *	—	5	5
Belgium *	—	10	10
Italy *	—	53	53
Netherlands *	—	11	11
	1,295	1,090	2,385

* Joined Consortium in 1962.
Source: Official Statistics.

scale. The 450 million people living in India make up a third of the population of the developing world. If aid is judged on a per capita basis, it works out at 30 cents a head—less than aid to Pakistan, much less than aid to Formosa or to some of the troubled successor States of Indo-China. One must assume that the success of an alternative, non-totalitarian method of development is worth something in the world-wide competition with Communism—that competition will continue in the poorer parts of the world whichever version of Communism prevails, pacific or violent, Russian-style or Peking-style. One must assume that the preservation of the open society in Asia has an absolute value for people who claim freedom for their way of life. With such issues at stake, it is not folly or "squandermania" or "pouring good money after bad"

(269)

to undertake the full support of the Indian balance of payments during the coming years of strain—even if another billion dollars are involved. The costs which some of the possible alternatives might entail—the infiltration of India, the collapse of its economy, its dissolution into warring local dictatorships, a repetition of the Chinese disintegration between the wars—would demonstrably be much higher in the long run or, perhaps, as the Korean War demonstrated, in the not so very long run.

However, one has to admit that the climate for greater aid is not promising. The United States Congress has always felt fairly grudging about spending their electors' money on nonvoters abroad. Fear of Communism, dedicated Administration leadership have kept them on the straight and narrow path for a decade. But, as the years go by, a new factor is entering in—a growing desire to see results. The results may be political—warm friends secured for the United States. They may be economic— demonstrably rapid growth. They are usually wholly unrealistic, either because it is always difficult for the poor to love the rich or because the difficulties of early development are simply not understood in wealthy, industrialized countries.

Could more be done to lessen this malaise? One wishes that aid could be removed from the narrow categories of giving and taking and put into the context of a joint attack on world poverty. It is always an uneasy business—acknowledging debts and being grateful for help, especially when the gratitude can be given all sorts of political overtones. The effusive thanks which some Western donors would like from some Eastern recipients smacks of bending the knee to Western neo-colonialism.* In fact, some

* Communist aid, which amounts to just under a billion dollars over the last decade, lacks these overtones since Russia never exercised colonial

Indian leaders have felt obliged to go as far as direct dis-
courtesy in order to prove the purity of their non-alignment. Somewhere between these extremes it should be
possible to establish reasonable terms for a dialogue which,
one must hope, will continue for at least another decade
and ought clearly to be less beset with snubs, misunder-
standings and hurt feelings. The only context in which
this might happen would be a joint acceptance of the fact
that the misery of so many millions of men and women is
a load which the human race should not be asked to carry
and that it is as much in the Western interest as in India's
to see that, in Lincoln's words, "the burdens are at last
lifted from the shoulders of all mankind."

Before leaving the issue of foreign aid for the moment,
one further point should be made. Even if, for the reasons
already described, an increase in aid-giving, even to
counter the emergency, does not prove possible, some of
the strain could be taken off the Indian economy if more
of the aid were not tied to particular projects. Two-thirds
of Britain's aid, four-fifths of America's is earmarked for
further expansions in productive capacity. Some of the
linkages—one thinks of new power stations, for instance
—are, no doubt, indispensable. But might not greater flexibility with the rest ensure that more of the existing plant
works to capacity before further extensions are planned?
Capacity working is the speediest way of increasing the
rate of growth. It was, for instance, profoundly disturbing
to be told for over two years that the investment had now
been made to ensure that the public sector produces its
full quota of coal and yet, for two years, to find output
static or falling. Investment which leads to 60 per cent
capacity working has an element of dis-investment. At

control in India and, so far, is still able to present itself as a proletarian
made good, not as a bourgeois.

present, India's first need is aid in general support of the balance of payments which would permit a larger flow of materials and components to existing factories.

The degree to which foreign investment can fill the gap in foreign exchange is not great. Although between 1948 and 1960, foreign business investment rose from $543,-480,000 to $1,282,470,000 and, since 1957, the number of agreements for technical and financial participation has increased sharply, the Third Plan's estimate that foreign private investment would not bring in much more than $126 million a year is probably not too wide of the mark. India is attractive as a growing market. Its record in the repatriation of profits and capital is impeccable. Compensation is guaranteed in the case of expropriation. Recently, firms pioneering new ventures have been exempted for a period of years from the very heavy taxation imposed on companies. Yet the malaise which prevails in the Indian government's handling of private enterprise spills over into the foreign sector. On the government side, the distrust has deep historical roots. Much typical nineteenth-century investment did amount to exploitation, particularly in the field of minerals, for which the French have coined the phrase *le trouisme*. By this, they mean an investment policy which opens up a lode or a reef, removes the minerals with the help of a wholly foreign supervisory staff, exports the profits, the capital gains and most of the salaries, pays locally only unskilled labour and finally decamps, leaving behind nothing but some unemployed miners and, where the deposit was, *un grand trou*—one large hole. The sense that in foreign investment the entire benefit is exported, dies hard. And the lingering suspicion of exploitation puts an uncertain edge to the welcome given to foreign capital.

Developing governments have therefore to be reminded

of three things. The first is that the well-established foreign firm is an incomparable school for skills in the early stages of industrialization. The proviso is that local staff is trained, but "Indianization" is universal in private industry in India. The second fact is that foreign capital is scarce and shy. There is more demand than supply and if a government makes its terms too onerous, the capital will not flow. On this point, the Indian government has combined a welcome pragmatism with its sterner attitudes. The proscription of foreign majority holding of shares has been waived in some cases. An Investment Centre has been established in America to encourage foreign interests. Various official credit corporations are prepared for participation. This flexibility somewhat offsets the tough taxation and the "damn'd disinheriting countenance" of some Ministers.

It is especially for these men that the third point needs to be stressed—the degree to which, in the developing countries today, it is the governments, not the companies, that hold most of the cards. So much nineteenth-century investment took place in dependent territories without governments of their own. For nearly a century, major economic decisions were in alien hands. In such conditions it is hardly surprising that new governments do not always realize at once what powers political independence gives them and how the relationship of power has changed between the foreign entrepreneur and the local government. What, after all, does a foreign entrepreneur do? He invests his capital and builds his plant; at this point, a solid part of his resources are, as it were, a hostage in the country of his investment. He cannot ultimately control any part of his environment. The government of the country can and does. Of course, if governments go in for indiscriminate, uncompensated takeovers, they probably

(273)

will not secure any more investment. But this does not help the man who is already in. A truly independent government has powers of control over foreign investment which formerly were either exercised by colonial officials or not at all. The whole context of power has changed. The days of *le trouisme* are over.

Independent governments have vast powers of taxation. Since, physically, the plant of the foreign company is in their territory, they exercise ultimate control over conditions of work. They can regulate the speed with which profits and capital are repaid. They can profoundly affect the reactions of the labour force. It is the foreign investor who, once the investment is made, plays from relative weakness. If developing governments fully realized their strength, they could afford to be quite moderate in the way they use it—on the whole, the trend is in that direction.

On the other hand, there are very real difficulties which foreign enterprise has to appreciate. In the post-colonial world, there cannot be, long-term, a continuance of the Cuban pattern under Batista according to which a country ends up with large parts of key sectors in its economy under foreign control. Western firms could, at this stage, very profitably use all their skill and imagination to devise ways in which foreign investment can become a true and recognizable partnership. There are many routes—joint enterprises, local ownership of shares, participation by the State in private ventures, profit sharing with the local labour force. Here, too, the trend is towards greater co-operation, a greater process of getting "mixed up together." Such bodies as the World Bank, the IDA and the various credit institutions set up inside developing countries are all helping to produce a much greater variety of patterns of partnership.

The Indian government itself seems to be growing increasingly and sensibly pragmatic about the issue. To give a recent example, back in 1956, under the pressure of the Mysore State government, the Centre felt obliged to nationalize the private Kolar Gold Mining Company. Recently, the Central Provinces Manganese Ore Company fell into a dispute with the state governments of Madhya Pradesh and Maharashtra about the duration of its leases. Once again, the States' reaction appears to have been: nationalize. This time, however, the Centre has persuaded the local governments to enter into a quadrapartite partnership—Centre, Company and the two State governments—to continue the leases. The public authorities bought into the private venture but it controls management and sales.

If governments, confident of their powers, use them reasonably, if private investment recognizes the local interest in securing participation in equity and capital gains, agreements profitable to both sides are negotiable. There are some areas—the "commanding heights" again—where many governments (including General de Gaulle's) will wish to avoid majority holdings by outsiders. There are some activities—which create neither exports nor import substitutes—in which foreign participation and the resulting repatriation of profits would simply add to the problems of foreign exchange. But, in general, foreign enterprise is an unequalled school of managerial and technical skills, a source of productivity and further savings and, very often, a significant booster of exports as well as an original source of foreign exchange. The test here—as in domestic enterprises—is efficiency and productivity. They are too precious for any source to be overlooked.

The crucial issue in foreign exchange, however, centres on the exports by which India can pay its way. It is only in the last eighteen months that positive steps in export promotion have been taken—the establishment of trade centres abroad, incentives to exporters in such shapes as differential traffic rates at home and the right to retain part of the foreign exchange that has been earned, compulsory setting aside of textile quotas for export, the establishment of a small fund to finance raw materials for exporters. All these measures are too recent and some would say, still too small, to affect exports greatly, and, indeed, far from a six per cent increase a year being registered under the Third Plan, exports have hardly risen at all. It is clear that $1.365 billion is some kind of a threshold which it is very difficult to cross.

And the reasons are not in dispute. Over half of India's exports are "traditional"—tea, cotton goods and jute (Table XI). The new manufactured lines suffer severe competition from other Asian producers and from Communist exporters. If at this point it is necessary to go beyond the Indian scene and look at the state of the world market as it affects developing countries, it is simply because, in the field of rising exports, the possibilities do not depend upon countries like India. The scale and scope of the market will be determined largely by the West.

One of the new facts about international trade that has become visible only in the last year or so is the fact that nearly all the trading policies of the developed industrial Western world are in some measure tipped *against* the underdeveloped countries. Science and technology are partly responsible. Development in the chemical industry, substitutes, artificial fibres, plastics, have reduced the nineteenth-century dependence of the developed world upon the primary producer. The tremendous impulsion to development in other continents which, a hundred years ago, sprang from the Western countries' hunger for raw ma-

TABLE XI GENERAL COMMODITY PATTERN OF INDIAN TRADE
(*In Millions of U.S. Dollars*)

Domestic Exports	1960	1961	Imports	1960	1961
Tea	252	261.2	Non-electric machinery	386	484.9
Fabrics other than cotton *	159.6	176.4	Iron and steel	247.2	214.6
Cotton fabrics *	122.9	106.1	Chemicals	178.9	186.9
Fruit and vegetables	51.7	55.7	Cereals and preparations	377.2	185.4
Leather	53.8	54.6	Petroleum and products	164.6	167
Iron ore and scrap	44.9	52.1			
Raw cotton	22.5	39.3	Raw cotton	158.1	145.5
Tobacco and manufactures	33	33.2	Electric machinery	114.9	133.4
Non-ferrous ores and concentrates	34.7	28.1	Transport equipment	140.5	120.5
Textile yarn and thread	23.1	26.5	Copper	48.1	43.1

* Excluding narrow and special fabrics.
Source: *Monthly Statistics of the Foreign Trade of India.*

terials, has lost much of its energy. Imports in the West expand much more slowly than industrial growth.

From this flows the tendency of primary prices to be very weak in relation to manufactured goods and, therefore, for the terms of trade to turn against the developing world. More and more of their primary products have to be sold to buy a given quantity of manufactured imports. This trend is reinforced by technological developments inside the poorer countries. We have, perhaps, grown accustomed to the image of the American farmer with grain pouring out of his eyes, ears, nose and mouth; we swallow hard and accept the fact that the same farmer is going to reappear in Europe. Over-production of food is no longer a remote possibility. It is a fact if we only regard market conditions and not real human need.

Owing to the general wealth of America, the American farmer, via a very powerful lobby in Washington, can secure an income commensurate with his needs. The policy creates a vast surplus of food, which, in turn, makes possible such brilliant innovations as the disposal of American food under Public Law 480. But where the primary producers are poor and cannot be subsidized by fellow-citizens as poor as they are themselves, the problem of over-production of such things as coffee, tea, cocoa, groundnuts, rubber and bananas, threatens to undermine still further the incomes of poor countries. The threat is there already. But the reality may be worse. In every research station in West Africa one can meet some absolutely dedicated scientist who says, with shining eyes: "Now, with a very simple change in the seedling and a very simple application of fertilizer, we can increase production of these groundnuts—or tea or coffee or rubber—by 1000 per cent." When one says "Oh! but there is a world carry-over of so and so many tons already" the reply is often a blank look: "Is there? But let me tell you more about our methods." Nearly every tropical country has tea, coffee, sugar, groundnuts and rubber written into their development plans. What happens when all these plans, jet-assisted by science, take off together? A further fall in world prices seems the least disturbing of the possible results. Admittedly, political disorder can offset the expansion—as it has done in Indonesia. But one should scarcely plan for a world economy in which good prices are secured only by local disorder.

Terms of trade turning against the poor—that is the first problem. The second is that if primary producers try any working-up or processing of their raw materials or minerals before they are exported, the West claps on higher tariffs. The reaction is a clear dis-incentive to the developing world to begin the processing and working up of their own materials which is perhaps the first essential step towards their own effective industrialization. Then one should add that many tropical products are also subject to excise taxes inside Europe, which tends to keep down their consumption. And we must not forget quotas. In the first stages of development, manufactured exports tend to consist of textiles and simple engineering products. In keeping with the West's anti-processing policy, they invite high tariffs. In addition, if they succeed in penetrating Western markets beyond a certain point, quotas are introduced to protect the higher-cost Western producers.

Nor is it only Western policies that create difficulties. Communist foreign trade is not based upon any definable or observable costing system. A quite usual pattern appears to be to charge 5 per cent less than the nearest competitor. It is difficult to see how the Asian exporter can deal with this problem easily. He does not necessarily have behind him a government ready to give large State subsidies or consumers who will pay much more for goods at home so that they can be sold below cost abroad.

These are general world-wide difficulties. There is one specific problem that must be examined—the problem of the Common Market. We do not know how soon or even how General de Gaulle's veto on Britain's entry can be overcome. But we have to remember that, whether Britain goes in, or whether Britain stays out, the consequences for the trade of the developing world are likely to be far-reaching. True, 75 per cent of India's trade would not, in fact, be affected because it would have duty-free entry both into Britain and Europe. But in the vital field of textiles, there are bound to be repercussions. If Britain joined Europe, India would lose its preference on textiles and, more than that, Belgian and French producers would receive preference against India. But before anyone throws his hat in the air over the General's veto, he must remember that Indian textile exports to Britain are already limited by quota. If Britain, as a result of exclusion from the Common Market, could not improve on its present rather inadequate 2 to 2.5 per cent rate of growth and if, in 1971, when the changes in tariff would have been completed, British markets had hardly grown, then it is not likely that the quotas would give much greater access to Indian textiles than they do now.

If, to carry speculation rather further, one makes a fairly optimistic assumption about Britain's entry into the Common Market and assumes that Britain, along with the rest of the Common Market countries, would sustain a rate of growth of about 4 or 5 per cent a year, then it is possible that the *total* European textile market would, in fact, be so much bigger that, in spite of the abolition of the preferential system, there would be more openings for Indian textiles than there could be in a restrictive stagnant, though preferential, British Market.

The arguments are strong on balance for the belief that it is to the advantage of the developing world that the French veto should be overcome. Britain has, inescapably, world-wide commercial links with developing countries. The British could not go in and forget all these connections. They would, therefore, tend to reinforce those inside the Common Market who do not want to see it as a sort of private hunting-ground for the French farmer. A British reinforcement to Europe's outward-looking forces could be strong. In fact, the Deniau report produced by the Commission in Brussels after the collapse of the talks declared that it had already proved so. Moreover, Britain's entry would render more likely the drawing up of the world-wide agreements we need if we are to deal effectively with all the various issues in world trade —low primary prices, risks of glut, anti-processing tariffs and so forth—which add up to an immense barrier to the trade of all the developing nations. Britain in the Common Market would facilitate the kind of agreements with the United States which would be necessary to create new patterns of trade to help developed and developing alike.

What kind of agreements are these? First of all, readiness to back, support and provide, where necessary, the working capital needed to establish world-wide commodity agreements in any area where absolute surplus is becoming a problem. Coffee is already a case in point; tea and cocoa are on the way. Sugar is already included. So are various minerals, with various degrees of success. Such agreements imply discipline among exporters and do run risks of rigidity and monopoly. But the present unregulated market puts all the load on the poorest members.

A second area of agreement might begin with an expansion of the existing textile agreements in such a way that the textile producers in the developing world get a better chance. At the moment, the textile agreement at least represents the first attempt on the part of the developed world to get to grips with the problem. It is based upon quotas which largely reflect the developing countries' exports in the last few years, but with the proviso that the quota will increase by 5 per cent a year for the next five years unless insuperable difficulties occur. A shared loophole is hardly a royal road to further exports. Yet it is nonetheless the first breakthrough to a recognition that, if the Western world wants to have beneficial trading relations with the developing world, then steadily it has to enlarge its own market to their manufactures. Although the agreement is small, it may be the thin end of the wedge. Areas like the American South may perhaps follow Lancashire's pattern which has been to shift out of cheap textiles into quite other fields such as engineering. There has been here a certain "vacation of the field" which one would like to see generalized, the more developed nations moving on to more complex technologies and importing cheaply the simpler technologies which developing countries can most easily make.

Yet agreements such as these depend finally on continued prosperity in the Atlantic World. People do not maintain import prices and "vacate fields" when they are struggling with massive unemployment. The most important factor in maintaining the trade of the developing world will simply be the buoyancy and the expansion of the existing economy. If that economy comprising 200 million people in North America and something nearer 250 million in Europe and Britain, were able to grow fairly steadily at a rate of 4 per cent a year, this in itself would be the greatest spur to the growth of exports throughout the developing world. This kind of steady expansion is much more likely to take place if there are common institutions linking both sides of the Atlantic, working to keep expansion before the minds of governments, to provide the working capital of international trade and to prevent the problems of the balance of payment from stopping economies dead in their tracks, as Britain has tended to stop every three years since 1947. If the developed world can advance to more institutionalized expansion and prosperity, that would be the best guarantee of buoyant markets and, therefore, of expanding exports for everyone else.

At this point, one should underline the degree to which a profound convergence of interests exists between developed and developing lands. It has been a commonplace almost since Marx to point out that the modern industrial economy tends to choke itself on its own productivity. Marx thought exploitation would prevent the workers from ever becoming a market. The vote, trade unions, better technology belied him, and by 1914 quite a lot of Western workers had some stake in the economy. The next great block came in the thirties, when even a moderately prosperous working class provided too narrow a market to absorb new technologies, and mass unemployment set in.

Then the vast "public works" of the War and the expansion of "consumer durables" created a wholly new market which, in the forties and early fifties, enfranchised millions of new consumers round the Atlantic.

Now the machines may be catching up again. America and Britain have had long periods of stagnancy. Western Europe is less buoyant. Where is the next stimulus, the next enfranchisement of new consumers to occur? Is it fanciful to suggest that the millions of the developing world could make up the next great extension of the consumer's market and that new expansive policies for trade and aid, far from representing self-denial and sacrifice for the West, may be the condition of survival for their mixed market economies?

Seen in this light, a cooperative effort to see India through the emergency, to get a 4 to 5 per cent rate of growth established and to draw 450 million people to the first modest fringes of well-being is not a work of charity or condescension or paternalism or even political self-interest. It is a sane answer to the risks—of slump and misery and despair—which could still assail developed and under-developed lands alike. The portents of 1929 are not so wholly banished that the world's statesmen can afford to disregard falling demand among under-developed producers and slackening growth among the developed. Given this context, aid to India is not simply support for the Indian economy. It can be part of a wider strategy, to keep open reasonable hopes and modest perspectives for all mankind.

Chapter Seventeen

My Brother's Keeper

YET more than a material interest in sustained and expanding markets is at stake. What is fundamentally at issue is the moral vision and purpose of Western society, or perhaps the even harsher question whether its vision and purpose may not have simply ceased to be.

The mass consumption economies of the Atlantic world represent a wholly new phenomenon in human history. In them, not simply individuals, or groups, or classes but society as a whole is rich and expects to become richer. Instead of the old pyramid-like social structure with its enormous base of gross poverty tapering off to a tiny apex of wealth, we have a new spheroid pattern: narrow at the bottom among the very poor, narrow at the top for the very rich, and swelling out vastly in between for the steadily expanding ranks of the middle class. For most of this middle class, food and health, leisure and recreation, cleanliness and clothing, holidays and entertainment are on a scale that, even a score of years ago, only the wealthy could command. Nor is the position static. Virtually every Western government speaks of living standards doubled in the next decades—and no one doubts the possibility. In this, modern wealth is more startling than any previous pattern. Most wealthy families in the past hoped for not much more than to maintain their position. Today probably the majority live in the expectation of becoming better off.

But if our society enjoys the advantages in comfort and elbowroom of growing wealth, it cannot escape the temptations either; and one does not need to be much of a moralist or an historian to know what these temptations are. From the beginnings of recorded time, rich men and rich classes have had to face the risk of being so swamped in their own affluence that they lose any sense of purpose in life or any capacity for understanding imaginatively the woes of other less fortunate human beings. Triviality and a closed heart have proved the bane of careless wealth from the great banquet of Belshazzar down to the latest ducking of Hollywood starlets in swimming pools full of champagne. The fact that now whole communities share in the affluence does not make the temptations any less insidious. To Hamlet's bitter question:

> What is a man
> If his chief good and market of his time
> Be but to sleep and feed?

the answer is not more reassuring if millions of people are involved, not one or two. In fact, the scale of wealth

(286)

adds a new risk. In the past, the evident misery of the many put pressure on the conscience of the few, and where conscience was dumb, fear of the angry multitude provided some substitute. But in the West today, the engine of progress seems to lack the motor power of social discontent. "You never had it so good" is the theme of modern elections, "I'm all right, Jack" the motto of once militant trade unions. The millions who live in murderous destitution in the great cities of the East are voiceless, faceless men. Immediate reality is the new car, the new TV, the cosy suburban house. How can one look through the picture window with vision enough to see the starving men, bundled in rags, lying on Calcutta's pavements? Just so did the nobles of France ignore the peasants starving at their castle gates.

By a strange irony it is not the Christian West that speaks today about purpose and compassion. However twisted the motives behind Communist propaganda, however specious the promises, one appeal of Communism as a world force is clear: it talks the language of vision and brotherhood. Behind each local conquest of power lies the vista of a world made one by Communism and thus prepared to achieve the final aim of man and history—an apocalyptic society in which lion and lamb lie down together and "there shall be no more death nor sorrow nor crying, neither shall there be any more pain: for the former things are passed away." This millennial strain in Communist thought provides the framework for its facts and statistics. China hopes to catch up with British steel production and Russia to pull level with the United States; but behind these proximate aims is still the building of the New Jerusalem in which a liberated humanity will find its ultimate home. Perhaps the vision does fade a little as the revolution recedes. Our old friend writing to

Pravda that sputniks are all very fine, but what about a new apartment, speaks with the familiar earthly voice of ordinary humanity. But the vision is not dead. In China, especially, the ultimate vision of a re-created world gives energy to the peoples' desperate labours.

And by its new claim to lead the colored, poverty-stricken peoples of the world to victory by means of an austere, unbourgeois Communism, China will sound more loudly than ever the ethical choices placed on the affluent by the mere fact of wealth. For, in this new society, men are to live as brothers. The evils which Communists claim to attack in all traditional societies are the evils which spring from exclusiveness and unshared wealth: the tight monopolies of feudal landowning, the careless, isolated wealth of foreign enterprise in primitive surroundings, the corruption of middle-class politicians, and—on a global scale—the fantastic concentration of wealth in the West. Of course, envy and power-hunger play their part in all this. But no one should discount the strain of justice and brotherhood, or the appeal to the deepest of modern instincts: the equality of man with man. Even though, like George Orwell's pigs, some men end up "more equal than others," the first stages of Communist revolution do put down the mighty from their seats and exalt them of low degree.

Insensibly one uses the language of the Bible. But the link is obvious. Marx drew his messianic vision and his concern for social justice directly from the Christian vision of the West. No other civilization produced Christianity's dramatic sense of history as the unfolding of a more than human purpose. In the East, the dominant picture was of a world endlessly gyrating through the same vast cycles of existence. And just because the reality of created things seemed so slight in much of Eastern thought, the obligations of social justice and neighbourly concern never acquired the same overwhelming moral emphasis as in the Christian ethic. But in Christianity the man who loves his neighbour is quite simply the man who feeds him, shelters him, clothes him, and heals him. It is all very direct and physical, and lacking in "spiritual" overtones. Yet the food given to the least of the little ones is given to God Himself. One can therefore understand why Marx in the England of the 1840s—where children still laboured sixteen hours a day, and died at their looms—failed to see much connection between contemporary religion and social justice, and constructed instead his own secular version of Christianity's messianic dream.

In the event, there was more vitality in the West's tradition of humanity and justice than Marx could have foreseen. Within domestic society, a steady advance has been made toward greater neighbourliness; and even though the income tax may seem a rather remote and impersonal instrument of Christian justice, its effect has been to help to clothe and house and employ the many in strict accordance with Biblical precept. That in so doing it has also helped to underpin the new economy based on mass consumption underlines the possibility that those who seek first the Kingdom of God and its justice may find "all these things added unto" them.

But just as it took time for an active spirit of humanity and Christian justice to overleap the class boundaries of Western society, it is taking even longer for the vision of the West to extend beyond its national boundaries—except in terms of self-interest or self-defense—to the wider community of mankind. The physical oneness of the human race is underlined for us every day: in ever quicker transport, in instant communication, in the overarching, all-inclusive terror of atomic annihilation. But the ideal of humanity as a moral community owing to all its members the obligations of justice and love, this ideal is left to the Communists to exploit. They alone speak with conviction of the world brotherhood of the future. They alone claim to accept the full obligations of human solidarity. They alone seem to speak to the present misery and future glory of mankind. Forget the sophistry. Gloss over the force and the tyranny. Look only at the propaganda —and one might say that in the world at large it is Communism that chiefly expresses the profoundest aspirations of the West.

This is the ultimate challenge we face: to extend our vision of the good society to the whole family of man. Our wealth and comfort hold us back. We find it easier— as do the wastrels of any age—to "sit down to eat and rise up to play." We can, like the misers of every epoch, argue that even the smallest transfer of our superabundant wealth will face us with bankruptcy and ruin. It is easy for us, as it has been for the lazy and unaware of every generation, to pretend that nothing has changed, that the world is not in flames, that the old ways are better, and that, if the poor lack bread, they can eat cake. Societies, classes, families, all have tried these evasions in the past. Marie Antoinette playing shepherdess at Trianon when the peasants, not the sheep of France, were eating grass; Rome bemused with bread and circuses while the barbarians gathered at the gate; the Cretan kings drinking deep behind the walls of Knossos with Mycenean fleets waiting to take the city in the night—all these are symbols of the fate that awaits the complacent and the comfortable when they let their good fortune stifle their good will.

There is no reason to suppose that the fate of the Western peoples will be different if they carry on with their round of fun and distraction, their TV and their quiz shows, their golf and their tourism, while all across the world the pressures of poverty and despair steadily gather strength. One is reminded of Thomas Carlyle's desperate reaction after a day spent with a casual acquaintance "guffawing . . . prating, jargoning. To me through these thin cobwebs, Death and Eternity sat glaring." So they do today—in the apocalyptic horror of atomic destruction, in the equally apocalyptic Communist vision of a world made safe and just for man. If to these vast promptings of a greater destiny the Western peoples make no more response than "to pass by on the other side," they will not only endure the fate of Babylon or Carthage. They will deserve it.

But this is not the inevitable outcome for free man. He has opted for reform and greater justice within domestic society. He can do so again for the world at large. Once at least since the war have his policies and his visions been equal to the crisis. The Marshall Plan remains one of the greatest, most unsordid acts of statesmanship in the annals of man. Only it has not been repeated.

Today the time has come to take up again the threads dropped so casually a decade ago, to restore the Marshall approach as the operating principle in Western policy and apply it at once in a new co-operative venture with Asia's greatest democracy to ensure the success of India's Third Plan. This is the best and most immediate chance open to the West to make operative in world affairs the deepest moral convictions of Western life. Behind the Indian figures and statistics lie the realities of children without bread, men without work, women without hope. If these do not move us to action, the outer form of our society may survive—but its inner spirit will have withered away. Then, like the myriad proud civilizations upon which "the Sentence of the Watchers" has already gone

forth, we shall be carted off this great stage of the world
into the dust and debris of history, there to join the
melancholy line of past societies which, at the crucial
test, could not change and advance in time.

It is our fortune at this point of crisis to have all the
physical resources that are needed to create a new world
of opportunity. It is our tragedy that we may lack the
vision and the will.

Index

(293)

INDEX

Laissez faire doctrine, 35, 38, 49–51, 125–32
Land reform, 107–08, 129, 148–49, 191

Mao Tse-tung, 211
Markets, maintenance of, 47–48
Marshall Plan, 53–56, 291
Marx, Karl, 31, 41, 59–77, 283, 288–87
Mixed economy, 44–56
Mobilization of resources, 227
  India, 204–05
  World War II, 48–49
Monnet Plan, 55, 168

National Congress, India, 118–23, 206–07
National Defense Fund, 225
National Defense Work, 228
National Development Council, 153
Nationalism, 19, 27, 76, 85
Nationalization of industry, 178–79
North Eastern Frontier Agency, attack on, 212ff.

Plans, Indian; *see also* First, Second and Third Plans
  administration of, 226ff.
  agriculture, 181–94
  broad aims, 153–94, 251–52
  industry, 166–80
  infrastructure, 157–66
  public and private expenditures, 157
Politics, economic expansion determined by, 29, 84
Population:
  Chinese cycle, 18–19
  India, 108, 128, 143, 243ff.
  Japan, 244–45
Poverty, problem of, 11, 121, 141–52, 190, 291
Profit motive, 39–42, 250ff.
  definition, 35–36
  laissez faire and, 35–37
  Marx on, 61–62

Railways, India, 23, 130–31
Resources, use of, 36, 195–207
Roads and roadbuilding, 188
Rural development, 184–92
Russia; *see* Communism *and* U.S.S.R.

Savings and investment, 17–18, 27, 42
  forced savings, 144–46

Second Plan, India, 194, 196, 198–99, 220–21, 225, 242–43, 247
Social reform, demand for, 46–47
Stagnation of the economy, 61, 81, 90
  India, 133–34
  private enterprise and, 48, 50

Taxes and taxation, 47, 51, 195–98, 224, 253, 274
Technical assistance, 213, 223
Third Plan, India, 169–70, 194, 215–23, 243, 247, 266, 268–69, 272, 276, 291
  birth control, 143–44
  Community Development movement, 184–92
  financing, 197
  resources, 195–207
Trade, international, 54, 201–03
  shaped by political facts, 84
Transportation in India, 157–60

Underdeveloped countries, 26
Union of Soviet Socialist Republics (U.S.S.R.), 29–30, 71–73, 151
Unions, labour, 26–27, 39, 65, 76, 172–77
United Nations, 51–52, 216
United States, 34, 42, 123
  affluence of, 285–92
  aid given to India, 184, 233–34
  colonialism, 105
  economic development, 28

Value, labour theory of, 62–63

Welfare capitalism, 15, 44–56
Welfare programs, 174–75
  in colonial territories, 90–91
  provided by state, 47
Western Powers:
  economic revolution, 12, 41
  foreign aid to India, 200–01, 232–40, 268ff.
  ideological disagreement with Communism, 57–58, 73, 286–92
  mixed economy, 44–56
  mixed experimental societies, 31
  reasons for giving aid to India, 268–84
World Bank, 268, 274
World War II, 41–42, 48–49, 82

(295)